I0199811

IRISH
FOLK MUSIC

**Recent Titles in
Discographies**

Women in Jazz
Jan Leder, compiler

The King Labels: A Discography
Michel Ruppli, compiler

Thank You Music Lovers: A Bio-Discography of Spike Jones and
His City Slickers, 1941-1965
Jack Mirtle, compiler

John McCormack: A Comprehensive Discography
Paul W. Worth and Jim Cartwright, compilers

Count Basie: A Bio-Discography
Chris Sheridan, compiler

The Symphonies of Gustav Mahler
Lewis M. Smoley, compiler

V-Discs: First Supplement
Richard S. Sears, compiler

French Horn Discography
Michael Hernon, compiler

The Clef/Verve Labels: A Discography
Michel Ruppli, compiler

The Cliff Edwards Discography
Larry F. Kiner, compiler

Broadway on Record: A Directory of New York Cast Recordings of
Musical Shows, 1931-1986
Richard Chigley Lynch, compiler

The Blue Note Label: A Discography
Michael Cuscuna and Michel Ruppli, compilers

His Master's Voice/La Voce Del Padrone
Alan Kelly, compiler

IRISH FOLK MUSIC

A Selected Discography

Compiled by
Deborah L. Schaeffer

Discographies, Number 31

Greenwood Press
New York • Westport, Connecticut • London

Library of Congress Cataloging-in-Publication Data

Schaeffer, Deborah L.
   Irish folk music : a selected discography / compiled by Deborah L.
Schaeffer.
     p. cm.—(Discographies, ISSN 0192-334X ; no. 31)
   Includes index.
   ISBN 0-313-25312-9 (lib. bdg. : alk. paper)
   1. Folk music—Ireland—Discography. 2. Folk-songs—Ireland—
Discography. I. Title. II. Series.
ML156.4.F5S25 1989
016.7899'13617415—dc19   89-1886

British Library Cataloguing in Publication Data is available.

Copyright © 1989 by Deborah L. Schaeffer

All rights reserved. No portion of this book may be
reproduced, by any process or technique, without the
express written consent of the publisher.

Library of Congress Catalog Card Number: 89-1886
ISBN: 0-313-25312-9
ISSN: 0192-334X

First published in 1989

Greenwood Press, Inc.
88 Post Road West, Westport, Connecticut 06881

Printed in the United States of America

The paper used in this book complies with the
Permanent Paper Standard issued by the National
Information Standards Organization (Z39.48-1984).

10 9 8 7 6 5 4 3 2 1

Contents

Preface

SCOPE

This selective annotated discography focuses mainly on
recordings of Irish folk music from the 1970s forward. The
early 1970s represent the beginning of what has been called
the Irish folk music revival or renaissance. Several titles
from the 1960s, such as <u>O Riada</u>, <u>Sweeney's Men 1968</u>, and <u>The
Johnston's Anthology</u>, are included as examples of early
influences on this rebirth. The entire scope of the discography covers from the 1960s through spring 1987. However,
citations of recordings released since this cut-off date
appear in the notes section of the appropriate entries.

The discography is the first work exclusively to
address and evaluate recordings. Inclusion is based on
printed reviews of the recording or concert performance and
articles about the artist. Availability is also a factor in
selection. With minor exceptions, all entries currently are
in print. A majority are released on major domestic (U.S.)
folk labels, such as Green Linnet Records or Shanachie
Records, with representation from major Irish record labels--
Tara Records and Gael-Linn Records. This should facilitate
easy access to the recordings, especially in the United
States and Canada.

THE ENTRY

The discography section is arranged alphabetically by
principal artist. Recording titles in turn are arranged
alphabetically under the artist. Works without a stated main
artist are listed by title under Various Artists at the end
of the alphabet.

Entries include the following basic information: the
main artist, in bold face and centered above the entry; the
title, underlined; the year of release, if given; and the
record label and number. The artists, including members of
bands, guest artists, solo artists, and producers, and their
instruments are listed next. Information in this regard is
taken directly from the liner notes or the disc. All musicians and producers, including performing groups, appear in the
Artist Index. Contents for the recordings are given as

listed on the disc or in the liner notes. If an alternate
title or translation is provided, such titles appear paren-
thetically after the title. The phrase "also known as"
precedes the alternate title. No attempt has been made to
assign uniform titles for selections known by more than one
name. All contents titles, including alternates and translations, appear in the Title Index.

Annotations follow the basic discographic information.
All entries have been critiqued by the author except for
those with asterisks after the title. The annotations for
the starred entries were culled from reviews, liner notes, or
summary notes from record label catalogs. A code representing available formats--**LP** for record albums, **CS** for
cassettes, and **CD** for compact discs--appears in brackets
after the annotation. The Notes section includes additional
miscellaneous information on the recording and its artists.

ADDITIONAL FEATURES

Aside from the Artist Index and Title Index, this
volume includes a Glossary of musical terms in English and
Irish and a Directory of suggested sources for obtaining the
recordings.

Acknowledgments

Many individuals have assisted, advised, and supported me during the three years this book was in preparation. I would like to thank those who freely gave their time and expertise. My colleagues at Montana State University Libraries always have been available for consultation. They now know more about Irish folk music than they ever wanted and I appreciate their patience and emotional support. Thanks to Bruce Morton, who encouraged me to complete this book and pushed me out the door to get started. Kathy Kaya was my guinea pig for the content. She always was ready to read portions of the text and offer practical suggestions. Lea Lockerman assisted with word processing procedures and rescued this text more than once. Annmarie Evans typed thousands of cards for the indexes and was assisted with the input by Gwen Maxwell. Janet Stroncek provided technical guidance in various capacities and saved the day many times. Thanks also to Marj David for her encouragement.

Several individuals, including Maureen Shea Reader, Margaret Mackin, and Steve Clancy, lent their records for reviews. Wendy Newton and her staff at Green Linnet Records, Inc., provided access to information on recordings and artists associated with their label. The gang at Andy's Front Hall helped with accessing hard to find records. I would also like to thank Fiona Ritchie of the syndicated radio show "The Thistle and Shamrock" for her encouragement and suggestions on records and Shay MacGowan of the band Oisín for his help. Thanks also to Howard and Roz Larman, whose show "Folkscene" on KPFK-FM, Los Angeles, was an early inspiration, and to Paula Karr and Marj Delida for being good friends. I salute the staff at McCabe's Guitar Shop in Santa Monica, California, for sticking their necks out to bring many Irish performers to the West Coast. McCabe's is a first class operation. A big thank you to Greenwood Press for their patience and support, especially to Mary Sive and Marilyn Brownstein. I am grateful to Dave Perkins, General Manager of KGLT-FM, for his confidence in my abilities to create my radio program "The Celtic Tradition" and to my many listeners and radio colleagues, whose cards, letters, and comments have meant so much. My family and friends have had to endure hours of Irish, Celtic, and British music in

concert, on the stereo, and on radio for years. I appreciate
their attempts to understand my obsession with a culture that
was not mine. Thanks to Steve Takata for keeping up my
spirits during the book´s birth. Mo Ghrá Thú a Stiofáin.

And finally, to the musicians both Irish and non-Irish
alike who keep this tradition alive, I dedicate this book.

IRISH
FOLK MUSIC

Introduction

Currently, Irish folk music (and the wider field of
Celtic folk music) is experiencing an immense surge in popularity. This success has not been an overnight sensation nor
is it limited to the Irish shores and people of Irish
heritage. Over the last three decades traditional Irish
music has captured the interest of a worldwide audience of
varying backgrounds. This movement has been proclaimed the
Irish folk music revival or renaissance.

Irish folk music is a means of Irish self-expression
and nationalism. The tunes and songs have been handed down
from generation to generation as part of Ireland's oral
tradition. In addition, printed collections, such as O'Neill
and Petrie, (see reading list following this introduction)
are sources for materials. With the advent of the phono-
graph, Irish music reached a larger, more diversified
populace. Later, as both radio and television became more
affordable, this audience continued to expand.

The manner in which traditional music has been performed also has changed over the years. Prior to the 1920s
it usually was played by a soloist, who may or may not have
been accompanied. Musicians gathered informally in small
groups to play for dances or céilís, but this gathering did
not constitute a formal band. Céilís provided a popular form
of entertainment until the arrival of rock and roll in the
1950s.

The Irish folk music revival came into full bloom in
the 1970s and dynamically continues today. With the ballad
band craze of the fifties and early sixties, groups like the
Clancy Brothers and Tommy Makem provided an early influence.
This trend coincided with the American folk revival, in
which artists such as the Kingston Trio and Peter, Paul &
Mary were extremely popular. The Irish ballad bands also
signaled the beginning of group performing as a dominant part
of the field.

In the midst of the pub ballad bands, pioneer Seán Ó
Riada introduced a more traditional type of music. With his
band, Ceoltóirí Chualann, Ó Riada strived for a classical,

orchestral approach to Irish folk music, utilizing traditional instruments (bodhrán, uilleann pipes, fiddle, etc.)
with the harpsichord. Ó Riada continued as a major force
until his death in 1971. The renowned band the Chieftains
was born from Ceoltóirí Chualann in 1963, recording its first
lp the following year. The Chieftains' approach is more
purist than that of the ballad bands and its arrangements are
like those of a chamber orchestra. The group's high visibility in concert and on record has established it as a key com-
ponent in Irish music.

In the late 1960s subtle ballad groups, like Sweeney's
Men and the Johnstons, provided a link between the pub ballad
bands of the early part of the decade and the more intricate
folk groups that would arrive in the seventies. With the
formation of Planxty in 1972, the Irish revival went into
full swing. Planxty combined traditional music and original
compositions by band members with multi-layered, acoustic
instrumentation led by the uilleann pipes. The group had a
large following and the band members have continued to contribute to the field. Skara Brae, a family band from County
Donegal, offered an earnest side to Irish music. Mícheál,
Tríona, and Mairéad Ó Domhnaill and their cousin Dáithí
Sproule took traditional Gaelic songs and accompanied them
with the clavichord and jazzy acoustic guitars. Skara Brae's
vocal harmonies were an influence on groups like Clannad and
Na Casaidigh.

One of the most celebrated bands of the 1970s was the
Bothy Band. It provided an exciting mixture of traditional
music performed on various instruments, such as the flute,
clavinet, guitar, bouzouki, fiddle, and pipes. The band's
style was intense and showed the outside influences of jazz,
rock, classical, and pop music. The Bothy Band never toured
North America, but its five recordings remain popular worldwide. Other noted bands that became popular at this time
include Boys of the Lough, Clannad, and De Danann. All three
groups continue to perform and record.

Relativity and Moving Hearts serve as excellent
examples of Celtic fusion, a recent trend in Irish music.
Relativity performs both Irish and Scottish traditional
selections with added layers of instrumentation and high
technology to create a vibrant, modern sound. Its music has
been labeled "new age" by some, but that is misleading.
Relativity's music is intelligent and innovative and does not
suffer from the vacuity that plagues some new age artists.
Moving Hearts presents a fusion of Irish folk, jazz, and
rock. Its music is flavored with saxophone and percussion,
plus a liberal spicing of electric and electronic sounds.

Irish music also is present in rock and roll and pop
music. Clannad has shed most of its traditional fare for a
contemporary sound. Paddy Moloney and Seán Keane of the
Chieftains backed Mick Jagger of the Rolling Stones on a
recent solo effort. Kate Bush, an English performer, utilized the talents of Liam Ó Flynn and Donal Lunny on "Jig of
Life" from her album Hounds of Love. This selection is the
most captivating tune on the recording! Ulster rocker Van
Morrison collaborated with the Chieftains on a 1988 release,
Irish Heartbeat, whose freshness and warmth makes it the best

recording from the both artists in some time. A new bent is
the marriage between folk and rock as represented by the
Pogues. The raucous exuberance this London based band produces sets a new standard in the field.

        Innovation and diversification in Irish folk music
satisfies veteran fans and has attracted new listeners from
all walks of life and various ethnic origins. Additionally,
many Irish bands are signing with major American labels, an
act that enhances their visibility and marketability in North
America. The Irish folk music scene indeed is healthy and
the outlook is bright.

FOR FURTHER READING

Breathnach, Brendán. Folk music and dances of Ireland. Rev.
        ed. Dublin: Mercier Press, 1971.

Carson, Ciarán. Pocket guide to Irish traditional music.
        Belfast: Appletree Press, 1986.

Ó Canainn, Tomas. Traditional music of Ireland. London:
        Routledge & Kegan Paul, 1978.

Ó Lochlainn, Colm. The complete Irish street ballads.
        (Combines Irish street ballads, 1939, and More Irish
        street ballads, 1965). London: Pan Books, 1984.

O'Neill, Francis. Irish folk music: a fascinating hobby.
        Philadelphia: R. West, 1977. (reprint of 1910 ed)

O'Neill, Francis. Irish minstrels and musicians. Philadel-
        phia: R. West, 1977. (reprint of 1913 ed)

Petrie, George. Ancient music of Ireland: the Petrie col-
        lection of the ancient music of Ireland. Brookfield,
        VA: Gregg International, 1967.

Discography

1.　Aengus.　(1978)　　　　　　　　　　　　　Tara 2001

    ARTISTS:　Tony Small-guitar, vocals; Jackie Small-uil-
leann pipes, whistle, mandolin, fiddle; Garry O Briain-mandocello, fiddle; with Maurice Lennon-fiddle.　Produced by
Aengus.

        CONTENTS:　Jackson's Morning Brush/Moloney's
        Wife; The Bonny Blue Handkerchief; The Con-
        gress/The Floggin' Reel; When the Cock Crows;
        The Card Game; Barney Brallaghan/Drops of
        Brandy; The Peacock's Feather/Jim Dillon's;
        Seven Irish Boys; The Maid Behind the Bar; Maid
        of the Spinning Wheel/Humours of Ennistymon; In
        Praise of the City of Mullingar; Flax in
        Bloom/The Boyne Hunt/The Bucks of Oranmore

Aengus, a trio from the west of Ireland, consists of Tony and
Jackie Small from Galway, and Garry O Briain, a Dubliner, who
resides in County Clare, where he is involved with collecting
and preserving its local music and lore.　Together, the
Smalls and O Briain present a spirited and confident performance of dance tunes and songs.　Jackie shows his expertise
throughout the album, but especially on "When the Cock
Crows."　Tony contributes four enjoyable songs, and O Briain
furnishes skilled accompaniment on mandocello.　Joining
Aengus for this album is Stockton's Wing's fiddler, Maurice
Lennon, who was the 1977 All-Ireland Senior Fiddle Champion.
Lennon performs a fine solo, "The Maid Behind the Bar," in
addition to his competent accompaniment.　**[LP, CS]**

    NOTES:　Tony Small was a member of Wild Geese, which
recorded on the West German Joke label in the mid and late
1970s.　Their albums include Quay of Galway Town (Joke 201),
their first album (1976), and Flight 2 (Joke 207) (1978).
Jackie Small is very active in the field and can be heard
playing fiddle with Dolores Keane and John Faulkner on Sail
Óg Rua (Green Linnet SIF 3033).　Garry O Briain provides
accompaniment on Buttons and Bows lps, Buttons and Bows

(Green Linnet SIF 1051), and <u>The First Month of Summer</u> (Green Linnet SIF 1079). He is currently a member of Skylark, which recorded <u>Skylark</u> (Claddagh CC 46).

PATRICK BALL

2.   <u>Celtic Harp: The Music of</u>
        <u>Turlough O'Carolan</u>. (1983)   Fortuna FOR 005

   ARTISTS: Patrick Ball-Irish harp. Produced by Dan Drasin.

   CONTENTS: Carolan's Quarrel with the Landlady;
   Maurice O'Connor; Blind Mary; Carolan's Receipt
   for Drinking; Carolan's Ramble to Cashel;
   Carolan's Welcome; Young William Plunkett;
   George Brabazon; Lady Athenry/Fanny Poer; Give
   Me Your Hand; Lady Maxwell; Dermott O'Dowd/The
   Queen's Dream; Mrs. Judge; Carolan's Farewell
   to Music; Sheebeg Sheemore

This refreshing album is the first in a series of solo
recordings by American harper and storyteller Patrick Ball,
who performs exquisitely on the wire-strung Irish harp. The
overall sound quality is crystal clear with a vibrant resonance. Playing the traditional Irish harp, in contrast to
the gut-strung or nylon-strung, neo-Irish harp, is more
difficult, in that the former is played with the fingernails,
which produces a bell-like tonal quality. Ball performs many
well-known Carolan compositions, including "Carolan's Welcome," "Blind Mary," and "Carolan's Farewell to Music." All
the selections are flawlessly executed. **[LP, CS, CD]**

PATRICK BALL

3.   <u>Celtic Harp, Volume Two:</u>
        <u>From a Distant Shore</u>. (1983)   Fortuna FOR 011

   ARTISTS: Patrick Ball-Celtic harp. Produced by Dan Drasin.

   CONTENTS: Come Live with Me and Be My Love
   (England); Greensleeves (England); The Black-
   thorn Stick (Ireland); Down by the Sea (Wales);
   John O'Connor (Ireland); The Grenadier and the
   Lady (Ireland); Londonderry Air (Ireland); The
   Ram on Arthur's Mountain (Contemporary)/Lulla-
   bye (Wales); Three Ravens (England); The Road
   to Lisdoonvarna/The Lark on the Strand (Ire-
   land); The Munster Cloak (Ireland); The Star of
   the County Down (Ireland); Ode to Whiskey
   (Ireland); Dr. John Hart (Ireland); Caitlin
   Triall (Ireland)/ Farewell (The Hebrides); The
   Ash Grove (Wales)

Ball's second album combines the traditional tunes from
Ireland, (many from harper Turlough O'Carolan) with traditional pieces of England, Wales and the Hebrides. A contem-

porary tune written by Lawrence Davis is also included. [LP, CS, CD]

PATRICK BALL

4.   Celtic Harp, Volume III:
        Secret Isles. (1985)   Fortuna FOR 029

     ARTISTS: Patrick Ball-Irish harp. Produced by Dan Drasin.

       CONTENTS: Planxty Burke/Bumper Squire Jones; Carrickfergus; Susie McGuire/Bridget Geary; Lord Inchiquin; Carolan's Favorite Jig; Song of the Water Kelpie/The Sheep Under the Snow; Planxty Irwin; The Foggy Dew; Squire Wood's Lamentation; Carolan's Concerto; Eleanor Plunkett; Dark Woman of the Glen

Volume Three of Ball's excellent continuing series of Irish harp recordings consists of traditional Irish and Manx tunes, plus eight selections composed by Turlough O'Carolan (1670-1738), the best known Irish harper. It is a shame that only two tunes from the tradition of the Isle of Man were included, as both "Song of the Water Kelpie" and "The Sheep Under the Snow" are marvelous. However, Ball earns another A+ for this collection of striking performances. [LP, CS, CD]

DEREK BELL

5.   Carolan's Favourite: the Music
        of Carolan, Volume 2. (1979)   Shanachie 79020

     ARTISTS: Derek Bell-Irish harp, neo-Irish harp; with Paddy Moloney-uilleann pipes, tin whistle, bodhrán; Seán Potts-tin whistle; Michael Tubridy-flute; Seán Keane-fiddle; Martin Fay-fiddle; Kevin Conneff-bodhrán; The New Irish Chamber Orchestra. Produced by Alan Tongue.

       CONTENTS: Aedh Ó Domhnaill (Hugh O'Donnell)/All Alive/Maíre Ní Néill ((Mary O'Neill) and also known as Carolan's Favourite Jig))/Carolan's Fancy; Squire Wood's Lamentation on Ye Refusal of His Halfpence; Seán Jones/Robert Jordan; Lady St. John/Donnchadha Ó Conchubhair (Denis O'Conor); David Poer/Seámus Óg Pluincéad (James Plunkett); Cian Ó hEaghra (Cian O'Hara)/Marbhna Thoirdhealbhach Óg Mhic Donnchadha (Lament for Terence Mac Donough); Bantighearna Dhíolúin (Lady Dillon); Micheal Ó Conchubair (Michael O'Connor); Brighid Crúis (Bridget Cruise)/Carolan's Welcome/Madame Keel; Coirnéal Pamár (Colonel Palmer)/The Right Reverend, the Lord Bishop Mac Mahon of Clogher/Ó Floinn (O'Flinn); Seán Ó hAirt, An Tighearna Oirmhidneach Easpoig Achadch Conaire (The Right Reverend John Hart, the Lord Bishop of Achonry)/Catríona Ó Mordha (Katherine O'More); Bettí

Níc Dhiarmada Ruaidh (Elizabeth Mac Dermott
Roe)/Anna Bean Mhic Dhiarmada Ruaidh (Anna Mac
Dermott Roe); Carolan's Variations on "Cock up
Your Beaver"

Derek Bell is a virtuoso harper, who joined the Chieftains in
the mid-1970s. Classically trained, Bell began to play the
harp in his late thirties, becoming a solo performer with the
BBC Northern Ireland Orchestra in Belfast. His performances
as a member of the Chieftains and as a solo artist are
imaginative, possessing both a lovely simplicity and baroque
intricacy, depending on the music. In contrast to his serious appearance, Bell is a droll comic and an audience favorite on stage. This album is both Bell's second solo record
and his second album devoted to the works of Turlough O
Carolan, Ireland's renowned 18th century harper. As with its
predecessor, Carolan's Receipt (Shanachie 79013), this recording is beautifully performed. Bell is assisted by the
Chieftains and the New Irish Chamber Orchestra. Extensive
background notes on each selection are included. [LP, CS]

                          DEREK BELL

6.   Carolan's Receipt. (1975)   Shanachie 79013

     ARTISTS: Derek Bell-Irish harp, neo-Irish harp,
tiompán; with Paddy Moloney-uilleann pipes, tin whistle,
bodhrán; Seán Potts-tin whistle; Michael Tubridy-flute; Seán
Keane-fiddle; Martin Fay-fiddle. Produced by Paddy Moloney.

     CONTENTS: Sídh Beag agus Sídh Mor; Carolan's
     Receipt (also known as An Dochtúir Seán Staf-
     ford (Dr. John Stafford)); Lady Athenry (Ban-
     tighearna Áltha an Ríogh); Fanny Poer ((Fanny
     Poer) and also known as Mrs Trench of Garbal-
     ly); Máire Dhall (Blind Mary); Sir Festus a
     Búrca (Sir Festus Burke); 'Rúisg, a bhean na
     tabhairne' (Carolan's Quarrel with the Land-
     lady)/Carolan's Ramble to Cashel; Mrs. Poer
     (also known as Carolan's 'Concerto'); Seán Ó
     Conchubhair (John O'Connor)/A h-uiscí chroidhe
     na n-anamann (The Ode to Whiskey); Seóirse
     Brabston (George Brabazon); Máible Ní Chealla-
     igh (Mabel Kelly); Madam Maxwell/Carolan's
     Nightcap/Lady Gethin; Brighid Crúis (Three
     Brighid Crúis airs); Seán Ó Raighilligh (John
     O'Reilly); Carolan's Farewell to Music

Bell's first solo album is also the first recording devoted
entirely to the work of blind harper, Turlough   O'-
Carolan. Carolan's music mixes 17th century Italian baroque
with Irish traditional music and the ancient Irish harp from
a previous era. Its beauty and complexity is breathtaking.
In addition, Carolan's Receipt is the first recording, on
which a metal strung Irish harp is used by an Irish harper.
The harp's tonal quality is bell-like and similar to the
harpsichord. Bell also plays the gut-strung, neo-Irish harp
and a tiompán, which could be called, more or less, an Irish
hammered dulcimer. The Chieftains provide accompaniment on a
few selections, but most are unaccompanied. [LP, CS]

DEREK BELL

7.   Derek Bell's Musical
       Ireland. (1984)   Shanachie 79042

ARTISTS: Derek Bell-Irish harp, neo-Irish harp,
tiompán, oboe cor anglais, gong; with Seán Potts-tin whistle;
Peadar Mercier-bodhrán, bones; New Irish Chamber Orchestra.
Produced by Alan Tongue.

> **CONTENTS:** She Moved through the Fair; The Boys
> of Bluehill/Hillsborough Castle/The Greencastle
> Hornpipe; Carrickfergus (also known as Do Bhí
> Bean Uasal (There was a Lady)); An Caitín Bán
> (The Little White Cat); The Gartan Mother's
> Lullaby; Im Aonar Seal (Alone and Lonely);
> Sliabh Geal gCua (Bright Sliabh gCua); Down by
> the Sally Gardens; Eibhlín a Rúin ((Eileen
> Aroon) and also known as Eileen My Secret
> Love); The Piper through the Meadow Straying;
> Marbhna Luimní (Limerick's Lamentation); Ag
> Críost an Síol (Christ the Seed); Is Trua Gan
> Peata Mhaoir Agam (I Wish the Shepherd's Pet
> were Mine)

Originally recorded in 1982 for Claddagh Records, Bell's
fourth solo album departs from his studies of Turlough
O'Carolan. He has recorded traditional tunes, some of which
have been included in classic printed collections of Irish
tunes and songs by George Petrie and Herbert Hughes, among
others. Arranged by Bell and Alan Tongue, the contents also
include "Ag Críost an Síol," a selection from a folk mass by
the late Seán O Riada, whose group, Ceoltoírí Chualann,
spawned the Chieftains. The album's overall sound is
unpretentious, and is lovely in its simplicity. The uilleann
pipes, a common feature on a Bell album, are not missed in
the arrangements. Each cut is basic, but beautifully performed. "Eibhlín a Rúin" is a very interesting piece, in
which Bell has chosen to play the original tune, then follow
it with two variations played on the neo-Irish harp ("Robin
Adair" and Cornelius Lyon's variation). He ends the medley
by repeating the orignal on the metal-strung Irish harp.
Another outstanding number is "Marbhna Luimní," an ancient
lament based on the defeat of the Irish army at Limerick in
1691. Attributed to County Cavan harper, Myles O'Reilly, it
is believed that Thomas Connellan took the tune to Scotland,
where it is popularly known as "Lochaber No More." [LP, CS]

NOTES: Bell has recorded one other solo album, Derek
Bell Plays with Himself (Claddagh CC 54).

THE BOTHY BAND

Dazzling, innovative, electrifying, vibrant, ... These and
many more complimentary terms have been utilized to describe
the progressive Irish group, the Bothy Band. Although together for only four years, the band recorded a quartet of
lps, which are still highly regarded after nearly ten years.

These four recordings have been reissued domestically by
Green Linnet Records.

The Bothy Band was born from an informal gathering of musicians organized by Tony MacMahon, a TV and radio producer and
accordionist, for a radio show on Irish National Radio. The
group consisted of Paddy Glackin (fiddle), Donal Lunny (bouzouki and vocals), Matt Molloy (flute), Tríona Ní Dhomhnaill
(clavinet and vocals), Paddy Keenan (pipes), Mícheál Ó Domhnaill (guitar), and MacMahon. They started to play regularly
on the weekends in halls and clubs, and for a time were
called Seachtar or 7. MacMahon returned to producing after a
time. Seachtar became the Bothy Band and made its first
official appearance in February 1975 at Trinity College,
Dublin. The magic had begun! Few personnel changes
occurred. Glackin left to finish college and was replaced by
Tommy Peoples, who was later replaced by Kevin Burke in May
1976.

The band's style can be described as inventive. It took
traditional Irish material, both songs and tunes, and infused
the music with touches of jazz, classical, and rock music.
The intense passion and multiple layers of the arrangements
created a vibrancy unmatched by other bands who have attempt-
ed to emulate the Bothy's style. The melody is carried by
three lead instruments--fiddle, flute, and pipes--which are
played as solos or in combination with one another. Bodhrán,
clavinet, bouzouki, and guitar provide rhythm. Mícheál Ó
Domhnaill and Tríona Ní Dhomhnaill, whose material originates
from their aunt Neillí's vast song collection, share vocals.

The Bothy Band played their final concert in August 1979 at
the Ballisadare Festival in Sligo. The members did not
retire from the field and are still very active. Molloy is a
member of the Chieftains, while Lunny has played with the
rejuvenated Planxty and Moving Hearts, in addition to
producing several recordings and scoring the Irish film "Eat
the Peach." Keenan and Burke recorded several solo lps.
Burke and Ó Domhnaill released two well-received albums as a
duo, and Burke is currently a member of Patrick Street.
Tríona Ní Dhomhnaill performs with the Irish American band,
Touchstone, in addition to working with her brother, Mícheál,
in Relativity. Mícheál also has recorded on Windham Hill
Records with Bill Oskay and is an active producer.

8.   Afterhours. (1978)   Green Linnet SIF 3016

     ARTISTS: Kevin Burke-fiddle; Paddy Keenan-uilleann
pipes, whistle, low whistle; Donal Lunny-vocals, bouzouki,
guitar, bodhrán; Matt Molloy-flute; Tríona Ní Dhomhnaill-

vocals, clavinet, harmonium, bodhrán; Mícheál Ó Domhnaill
vocals, guitar, harmonium, organ. Produced by The Bothy
Band.

          CONTENTS: The Kesh Jig/Give Us a Drink of
          Water/Famous Ballymote; The Butterfly; Casadh
          an tSúgáin; Farewell to Erin; The Heathery
          Hills of Yarrow; The Death of Queen Jane; The

Pipe on the Hob/The Hag at the Churn; The
Priest/Mary Willie's/This is My Love, Do You
Like Her?; How Can I Live at the Top of a
Mountain; Rosie Finn's Favourite/Over the Water
to Charlie/The Kid on the Mountain; The Green
Groves of Erin/The Flowers of Red Hill

Afterhours, the group's final lp, was recorded live in Paris
in June 1978, and includes both material previously recorded
on its three studio albums and several new selections. The
sound quality, a problem with many live recordings, is very
good. In addition, the audience reaction has not been completely deleted from the record, which gives a better representation of the band's overall concert performance. A
little interplay between the group and the crowd would have
lent a little more intimacy, but the audience's enthusiasm is
unmistakable. Top instrumental honors go to "Farewell to
Erin," starring Kevin Burke on fiddle, and the wild "The
Piper on the Hob/The Hag at the Churn" set. Vocals are also
highlights with Tríona's unaccompanied "How Can I Live at the
Top of a Mountain," and Mícheál's tragic "The Death of Queen
Jane" the best of the four. **[LP, CS]**

9.   The Best of the
           Bothy Band. (1981)   Green Linnet SIF 3001

   ARTISTS: Tommy Peoples, Matt Molloy, Paddy Keenan,
Donal Lunny, Tríona Ní Dhomhnaill, Kevin Burke, and Mícheál Ó
Domhnaill.

   CONTENTS: The Salamanca/The Banshee/The Sai-
   lor's Bonnet; Pretty Peg/Craig's Pipes; The
   Blackbird; The Maids of Mitchelstown; Casadh an
   tSúgáin; Music in the Glen; Fionnghuala; Old
   Hag You Have Killed Me; Do You Love an Apple?;
   Rip the Calico; The Death of Queen Jane; The
   Green Groves of Erin/The Flowers of Red Hill

The best of the very best! Taken from their four albums,
many of these tunes and songs have become classics. **[LP, CS]**

10.   The Bothy Band Band 1975. (1975)   Green Linnet SIF 3011

   ARTISTS: Paddy Keenan-uilleann pipes, whistle; Donal
Lunny-bouzouki, vocals; Matt Molloy-flute, whistle; Tríona
Ní Dhomhnaill-harpsichord, bodhrán, vocals; Mícheál Ó Domh-
naill-guitar, vocals; Tommy Peoples-fiddle. Produced by
Donal Lunny and Mícheál Ó Domhnaill.

   CONTENTS: The Kesh Jig/Give Us a Drink of
   Water/The Flower of the Flock/Famous Ballymote;
   The Green Groves of Erin/The Flowers of Red
   Hill; Do You Love an Apple?; Julia Delaney;
   Patsy Geary's/Coleman's Cross; Is Trua Nach
   Bhfuil Mé in Éirinn; The Navvy on the Line/The
   Rainy Day; The Tar Road to Sligo/Paddy Clan-
   cy's; Martin Wynne's/The Longford Tinker;
   Pretty Peg/Craig's Pipes; Hector the Hero/The
   Laird of Drumblaire; The Traveller/The Humours

of Lissadell; The Butterfly; The Salamanca/The
Banshee; The Sailor's Bonnet

The Bothy Band's impressive debut contains electrifyingly
performed traditional tunes and songs. A non-stop dynamism,
the recording's highlights include "Julia Delaney," and
"Hector the Hero/The Laird of Drumblair," featuring the
powerful fiddling of Tommy Peoples. Paddy Keenan on Irish
pipes gives a stellar performance with "Patsy Geary's/Cole-
man's Cross." Matt Molloy's flute shines on "The Travel-
ler/The Humours of Lissadell." The ensemble is excellent on
"The Kesh Jig/Give Us A Drink of Water/The Flower of the
Flock/Famous Ballymote," "Martin Wynne's/The Longford Tinker," and "The Butterfly." Vocally, the Ó Domhnaills are in
fine form with three numbers. Tríona uses her lilting style
and rich interpretation to bring "Do You Love an Apple" and
"Pretty Peg" to life. Mícheál offers the quiet, evocative
Irish song, "Is Trua Nach Bhfill me in Éirinn." **[LP, CS]**

11.   <u>Old Hag You Have
       Killed Me</u>. (1976)   Green Linnet SIF 3005

       ARTISTS: Matt Molloy-flute, whistle; Paddy Keenan-
uilleann pipes, whistle, low whistle; Kevin Burke-fiddle;
Tríona Ní Dhomhnaill-vocals, clavinet, harmonium; Mícheál Ó
Domhnaill-vocals, guitar; Donal Lunny-vocals, bouzouki, guitar, bodhrán. Produced by Donal Lunny and Mícheál Ó Domhnaill.

       CONTENTS: Music in the Glen; Fionnghuala, The
       Kid on the Mountain; Farewell to Erin; Tioch-
       faidh An Samhradh (Summer Will Come); The
       Laurel Tree; 16 Come Next Sunday; Old Hag You
       Have Killed Me; Calum Sgaire; The Ballintore
       Fancy; The Maid of Coolmore; Michael Gorman's

The Bothy Band performs a mixture of driving Irish tunes with
several splendid songs. This lp also introduces the talents
of fiddler, Kevin Burke, who replaces Tommy Peoples. The
multi-layered ensemble tunes are excellent. "Music in the
Glen" serves to musically introduce the band. Each of the
three leads--Burke, Paddy Keenan, and Matt Molloy--solo in
the midst of an energetic rhythm section. Another example,
"The Kid on the Mountain," stars Molloy on flute. On
"Michael Gorman's" each layer of instrumentation gradually
joins to create a free-wheeling abandon. The entire band is
outstanding throughout the recording, and Keenan is absolutely amazing on pipes. The Ó Domhnaills offer five vocal
gems. "The Maid of Coolmore," exquisitely performed by
Tríona, is lovely and mesmerizing. Vocal harmonies and
Mícheál's lead set "Calum Sgaire" apart from the crowd.
Tríona gives charm to "16 Come Next Sunday" and Mícheál's
plaintive vocals on "Tiocfaidh An Samhradh (Summer Will
Come)" fill it with longing. The show stopper, "Fionnghu-
ala," contains the unique sounds of Scottish mouth music.
Its fast pace and harmonies make it a wonderful classic.
[LP, CS]

12.   Out of the Wind
      Into the Sun. (1977)   Green Linnet SIF 3013

      ARTISTS: Paddy Keenan-uilleann pipes, low whistle, B$_b$
chanter; Matt Molloy-flute, whistle; Kevin Burke-fiddle;
Tríona Ní Dhomhnaill-vocals, clavinet, harmonium, electric
piano; Donal Lunny-bouzouki, guitar, bodhrán, synthesizer;
Mícheál Ó Domhnaill-guitar. Produced by Donal Lunny and
Mícheál Ó Domhnaill.

      CONTENTS: The Morning Star: The Morning
      Star/The Fisherman's Lilt, The Drunken Land-
      lady; The Maids of Mitchelstown; Rip the Cali-
      co: The Leitrim Fancy, Round the World for
      Sport (also known as Sword in Hand), Rip the
      Calico, Martin Wynne's Reel, The Enchanted
      Lady, The Holy Land; The Streets of Derry (also
      known as Derry Gaol); The Pipe on the Hob/The
      Hag at the Churn; The Sailor Boy (also known as
      My Boy Willie); The Blackbird; The Strayaway
      Child; The Factory Girl; Slides: The Priest,
      Mary Willie's, This is My Love, Do You Like
      Her?

The band produces another excellent recording with its third
and last studio album. All the material is traditional
except for the marvelous six part jig, "The Strayaway Child,"
written by the late Sligo fiddler, Michael Gorman, and
"Wynne's," a reel by Martin Wynne in the "Rip the Calico"
set. Most of the exceptional tunes are arranged in sets with
"The Pipe on the Hob" and "Rip the Calico" sets fine examples
of the group's prowess. Contrasting these vigorous tunes is
the more sedate reel, "The Maids of Mitchelstown," which
utilizes Molloy's flute for the melody and Burke's sweet
harmony on fiddle. One disappointment is that at least one
song by Mícheál Ó Domhnaill is not included. His sister,
Tríona sings three selections with the striking "The Factory
Girl" the most satisfying. **[LP, CS]**

      NOTES: Recordings by Bothy Band members include Tommy
Peoples' solo lps, The High Part of the Road (Shanachie
29003) and The Iron Man (Shanachie 79044) and Kevin Burke's
If the Cap Fits... (Green Linnet SIF 3009), Sweeney's Dream
(Folkways 8876), and Up Close (Green Linnet SIF 1052). Burke
and Mícheál Ó Domhnaill recorded Promenade (Green Linnet SIF
3010) and Portland (Green Linnet SIF 1041) as a duo. Burke
is also active with Patrick Street. Paddy Keenan has two
solo lps, Paddy Keenan (Gael-Linn CEF 045) and Poirt an
Phíobaire (Gael-Linn CEF 099). Donal Lunny recently
released his first solo lp, Donal Lunny (Gael-Linn CEF 133),
and he appears on The Gathering (Greenhays GR 705). Lunny is
a busy producer and was a founding member of both Planxty and
Moving Hearts. He also composed the soundtrack to the Irish
film "Eat the Peach." Tríona Ní Dhomhnaill has one solo lp,
Tríona (Green Linnet SIF 3034), and has performed with Skara
Brae, Touchstone, and Relativity. She contributes accompaniment on Notes from My Mind by Seamus Connolly (Green Linnet
SIF 1087), Mairead Ní Dhomhnaill (Gael-Linn CEF 055), her
sister's recording, Something of Time (Windham Hill WH 1057)
by Nightnoise, Celtic Folkweave (Polydor 2908 013), and Fresh
Takes (Green Linnet SIF 1075) by Whelan & Ivers. Matt Molloy

currently is a member of the Chieftains and also played with
the rejuvenated Planxty. He has several solo lps, Matt
Molloy (Green Linnet SIF 3008), The Heathery Breeze (Shanachie 79064), and Stony Steps (Green Linnet SIF 3041).
Molloy also appears on The Gathering (Greenhays GR 705) and
was a part of the trio of Molloy/Peoples/Brady, whose album
by the same name is a classic (Green Linnet SIF 3018).
Finally, Mícheál Ó Domhnaill is active in producing and
accompaning and was a part of Skara Brae. He recorded Celtic
Folkweave (Polydor 2908 013) with Mick Hanly and is currently
working with Relativity. Ó Domhnaill also records with
Nightnoise, which has two lps, Nightnoise (Windham Hill WH
1031) and Something of Time (Windham Hill WH 1057). The band
also appears on the Christmas recording, A Winter's Solstice
(Windham Hill WH 1045).

BOYS OF THE LOUGH

For more than fifteen years Boys of the Lough has provided
audiences and listeners with solid, straightforward, professional performances. The band's tastefully arranged music is
striking, polished, and energetic. Aly Bain, the outstanding
Shetland fiddler, Ulsterman, Cathal McConnell, with his
evocative vocals and flawless flute and tin whistle, and Dave
Richardson of Northumbria, the marvelous multi-talented
instrumentalist, make up the core of the band, which has
included Robin Morton, co-founder of Boys of the Lough, the
renowned Scottish minstrel Dick Gaughan, and Richardson's
brother, Tich. The band has survived numerous line-up
changes and has managed to bounce back from these personnel
changes with an even fresher sound than before. Lesser
groups would have split, but the Boys have persevered.

13.   The Boys of the Lough. (1973)   Shanachie 79002

    ARTISTS: Cathal McConnell-vocals, flute, whistle;
Robin Morton-vocals, bodhrán, concertina; Aly Bain-fiddle;
Dick Gaughan-vocals, guitar, mandolin. Produced by Bill
Leader.

        CONTENTS: The Boys of the Lough/Slanty Gart;
        In Praise of John Magee; Wedding March from
        Unst/The Bride's a Bonny Thing/Sleep Sound i'
        da Moarnin' (also known as Out and In the
        Harbour and also as The Gutters of Skeld);
        Farewell to Whiskey; Old Joe's Jig/Last Night's
        Joy; The Granny in the Corner; The Old Oak
        Tree; Caoineadh Eoghain Rua (Lament for Owen
        Roe)/The Nine Points of Roguery; Docherty's
        Reel (also known as The Killarney Boys of
        Pleasure)/The Flowing Tide; Andrew Lammie;
        Sheebeg and Sheemore/The Boy in the Gap/
        McMahon's Reel; Jackson and Jane; The Shaalds
        of Foulla (The Fields of Foulla)/Garster's
        Dream/The Brig

The band's debut album is a delightful recording. Gaughan
scores with two electrifying vocals, "Andrew Lammie" and
"Farewell to Whiskey." The rapport between the musicians is

evident on all the selections. They complement each other
well and all four are given an opportunity to shine in their
own right. Bain is absolutely remarkable on fiddle. He has
such a love for the music of his native Shetland and a deep
understanding of Ireland's musical traditions. Morton and
McConnell are at their best with the humorous "In Praise of
John McGee." The lovely air, "Caoineadh Eoghain Rua," performed by the latter duo on flute and concertina, and the
following tune, "Nine Points of Roguery," are classics. **[LP,
CS]**

14.   Far From Home. (1986)   Shanachie 79065

   ARTISTS: Aly Bain-fiddle; Cathal McConnell-flute,
whistle; Dave Richardson-concertina, cittern, mandoline; Tich
Richardson-guitar. Produced by Peter Harris and Dave Richardson.

   CONTENTS: Far from Home/Hurlock's Reel/Da
   Peerie House Ahint Da Burn/Da Merrie Boys of
   Greenland; The Gates of the Yellow Town/The
   Eagle's Whistle; Petticoat Loose/The Geese in
   the Bog/The Connaughtman's Rambles; Da Slockit
   Light/Crossing the Minch/The Laird of Drum-
   blair/The Fairy Dance; The Barrowburn Reel; The
   Ballydesmond Polka/Polka No. 1/Polka No. 2; The
   Hanged Man's Reel; The Mason's Apron; For
   Ireland I'd Not Tell Her Name.

Far From Home captures the band live on its 1984 world tour.
This all instrumental lp presents a collection of exuberant
tunes by these dynamic musicians. Top honors go to "Da
Slockit Light/Crossing the Minch/The Laird of Drumblair/The
Fairy Dance," featuring Aly Bain in expert form on these
fiddle tunes. McConnell is amazing on whistle with "The
Mason's Apron." The Richardson brothers, Tich and Dave,
provide solid accompaniment throughout. The album ends with
the beautiful air, "For Ireland I'd Not Tell Her Name," a
perennial favorite. This recording is dedicated to the
memory of Tich Richardson, who was killed in an automobile
accident in Scotland in 1984. **[LP, CS]**

15.   Farewell and Remember Me. (1987)   Shanachie 79067

   ARTISTS: Aly Bain-fidle; Cathal McConnell-flute,
whistle, vocals; Dave Richardson-concertina, mandolin, cittern; Christy O'Leary-uilleann pipes, whistle, vocals; John
Coakley-guitar, piano, bodhrán, mandolin, fiddle; with Ron
Shaw-cello. Produced by Peter Harris and Boys of the Lough.

   CONTENTS: Sean Bui/Tommy Peoples'/The Lark in
   the Morning; The Leitrim Queen; Lucky Can Du
   Link Ony/Pottinger's/Billy Nicholson; Farewell
   and Remember Me; Angus Polka No. 1/Angus Polka
   No. 2/Donegal Barn Dance; An Spailpín Fánach/
   The One-Horned Buck; Valentia Harbour (also
   known as The Story of the Books)/The Jug of
   Punch/MacArthur Road; Lovely Ann; The Holly

Bush/The New Ships Are Sailing; The Waterford
Waltz/The Stronsay Waltz

The Boys' new lineup successfully blends enjoyable songs and
spirited dance tunes mostly from Ireland and the Shetlands.
Cathal McConnell and Christy O'Leary share vocal chores with
four outstanding songs. The best of these are McConnell's
unaccompanied "Lovely Ann," and O'Leary with a song from the
late 1700s, "An Spailpín Fánach." Instrumentally, selections
range from the animated Shetland reels, "Lucky Can Du Link
Ony/Pottinger's/Billy Nicholson," to the graceful air,
"Valentia Harbour," which is splendidly performed on pipes by
O'Leary. Other notable tunes include "The Holly Bush/The New
Ships are Sailing," which prominently features O'Connell on
flute and O'Leary on pipes, and "Angus Polka No. 1/Angus
Polka No. 2/Donegal Barn Dance," a fine vehicle for fiddler,
Aly Bain. **[LP, CS, CD]**

16.   Good Friends-Good Music. (1977)   Philo PH 1051

   ARTISTS: Robin Morton-bodhrán, concertina; Aly Bain-
fiddle; Cathal McConnell-flute, whistle; Dave Richardson-
cittern, mandolin, banjo; with Tony McMahon-accordion; Barney
McKenna-banjo; Vincent Griffin-fiddle; Finlay MacNeill-vocal,
Highland pipes; Tom Anderson-fiddle; Willie Johnson-guitar;
Jimmy Cooper-dulcimer; Louis Beaudoin-fiddle; Willie Beau-
doin-guitar; Sylvia Blaise-piano; Jay Ungar-fiddle; Lyn
Hardy-guitar; Kenny Hall-mandolin, guitar; Eamon Curran-uil-
leann pipes; Robbie Hughes-uilleann pipes; Dierdre Shannon-
fiddle; Tommy Gunn-fiddle, lilting; Brendan Gunn-fiddle; Tony
Smith-fiddle; Pat Hanly-flute; John Joe Morgan-flute.
Produced by Boys of the Lough.

      CONTENTS: Breton Wedding March/The Wild Irish-
      man (also known as O'Rourke's Reel)/The
      Scholar; Down the Broom/The Gatehouse Maid;
      Gaelic Mouth Music; Farewell to Gilbraltar/Cap-
      tain Horne/The High Road to Linton; Far from
      Home/Da Road to Houll; Hillswick Wedding/Ro-
      bertson's Reel; Cadam Woods (also known as
      Mystley Castle)/The Bonnie Lass of Bon Accord;
      La Grande Chaîne/The Newlyweds' Reel; Kitchen
      Girl/The New Riggit Ship; Canadian Waltz;
      Hop-High Ladies; Dennis Murphy's Hornpipe/Lea-
      ther Britches (also known as McDonald's Reel
      and also as Slanty Gart); The Humours of Ennis-
      tymon/The First House in Connaught/Roll Her in
      the Rye-Grass; Kitty's Gone A-Milkin/Master
      McDermott's Reel; The Flail/Paddy Doory's
      Jig/The Pride of Leinster; The Midsummer's
      Night (also known as Mrs. McKnight's Reel)/The
      Tinker's Daughter/The Crock of Gold

One of the band's best albums to date. A unique anthology of
performers who have influenced Boys of the Lough are in the
spotlight with the group playing a secondary role on the
selections. Performances by Tom Anderson, Finlay MacNeill,
Willie Johnson, John Joe Maguire, Tommy Gunn, Kenny Hall,
Louis Beaudoin and Jimmy Cooper are the highlights. **[LP,
CS]**

17.   In the Tradition.   (1981)   Flying Fish FF 263

   ARTISTS: Aly Bain-fiddle; Cathal McConnell-flute,
whistle, vocals; Dave Richardson-concertina, mandolin, cittern, banjo; Tich Richardson-guitar, acoustic bass guitar.
Produced by Boys of the Lough.

   CONTENTS: Out on the Ocean/Padeen O'Rafferty/
   Isabelle Blackley; Kiss Her under the Cover-
   let/The Lads of Alnwick; The Road to Cashel/
   Paddy Kelly's; Lord Gregory (also known as The
   Lass of Roch Royal); Dark Woman of the Glen
   (Bean Dubh a'Ghleanna); J. O. Forbes Esq of
   Corse/The Hawk/Charles Sutherland; Eddie
   Kelly's/The Green Fields of Glentown; The
   Eclipse/The Tailor's Twist; Biddy from
   Sligo/The Sunset/Peoples' Reel; Padriag
   O'Keefe's/Con Cassidy's; The Sea Apprentice;
   Miss McDonald; For Ireland I'd Not Tell Her
   Name (Ar Éirinn ní 'neosfainn cé hí)

Another winning combination of dance tunes and songs from
this Scots, Irish and Northumbrian band. In the Tradition,
the group's ninth album is a fine example of its work. The
variety of selections from jigs, reels and hornpipes to slow
airs and songs is well-chosen. "Lord Gregory," a ballad
included in Alan Lomax's collection of Childe ballads,
(recorded on Topic Records 12T160), the Scottish set of
tunes, "J. O. Forbes Esq of Corse/The Hawk/Charles Sutherland," and two airs, "Dark Woman of the Glen" and "For Ireland I'd Not Tell Her Name," are the finest works. The
latter air, popularized by Seán O'Riada and Ceoltóirí Chualann, is traditionally believed to be the aisling type of
poetry commmon in the 18th century. The young girl in the
poem is allegorical Ireland. **[LP]**

18.   Live at Passim. (1975)   Philo 1026

   ARTISTS: Cathal McConnell, Aly Bain, Robin Morton,
Dave Richardson.   Produced by Boys of the Lough.

   CONTENTS: The Kincora Jig/Behind the Haystack;
   The Day Dawn/Pit Hame da Borrowed Claes/Da
   Fashion o'da Delting Lasses/Da Peerie House
   under da Hill; General Guinness; The Boys of
   Twenty-Five/The Boyne Hunt/Chase Her through
   the Garden; The Flower of Magherally; The Hound
   and the Hare; The Cameron Highlanders/The
   Balkan Hills/The Atholl and Breadalbane Gathering; The New Set: The Golden Slipper, The
   Streamstown Jig, Johnny McIljohn's Reel, Sonny's Mazurka; The Shores of Lough Bran; Ar
   Eirinn Ni'neosfainn Ce Hi (For Ireland I'd Not
   Tell Her Name)/The Whinny Hills of Leitrim
   (also known as Leitrim Town)/Another Jig Will
   Do; The Darling Baby; The Nine Points of Roguery (also known as The Black Mare of Fan-
   nad)/The Oak Tree

Recorded live at Passim, a club in Cambridge, Massachusetts,
Boys of the Lough proves to be as vibrant in person as it is
on disc. Eight tightly woven instrumental sets are offset by
a pair of vocals from both McConnell and Morton. McConnell's
"The Flower of Magherally" and "The Shores of Lough Bran" are
quite lovely, while Morton treats the audience to two comical
pieces, "The Darling Baby," and "General Guinness," a liquid
officer of the first rank. Live at Passim does justice to
the band and capturing it in good form. [LP]

19.   Lochaber No More. (1976)   Philo 1031

     ARTISTS: Dave Richardson-cittern, mandolin, banjo,
concertina; Aly Bain-fiddle; Cathal McConnell-flute, whistle,
vocals; Robin Morton-bodhrán, concertina, vocals. Produced
by Boys of the Lough.

          CONTENTS: Lochaber No More; The Laird O'Drum-
          blair/Millbrae; The Blantyre Explosion; The
          Blarney Pilgrim/Jackson's Jig; The Mountain
          Streams Where the Moorcock's Crow; The Trowie
          Burn; Haughton House/Kataroni/Da Back Reel; One
          Thing or the Other; A 'Da Ships are Sailin'/
          Shelder Geo/Tame Her When da Snaw Comes; The
          Bonny Blue-Eyed Lass; Jackie Donnan's Mazurka/
          Bonnie Charlie; Farewell to Ireland

On this fourth album the music of Scotland and the Shetland
Islands is emphasized. Selections of note include "The
Blantyre Explosion," "Farewell to Ireland," the "Haughton
House" set, and the title track, "Lochaber No More," which is
a piping tune played as a lament at funerals. [LP]

20.   Open Road. (1983)   Flying Fish FF 310

     ARTISTS: Aly Bain-fiddle; Cathal McConnell-flute,
whistle, vocals; Dave Richardson-concertina, mandolin, cittern; Tich Richardson-guitar, acoustic bass; with Savourna
Stevenson-harp. Produced by Boys of the Lough and Peter
Harris.

          CONTENTS: Calliope House/Gerry O'Connor's Jig
          in A/The Setting Sun; Harvest Home/Toss the
          Feathers; The Clay of Kilcreggan; On Raglan
          Road; The Dying Year/Madame Vanoni; Big Terry
          McAloon's/Tommy People's/Jenny Dang the Weaver;
          The Flower of the Quern/The Bonawe Highlanders/
          Earl Grey/The Spey in Spate; Trotting to Larne/
          The Black Cock of Whickham; Lough Erne; The
          Gates of the Yellow Town (Geaftai Bhaile Bui)/
          The Eagle's Whistle; Petticoat Loose/The Geese
          in the Bog/The Connaughtman's Rambles

The Boys' tenth album contains more slower pieces than usual.
Some tunes are enhanced by guest artist, Savourna Stevenson,
on harp. In contrast to the airs, Aly Bain excels with the
1930s Scots set, "The Dying Year/Madame Vanoni," and the
Richardson brothers add a touch of their Northumbrian heritage to the album's lively instrumentals. [LP]

21.   The Piper's Broken Finger. (1976)   Philo PH 1042

   ARTISTS: Robin Morton, Dave Richardson, Cathal McConnell, Aly Bain; with Finlay MacNeill-highland pipes; Gilles Losier-piano. Produced by Boys of the Lough.

   CONTENTS: Lady Anne Montgomery/The Highland Man that Kissed His Grannie/O'Connor Donn's; The Greenland Man's Tune/Da Forefit o' da Ship/Heave and Go; O'Reilly from the County Cavan; Colonel Robertson/The Atholl Highlanders; The Shamrock Shore; Da Sixereen/Gordon's Favourite; The Lament for Limerick; Millbank Cottage/Sandy Duff/The Ale is Dear; The West of Ireland; Johnny Will You Marry Me (also known as The Braes of Mar); The Rushes Green; The Torn Petticoat/The Piper's Broken Finger/The Humours of Ballyconnell (also known as Captain Rock); The Old Favourite/Bobby Gardiner's Jig

The band is joined by piper Finlay MacNeill, who broke his finger during the recording session. Hence, the title! [LP, CS]

22.   Regrouped. (1980)   Flying Fish FF 225

   ARTISTS: Aly Bain, Cathal McConnell, Dave Richardson, Tich Richardson, with Len Graham and Martin O'Connor. Produced by Boys of the Lough.

   CONTENTS: The Star of Munster; Owen Hacket's Jig/The King's Favourite/The Rocking Chair; Willie O; The Bamboo Flute/Albert House/Annalese Bain; The Castle/Mulqueen's; Anac-cuain/ The Humours of Ballinahinch (also known as Mullen's Fancy)/The Floggin; I'll Buy Boots for Maggie/O'Connor's Polka; Moorlough Mary; The City of Savannah/The Acrobat/Off to California; Da Tushkar/Susan Cooper/Millbrae; Jog Along/The Cup of Tea Set

The band's eighth album introduces new member, Tich Richardson, Dave Richardson's brother, who replaces Robin Morton, an original member who left the band in 1979. Tich's guitar accompaniment adds a new dimension to the group's arrangements, giving many selections rhythmic support similar to the piano so often used in Scottish tunes. Also joining Boys of the Lough are guest artists, Martin O'Connor, an accordionist from Galway, and Len Graham of County Antrim, a singer and bodhrán player. Graham sings a duet with Cathal, "Jog Along," and provides the driving force on bodhrán for the reel set, "The Castle/Mulqueen's." O'Connor's accordion is very haunting on "Anac-cuain" and gives an added layer on two polkas he taught the band, "I'll Buy Boots for Maggie/O'Connor's Polka." As always Boys of the Lough exudes talent and professionalism in its performances. [LP]

   NOTES: Martin O'Connor has recorded The Connachtman's Rambles for Green Linnet (SIF 3012). He performs with De Danann.

23.   <u>Second Album</u>. (1974)   Rounder Records 3006

    ARTISTS: Aly Bain, Robin Morton, Cathal McConnell,
Dave Richardson; with Alison Kinnaird-Scottish knee-harp,
clarsach (or Scottish harp). Produced by Bill Leader, Henry
Miller and Walter Koehli.

    CONTENTS: Da Lerwick Lasses/Da Scalloway
Lasses/Da Underhill/Da Galley Watch; An Goirtin
Eornan (The Little Field of Barley); Sally
Monroe; Patsy Campbell; The Gravel Walk; Lough
Erne; The Gold Ring; The Halting March (also
known as The Pikeman's March); Lovely Nancy;
Merrily Kiss the Quaker's Wife (also Merrily
Kiss the Crater)/Padriac O'Keefe's Slide; A Yow
Cam' ta Wir Door Yarmin' (A Ewe Came to Our
Door Bleating)/Christmas Day ida Moarnin'; The
Lass with the Bonny Brown Hair; Lowrie Tar-
rell/The Mason's Apron

This album introduces Dave Richardson, the first Englishman
to perform with the group. He brings tunes from his native
Northumbria and plays wonderfully on various stringed instruments. Alison Kinnaird, the wife of Robin Morton, joins the
band for this album. The two tunes for which she provides
harp accompaniment, "The Halting March" and "An Goirtin
Eornan" are only two of the album's highlights. **[LP]**

24.   <u>To Welcome Paddy Home</u>. (1985)   Shanachie 79061

    ARTISTS: Aly Bain-fiddle; Cathal McConnell-flute,
whistle, vocal; Dave Richardson-concertina, mandolin, tenor
banjo, cittern; Christy O'Leary-uilleann pipes, harmonica,
whistle, vocal; John Coakley-guitar, piano. Produced by
Peter Harris and Boys of the Lough.

    CONTENTS: When Sick is it Tea You Want?/Done-
gal Highland/Johnny McIljohn's No. 1/Johnny
McIljohn's No. 2; To Welcome Paddy Home; Miss
Rowan Davies; The Antrim Rose/Miss McGuinness/
Brereton's; The Tombigbee Waltz/The Ennis
March; Cape Breton Wedding Reel No. 1/Cape
Breton Wedding Reel No. 2/Cape Breton Wedding
Reel No. 3; Alexander's/The Green Cockade; The
Rose of Ardee; The Teelin March/Father O'Flynn;
Eugene Stratton/The Constitution/President
Garfield's

For the first time in the band's history it is a quintet.
After the death of Tich Richardson the remaining members
decided to change the Boys' sound to include Irish pipes and
piano accompaniment. It is also the first time these instruments have been included on a regular basis. Enter, Christy
Leary of Kerry and John Coakley from Cork. They help provide
a fuller sound, giving the band greater depth. The album is
mostly Irish tunes and songs, plus a wonderfully spirited
Cape Breton set. The fullness of the added instrumentation
is especially evident on the "Breton Wedding Reels," "Miss
Rowan Davies," and the reel set, "The Antrim Rose/Miss
McGuiness/Brereton's." O'Leary tastefully sings the title

track, but it is McConnell's moving song, "The Rose of
Ardee," that is the show stopper; Coakly admirably accompanies him. **[LP, CS]**

25. <u>Wish You Were Here: Highlands
     and Islands Tour</u>.   Flying Fish FF 070

    ARTISTS: Dave Richardson, Aly Bain, Robin Morton,
Cathal McConnell. Produced by Boys of the Lough.

    CONTENTS: The Barmaid (also known as The Maid
Behind the Bar)/Chase Her Through the Garden;
The Lark's March; The Red Haired Man's Wife
(Bhan an Fhir Rua); The Resting Chair/Leaving
Glenurquhart/The Fairy Dance (also known as Old
Molly Hare); The Full-Rigged Ship/Naked and
Bare/The Graemsay Jig; An Chuifhionn (The Cool-
in)/The Athol Highlanders' Farewell to Loch
Katrine/Lady Mary Ramsay/The Spey in Spate;
Mickey Docherty's Slip Jig/The West Clare
Reel/Gorman's Two-Step; On Board of the Vic-
tory; Lady Livingstone/The Iron Man/The Humours
of Tulla; Mary McMahon/The Galway Rambler/The
Castlebar Tramp; The Glasgow Police Pipers/The
Curlew; The Green Fields of America/The Bag of
Potatoes/Puck's Reel

An in-concert album from the band's tour of the village halls
of the Highlands and Islands of Scotland in late summer of
1978. The date is not on the album, but since Robin Morton
left the group in early 1979, and the last album was recorded
in 1977, it can be estimated that the tour occurred in 1978.
[LP]

    NOTES: Boys of the Lough released <u>Sweet Rural Shade</u>
(Shanachie 79068) in 1988. Solo lps from the band include
Cathal McConnell's <u>On Lough Erne's Shore</u> (Topic 12TS 377),
and McConnell and Morton's <u>An Irish Jubilee</u> (Topic 12T 290).
Aly Bain has recorded <u>Silver Bow</u> (Topic 12TS 281), <u>Shetland
Fiddling, Volume Two</u> (Topic 12TS 379), both with Tom Ander-
son, <u>Aly Bain</u> (Whirlie 001), a 1984 release, and <u>Aly Bain and
Mike Whellans</u> (Trailer 2022).

PAUL BRADY

26. <u>Welcome Here Kind   Green Linnet SIF 3015
     Stranger</u>. (1978)

    ARTISTS: Paul Brady-mandolin, whistle, guitar, har-
monium, bouzouki, vocals; with Tommy Peoples-fiddle; Noel
Hill-concertina; Andy Irvine-hurdy gurdy, mandolin, harmonica; Donal Lunny-bouzouki. Produced by Donal Lunny and Paul
Brady.

    CONTENTS: Don't Come Again; I Am a Youth
that's Inclined to Ramble; Jackson and Jane;
The Lakes of Pontchartrain; The Creel; Out the
Door and Over the Wall; Young Edmund in the

Lowlands Low; The Boy on the Hilltop/Johnny
Goin' to Céilidh; Paddy's Green Shamrock Shore.

Paul Brady, a member of two early Celtic revival groups, the
Johnstons and Planxty, is a very polished musician and singer
with an expressive and unique vocal style. Welcome Here Kind
Stranger, his first solo album, (originally on the Mulligan
Music label), was released shortly after the acclaimed record
Brady made with Planxty mate, Andy Irvine, Andy Irvine and
Paul Brady, also a reissue on Green Linnet (SIF 3006).
Brady's vocals are the highlights of this outing. His interpretations and style are warm and innovative. One of the
best is "The Lakes of Pontchartrain." In addition to his
enchanting vocals, Brady's guitarwork is marvelous, but he
does not limit himself to the guitar for accompaniment. On
"The Creel," for example, Brady has utilized multitracking,
enabling him to play guitar, bouzouki, mandolin, plus
vocals. "Out of the Door and Over the Wall" finds Brady
performing on tin whistles and bouzouki. The overall sound
and solid Balkan flavor of this tune is striking. Paul Brady
is currently recording contemporary works, but with the
reissue of his albums, his important contributions to the
Irish music scene can be enjoyed once again. [LP]

NOTES: Paul Brady has recorded several contemporary
albums, which include Hard Station (1981) on the British
Polydor label, Full Moon (Demon Fiend 34), the 1983 True to
You, which was domestically released on Atlantic's 21 Records
(90504), Back to the Centre (Phonogram (Mercury) MERH 86),
and Primitive Dance (Mercury MERH 106). Brady also has
worked on the soundtracks of "Cal," collaborating with Mark
Knopfler of Dire Straits, and "Eat the Peach," in which he
worked with Donal Lunny. Two of Brady's compositions,
"Steel Claw" and "Paradise is Here," have been recorded by
Tina Turner. He also appears on the folk recording, The
Gathering (Greenhays GR 705) and Paul Brady and John Vesey
(Shanachie 29006).

ÉAMON DE BUITLÉAR AGUS CEOLTÓIRÍ LAIGHEAN

27.   An Bóthar Cam (The Crooked Road).   Gael Linn 035

ARTISTS: Seán Ó Liatháin-vocals; Diarmuid O´ Súillea-
bháin-vocals; John Kelly-fiddle; Paddy Glackin-fiddle; James
Kelly-fiddle, concertina; Peter Phelan-uilleann pipes; Mí-
cheál Ó hAlmháin-flute, whistle; Aileen McCrann-harp; Paddy
O´Brien-accordion; Mary Bergin-flute, whistle; Éamon de
Buitléar-bodhrán, accordion. Recorded by Pat Hughes.

CONTENTS: An Bóthan Cam (The Crooked Road)/
Diúc Laighean agus a Bhean (The Duke of Leinster and His Wife); Sláinte Bhreá Hewlett (A
Fine Toast to Hewlett); Airgead Réalach (Sixpenny Money); Máthair Mo Chéile (My Mother-
in-Law); Neil Spóirtiúil (Sporting Nell)/Ámhar
´sa nGrá (Lucky in Love); Seán Ó Duibhir
a´Ghleanna (John O´Dwyer of the Glen); Murtach
Mac Cana (Murtagh McCann); Dé Bheatha- sa, a
Pheaití (God Welcome You, Patty!); Drúcht na
Maidne (The Morning Dew); Amhrán a´Steaimpí

(The Song of the Stampy); Na Cosáin Ghriothail
(The Gravel Walks); A Ghrá, Luigh Láimh Liom (O
Love, Lie Beside Me)

Ceoltóirí Laighean is a loosely formed group of musicians,
lead by Colonel Éamon de Buitleár, who was a member of Seán Ó
Riada's Ceoltóirí Chualann. Recorded live in Dublin at
University College, <u>The Crooked Road</u> consists of jigs, dance
tunes and songs. The overall sound quality leaves something
to be desired, and the selections are fairly standard, but
the performers are good. Highlights include two songs from
vocalists Ó Liatháin and Ó Súilleabháin, "Welcome Back
Patsy," and "The Song of Stampy." The best instrumental
selections are the lively reels, especially the well-performed "The Morning Dew" and "The Gravel Walk." Liner notes
on the musicians, background on each selection, and lyrics to
the songs are in both English and Irish. (No date is given).
[LP]

JOE BURKE

28.   <u>The Tailor's
       Choice.</u> (1983)   Green Linnet SIF 1045

   ARTISTS: Joe Burke-flute, tin whistle, accordion;
with Máire Ní Chathasaigh-harp; Kathleen Guilday-harp; Lori
Feeley-flute; Mike Rafferty-flute; Brian Conway-fiddle.
Produced by Joe Burke.

   CONTENTS: Bean Dubh An Gleanna (Dark Woman of
   the Glen); The Mills Are Grinding/Paddy
   Doorhy's; Cuaichín Ghleann Neifinn/The Green
   Blanket (also known as The Ewe Reel); The Dean
   Brig of Edinburgh (also known as Miss Gray of
   Carse); Jack Coughlan's Fancy; The Coolin (An
   Chuilfhionn); Sean Reid's Fancy/The Kerry Reel;
   Mama's Pet/The Tailor's Choice; Blind Mary
   (Máire Chaoch); The Humours of Quarry Cross/
   Jackson's Bottle of Brandy; Roísín Dubh; The
   Fort of Kincora/Caroline O'Neill's; Raibh Tú ag
   an gCarraig (Were You at the Rock); The Lime-
   stone Rock/The Banshee Reel; O'Rahilly's Grave

Joe Burke changes the emphasis of his music on his second
album from the accordion to the flute. Burke's style is
unpretentious and competent. The listener is treated to
dance tunes and airs mostly from Galway, some of which were
recorded in the 1930s by the Ballinakill Band of East Galway. Distinctive tunes include the lovely opening air, "Bean
Dubh An Gleanna (Dark Woman of the Glen), "Jack Couglan's
Fancy," a wonderful reel named for this Galway flute player,
and the accordion piece, "The Dean Brig of Edinburgh," a slow
Scottish strathspey accompanied nicely by the harp. Máire Ní
Chathasaigh and Kathleen Guilday provide good harp accompaniment on both the slower airs and the faster reels and jigs.
Lori Feeley is excellent with the flute harmonies throughout
the album, especially on "The Coolin." [LP, CS]

   NOTES: Joe Burke also recorded an album with fiddler
Johnny Cronin, <u>Cronin & Burke</u> (Shanachie SH 29005), which

is currently out of print, and <u>Funny Reel</u> (Shanachie 29012)
with Andy McGann.

JOE BURKE WITH CHARLIE LENNON

29.   <u>Traditional Music of
      Ireland</u>. (1983)   Green Linnet SIF 1048

    ARITSTS: Joe Burke-accordion; with Charlie Lennon-
piano. Produced by Joe Burke.

      CONTENTS: The Bucks of Oranmore/The Wind that
      Shakes the Barley; The Dogs Among the Bushes/
      Gorman's; Trip to the Cottage/Tatter Jack
      Walsh; Minny Foster/The Banks; Sporting Nell/
      The Boyne Hunt; Murray's Fancy/The Smell of the
      Bog; Patsy Tuohey's Reel/Molly Bán; The College
      Groves/The Flogging Reel; Jackson's Reels; The
      Grey Goose/Sixpenny Money; Bonnie Kate/Jenny's
      Chickens; Galway Bay/The Contradiction; Pat
      Burke's/Fraher's; The Longford Spinster/Paddy
      Lynn's Delight

A reissue of a 1973 Shaskeen recording (OS 361), this album
is considered by critics to be a "collectors item." It is an
important part of Irish music tradition, as it exemplifies
the button accordion's contributions to the field. The album
and Burke's performance on the button accordion has helped to
increase the instrument's popularity and reputation. The
record contains standard material and solid performances by
Burke and his piano accompanist, Charlie Lennon. They are
both naturals and play straightforward music. The reels are
the best tracks, especially "Jackson's Reels," "Patsy
Tuohy's/Molly Bán," and "The College Groves/The Flogging
Reel." **[LP, CS]**

JOE BURKE, MICHAEL COONEY, TERRY CORCORAN

30.   <u>Happy to Meet & Sorry
      to Part</u>. (1986)   Green Linnet SIF 1069

    ARTISTS: Joe Burke-accordion; Michael Cooney-tin
whistle, uilleann pipes; Terry Corcoran-guitar, vocals.
Produced by Joe Burke.

      CONTENTS: Dowd's No. 9/The Galway Rambler;
      Daleystown Hunt/The Carraroe Jig; Bonaparte's
      Retreat; Captain Kelly's/Jennie's Wedding; The
      Maid on the Mountain; The Bells of Tipperary/
      Miss Galvin's; Father O'Flynn/Haste to the
      Wedding; Kitty Gone a'Milking/Lucky in Love/
      Corney is Coming; Rogaire Dubh (Black Rogue)/
      Split the Whisker; The Boyne Hunt/Come West
      Along the Road; Brian Boru's March/Sporting
      Paddy/The Traveler; I Buried My Wife and Danced
      on Top of Her/Will You Come Home With Me?; The
      High Reel/Geoghegan's; Cherish the Ladies;
      Dunlavin Green; The Star of Munster/The Black-

berry Blossom; Happy to Meet & Sorry to Part/
Paddy in London; Aggie Whyte's/Miss Thorton

A spirited collection of dance tunes and songs populate this
album, which was recorded in Memphis. The fine trio of
musicians complement each other very well. Burke, known for
his proficiency on button accordion and his large and varied
repertoire, is accompanied on pipes and whistle by Michael
Cooney, an All-Ireland Champion from County Tipperary, and
Dubliner, Terry Corcoran, who in addition to providing lively
guitar back-up, also performs two songs. The dance tunes,
(34 tunes in 18 tracks), are all tastefully performed.
Highlights include a fine performance on pipes by Cooney on
"The Bell of Tipperary/Miss Galvin's Reel," the difficult
five-part jig, "Cherish the Ladies," "Brian Boru's March,"
and the title track, "Happy to Meet & Sorry to Part." [LP,
CS]

KEVIN BURKE

31.   If the Cap Fits.... (1978)   Green Linnet SIF 3009

ARTISTS: Kevin Burke-fiddles; with Gerry O'Beirne-
slide guitar; Paul Brady-mandolin, piano; Peter Brown-flute
and uilleann pipes; Donal Lunny-bouzouki; Jackie Daly-accordion; Mícheál Ó Domhnaill-guitar. Produced by Donal Lunny.

CONTENTS: A Kerry Reel/Michael Coleman's/The
Wheels of the World/Julia Delaney; Dinny Dela-
ney's/The Yellow Wattle; The Mason's Apron/
Laington's Reel; Paddy Fahy's Jig/Cliffs of
Moher; The Star of Munster/John Stenson's
no. 1/John Stenson's no. 2; Biddy Martin's/Ger
the Rigger/Bill Sullivan's Polka; Caisleán na
nÓr/Bobby Casey's Hornpipe; Toss the Feathers/
The College Groves/The Pinch of Snuff/The
Earl's Chair/The Woman of the House/The Girl
that Broke My Heart/The Drunken Tinker/Paddy
Cronin's?/McFadden's Handsome Daughter/The
Hunter's Purse/Toss the Feathers

Kevin Burke's first solo album gives him an opportunity to
demonstate his masterful abilities. He has employed tasteful
arrangements to the tunes and adroitly performs on fiddle.
Backed by some of the finest Irish musicians, Burke double
tracks his fiddling with accompaniment by bouzouki, guitar,
mandolin, piano, flute, pipes and slide guitar. He even
layers his own fiddling for a powerful effect. The fiddle
and accordion duets with Burke and Jackie Daly combine spirited harmonies. Side two is especially interesting. It
begins with two hornpipes, continuing into a monstrous medley
of intertwined jigs accompanied by various instruments that
fade in and out of the set, creating an unusual and powerful
piece. [LP]

KEVIN BURKE

32.   Up Close. (1984)   Green Linnet SIF 1052

ARTISTS: Kevin Burke-violin; Gerry O'Beirne-guitars, synthesizer; Matt Molloy-flute; Joe Burke-accordion; Phil Murphy-harmonica; Pip Murphy-harmonica; John Murphy-harmonica; Mark Graham-harmonica; Paul Kotapish-cittern, mandolin. Produced by Gerry O'Beirne.

CONTENTS: Lord Gordon's Reel; A Polka/A Finnish Polka/Jessica's Polka; The Thrush in the Straw/A Health to the Ladies/The Boys of the Town; Tuttle's Reel/The Bunch of Green Rushes/The Maids of Mitchelstown; The Shepherd's Daughter/Jerusalem Ridge/Michael Kennedy's

Reel; The Bloom of Youth/Molloy's Favourite/The Cabin Hunter; The Boys of Ballycastle/The Stack of Barley; The Raheen Medley; The Rambler/The Chapel Bell; The Peeler's Jacket/The Flax in Bloom/Eileen Curran; The Orphan/The Mist on the Mountain/The Stolen Purse

Whether playing solo or with accompanists, Kevin Burke's fiddling style is smooth, sensitive, vibrant, and imaginative. Up and Close contains selections with full-bodied arrangements, agreeable mixes of instruments, and solid performances by Burke and his accompanying musicians. Prominent tunes include two solo fiddling tracks ("The Orphan" and "The Boys of Ballycastle"), the wild harmonica accompaniment of "The Thrush in the Straw/A Health to the Ladies/The Boys of the Town," and "Jerusalem Ridge," a tune by Bill Monroe (the father of bluegrass). A good example of the harmonies between Burke and his backup musicians is "Lord Gordon's Reel" and "The Peeler's Jacket/The Flax in Bloom/Eileen Curran," which prominently features Joe Burke's accordion. [LP, CS]

NOTES: Burke has one other solo lp, Sweeney Dream, (Folkways 8876).

KEVIN BURKE AND JACKIE DALY

33.   Eavesdropper. (1981)   Green Linnet SIF 3002

ARTISTS: Kevin Burke-fiddle; Jackie Daly-accordion, concertina, melodeon; with Ignatius Commerford-guitar; Conal Ó Grada-flute; Paul Brady-piano; Philip Begley-piano; Francis Thoma-bodhrán. Produced by Kevin Burke and Jackie Daly.

CONTENTS: Victory Reel/London Lasses/Courting Them All; Scully Casey's Jig/The Eavesdropper; Johnny Leary's/Miko Russell's Slides; Rose in the Garden/Andy McGann's; Garrett Barry's; The Steeplechase/The Graf Spee; The Blackbird; Killoran's/The Hilltop/Jim Coleman's; Palm Sunday/The Burnt Old Man; O'Connell's Trip to Parliament/The Fairy Reel; An Páistín Fionn/The Atlantic Sound; O'Keeffe's/Trip to the Cottage

Burke and Daly expertly combine fiddle and accordion (concertina and melodeon, too) on this delightful album of dances. Highlights include Burke's fiddling on "Garrett Barry's" and Daly's solo concertina with "Johnny Leary's." Daly also plays the beautiful "The Blackbird" with guitar accompaniment, offering a nice contrast to the faster selections. Together the duo soar with flying fingers through the final set, "O'Keefe's/Trip to the Cottage." An energetic ending to a first-rate album. **[LP, CS]**

KEVIN BURKE AND MICHEÁL Ó DOMHNAILL

34.   <u>Portland</u>. (1982)   Green Linnet SIF 1041

   ARTISTS: Kevin Burke-fiddle; Mícheál Ó Domhnaill-guitar, harmonium, vocals. Produced by Kevin Burke and Mícheál Ó Domhnaill.

   CONTENTS: Maudabawn Chapel/The Wild Irishman/The Moher Reel; Éirigh a Shiúir; Breton Gavottes; The Rolling Waves/The Market Town/Scatter the Mud; Aird Uí Chumhaing; Paddy's Return/Willy Coleman's/Up in the Air; Lucy's Fling/S'iomadh Rud a Chunnaic Mi/Some Say the Devil is Dead; Is Fada Liom Uaim Í; Tom Morrison's/The Beare Island Reel; George White's Favourite/Dipping the Sheep

Kevin Burke and Micheál Ó Domhnaill follow up their award winning lp <u>Promenade</u> (Green Linnet SIF 3010) with this stunning recording. The duo presents a combination of lively dance tunes and Irish songs in an uplifting, joyous atmosphere mixed with a trace of melancholy. Burke and Ó Domhnaill blend well together, complementing one another's style. Burke is touted as one of the masters of the Irish fiddle and his highly lyrical style is consistently praised. He is in command with the animated dance sets, especially "Breton Gavottes," an almost unwordly piece. In addition to providing the rhythmic guitar accompaniment for Burke's fiddle, Ó Domhnaill offers three songs sung in the Irish language, and a short piece of Scots Gaelic mouth music, "S'iomadh Rud a Chunnaic Mi." The songs are hauntingly beautiful with Burke's sweet fiddle in the background. A standout is "Aird Uí Chumhaing," an ex-patriot's lament for his beloved childhood home, Aird Uí Chumhaing, on the northeast coast of Ireland. Lyrics and translations are provided for each song. Individually, Kevin Burke and Micheál Ó Domhnaill are preeminent artists in Irish folk music. Together they are a vibrant duo and <u>Portland</u> is an innovative and dynamic album. **[LP, CS]**

KEVIN BURKE AND MÍCHEÁL Ó DOMHNAILL

35.   <u>Promenade</u>. (1981)   Green Linnet SIF 3010

   ARTISTS: Kevin Burke-fiddle; Mícheál Ó Domhnaill-vocals, guitar, electric piano; with Tríona Ní Dhomhnaill-vocal harmony; Donal Lunny-bouzouki, bass bouzouki; Declan Sinnot-

electric bass, electric guitar. Produced by Gerry O'Beirne
and Mícheál Ó Domhnaill.

> **CONTENTS:** The Pigeon on the Gate, Lafferty's
> Reel/Matt People's Reel; Lord Franklin; Walsh's
> Hornpipe/The Old Torn Petticoat/The Old Torn
> Petticoat (Reel)/The Bank of Ireland; Coinleach
> Ghlas an Fhómhair; The Promenade; Ar a Ghabháil
> go Baile Átha Cliath domh; The Whole Chicken in
> the Soup/The Bird in the Bush/The New-Mown
> Meadow/The Silver Spear; The Reverend Brother's
> Jig/Sean Ryan's Jig

The first recorded collaboration between two former Bothy
Band members won the 1980 Gran Prix Du Disque at the Mon-
treaux Jazz Festival. It is a fine representation of Kevin
Burke's and Micheál O' Domhnaill's well-blended styles.
Chocked full of dance tunes highlighted by Burke's fiddle and
Ó Domhnaill's guitar accompaniment, the album also features
three evocative songs by Ó Domhnaill. "Ar a Ghabháil go
Baile Átha Cliath domh" is the strongest of the three, but
"Lord Franklin," a song depicting Lady Franklin's nightmare
of her husband's tragic fate during his search for the
Northwest Passage, is also very good. Ó Domhnaill is joined
by his sister, Tríona Ní Dhomnaill on harmonies. Burke
sparkles throughout the selections. His fiddling is
especially delightful on the final two medley cuts. The
title track, "Promenade," successfully captures the fusion of
folk and jazz in a quiet and soulful way. [LP]

> **NOTES:** This recording was originally released on
Mulligan Music in 1979. Micheál Ó Domnhaill is currently
working with Relativity and with Irish fiddler Bill Oskay in
Nightnoise. Kevin Burke presently is performing with Patrick
Street.

PADDY CARTY AND MICK O'CONNOR

36.   Traditional Music
        of Ireland. (1975)   Shanachie 29001

> **ARTISTS:** Paddy Carty-flute; Mick O'Connor-banjo.

> **CONTENTS:** Stone in the Field/West Wind; The
> Day I Met Tom Moylan/Ships A-Sailing; Paddy
> Kelly's/Mullingar Lea; Paddy Fahy's/Whelan's
> (also known as Morrison's Jig); Richard
> Dwyer's/Paddy Kelly's; Tit for Tat (also known
> as Limestone Rock)/Tommy Whelan's; Chicago
> Reel/Green Groves of Erin; Cornelius Curtin's
> Big Balloon/Queen of the Fair; The Wise Maid
> (also known as John Doughtery's)/Jenny's Wed-
> ding; Eileen Curan/Dowd's; Reel of Mullina-
> vat/Morrison's Reel; Dogs Among the Bushes/Ewe;
> Jug of Punch/Cottage Groves; Oh! Hag You Have
> Killed Me/Fraher's

Paddy Carty of Co. Galway won five All-Ireland Championships
and three Connaught medals on flute. He plays the more contemplative Galway style of Irish music, which contrasts with

the lively, danceable, and more popular Sligo style. Carty
has a smooth playing manner with exceptional breath control.
This album is a collection of reels and jigs accompanied on
tenor banjo by Londoner Mick O'Connor, the 1971 All-England
Champion. Every selection is well-performed. "The Day I Met
Tom Moylan," "Paddy Fahy's Jig," "Green Groves of Erin," and
O'Connor's banjo solo, "Oh! Hag You Have Killed Me/Faher's
Jig" are just a few standouts. It is too bad this fine album
is marred by poor sound quality. [LP, CS]

NOTES: This record is part of Shanachie's collector
series, which also includes Kathleen Collins (29002), Liz
Carroll and Tommy Maguire (29010), and Joe Burke & Andy
McGann with Felix Dolan (29012), to name a few.

CELTIC THUNDER

37.   Celtic Thunder.   (1981)   Green Linnet SIF 1029

ARTISTS: Linda Hickman-flute, whistle, vocals; Jesse
Winch-bouzouki, bodhrán, vocals; Steve Hickman-fiddle, harmonica, vocals; Terry Winch-accordion, vocals; Nita Conly-
guitar, vocals; with Brendan Mulvihill-fiddle; Mick Moloney-
tenor banjo, mandolin, vocals; Billy McComisky-accordion;
Andy O'Brien-guitar; Frank Emerson-vocals; Tony O'Riordan-
vocals. Produced by Mick Moloney.

CONTENTS: Mark Quinn's Polkas (includes The
Galway Belle, The Barren Rock of Aden); The
Deadly Wars; Sixpenny Money/The Blackthorn
Stick; Bold Thady Quill; All the Way to Bir-
mingham/Roaring Mary; The Best Years of Our
Lives; The Philippine Soldier; Woman of the
House/Paddy Lynn's Delight; Gem of the Roe;
Doug Lang's/My Brother Seamus/P.J. Conways's;
Johnny Doyle; The Wise Maid/The Cup of Tea/
Sheehan's

Celtic Thunder, an Irish American ensemble based in the
Baltimore/Washington, D. C. area, is a unique band boasting
five lead singers, who perform at least one lead vocal per
member and multi-part harmonies. Instrumentally, the group
presents lively dance sets, and is joined by The Irish Tradition for two exuberant and satisfying sets, "Sixpenny Money/
The Blackthorn Stick" and "The Wise Maid/The Cup of Tea/Shee-
han's Reel." Vocalist, songwriter, and accordionist Terry
Winch presently is exploring the Irish American experience,
having published recently a volume of poetry in honor of
Irish emigrant musicians, Irish Musicians, American Friends
(Tombouctou, 1985). For this album, he composed the
well-performed and moving song "The Best Years of Our Lives,"
which is based on his father's life. The remaining vocal
selections are less strong. [LP, CS]

NOTES: Celtic Thunder released a second recording,
The Light of Other Days (Green Linnet SIF 1086) in 1988.
Both Linda Hickman and Nita Conley have left the band. New
members include Rob Thornburgh (fiddle), Regan Wick (piano
and percussion), and Laura Murphy (vocals).

THE CHIEFTAINS

For more than twenty-five years the Chieftains has delivered
classic Irish folk music to audiences worldwide. The band is
probably the best known exponent of Celtic music today
although these unassuming gentlemen would be embarrassed to
admit it. Their music is well-arranged and concentrates on
the traditions of Ireland, Scotland, and Brittany. Recently
the repertoire expanded to include Chinese influences.

Members of the Chieftains knew one another casually in the
1950s, playing in duos and trios before they joined Seán Ó
Riada and Ceoltóirí Chualann in 1960. Paddy Moloney, Michael
Tubridy, Seán Potts, Martin Fay, and the late Davey Fallon
formed the original Chieftains in 1963, recording their first
lp in 1964. A five year gap occurred between this debut
recording and the next album. In fact, The Chieftains 1 was
actually an experiment for the group. Originally the members
had no intention of continuing as a band. But their experiment was a success and over the five year interval between
lps the Chieftains played various venues to an ever increas-
ing audience. During this period the musicians also continued their collaboration with Ó Riada until he disbanded
his group around 1970. With the break up of Ceoltóirí Chualann, Moloney and company further developed the Chieftains
and its music, although the bandmates did not give up their
regular jobs until the late 1970s.

It is interesting to note that ensemble performances were a
novelty in the 50s and 60s. The solo artist on fiddle,
pipes, and vocals was the norm. With the event of Ceoltóirí
Chualann, the Clancy Brothers, the Chieftains, and others,
group performing became a fixture, which dominates Irish
music today. The Chieftains gave a new definition to
ensemble performing with its classically arranged music
played on traditional instruments. The group's popularity
has grown extensively due to its high visibility in concerts,
on television, on recordings, soundtracks, etc. The Chieftains is at the pinnacle of its success.

All the major Chieftain albums are listed here. The original
release dates are given next to the titles rather than the
reissue dates. Most of the earlier works now are available
on Shanachie Records. In the notes at the end of the last
entry, the Chieftains soundtracks and albums by individual
band members will be listed.

38.   The Chieftains 1. (1964)   Shanachie 79021

      ARTISTS: Paddy Moloney-uilleann pipes, tin whistle;
Michael Tubridy-flute, concertina; Seán Potts-tin whistle;
Martin Fay-fiddle; David Fallon-bodhrán. Music arranged and
directed by Paddy Moloney.

            CONTENTS: 'Se Fáth mo Bhuartha/The Lark on the
            Strand/An Fhallaingín Mhuimhneach (Munster
            Cloak)/Trim the Velvet; An Comhra Donn/Murphy's
            Hornpipe; Cailín na Gruaige Doinne (The Brown
            Haired Girl); Comb Your Hair and Curl It/The
            Boys of Ballisodare; The Musical Priest/The

Queen of May; The Walls of Liscarroll; A
Dhruimfhionn Donn Dilis; The Connemara Stock-
ing/The Limestone Rock/Dan Breen's; Casadh an
tSúgáin (The Twisting of the Rope); The Boy in
the Gap; Saint Mary's/Church Street/Garrett
Barry/The Battering Ram/Kitty Goes A-Milking/
Rakish Paddy

This first Chieftain album, recorded in Dublin for the Claddagh label, is an excellent introduction to the band. At
this time the members were still working their day jobs and
playing in the evenings or on weekends. **[LP, CS]**

39.   The Chieftains 2. (1969)   Shanachie 79022

ARTISTS: Michael Tubridy-flute, concertina, tin
whistle; Seán Potts-tin whistle; Paddy Moloney-uilleann
pipes, tin whistle; Martin Fay-fiddle; Seán Keane-fiddle;
Peadar Mercier-bodhrán, bones. Music arranged and directed
by Paddy Moloney.

CONTENTS: Banish Misfortune/Gillan's Apples;
Planxty George Brabazon; Bean an Fhir Rua (The
Red Haired Man's Wife); Pis Fhliuch (also known
as O'Farrell's Welcome to Limerick); An Páistín
Fionn/Mrs. Crotty's Reel/The Mountain Top; The
Foxhunt; An Mhaighdean Mhara/Tie the Bonnet/
O'Rouke's; Callaghan's/Byrne's; Pigtown/Tie the
Ribbons/The Bag of Potatoes; The Humours of
Whiskey/Hardiman the Fiddler; Dónall Óg; Brian
Boru's March; Sweeney's/Denis Murphy's/The
Scartaglen Polka

The second Chieftain lp, recorded in Edinburgh, adds two
members, Dubliner Seán Keane, an All-Ireland Champion on
fiddle, and percussionist, Peadar Mercier from Cork. This
lineup would continue for several years. **[LP, CS]**

40.   The Chieftains 3. (1971)   Shanachie 79023

ARTISTS: Michael Tubridy-flute, concertina, tin
whistle; Seán Potts-tin whistle; Paddy Moloney-uilleann
pipes, tin whistle; Martin Fay-fiddle; Seán Keane-fiddle;
Peadar Mercier-bodhrán, bones; with Pat Kilduff-lilter.
Music arranged and directed by Paddy Moloney.

CONTENTS: Strike the Gay Harp/Lord Mayo (air)/
The Lady on the Island/The Sailor on the Rock;
Sonny's Mazurka/Tommy Hunt's Jig; Eibhlí Gheal
Chiúin Ní Chearbhaill/Delahunty's Hornpipe; The
Hunter's Purse; The March of the King of Laois;
Carolan's Concerto; Tom Bill's/The Road to
Lisdoonvarna/The Merry Sisters; An Ghaoth Aneas
(also known as I Have a Secret to Tell Thee);
Lord Inchiquin; The Trip to Sligo; An Raibh Tú
ag an gCarraig? (Have You Been to Carrick or
Have You Been at the Rock); John Kelly's/Mer-
rily Kiss the Quaker/Denis Murphy's Slide

Recorded in London, <u>The Chieftains 3</u> features the first
photograph cover of the band. On previous Irish releases
lithographs by Edward Delaney had graced the covers and
continue to do so today. The band is joined by Pat Kilduff
of the midlands, whose lively lilting can be heard on "The
Hunter's Purse." **[LP, CS]**

41.   <u>The Chieftains 4</u>. (1973)   Shanachie 79024

    ARTISTS: Michael Tubridy-flute, concertina, tin
whistle; Seán Potts-tin whistle; Paddy Moloney-uilleann
pipes, tin whistle; Martin Fay-fiddle; Seán Keane-fiddle;
Peadar Mercier-bodhrán, bones; with Derek Bell-harp. Music
arranged and directed by Paddy Moloney.

    CONTENTS: Drowsey Maggie; Morgan Magan; The
Tip of the Whistle; The Bucks of Oranmore; The
Battle of Aughrim; The Morning Dew; Carrick-
fergus; Hewlett; Cherish the Ladies; Lord Mayo
(march); Mná na h Éireann ((Women of Ireland)
and is also known as The Love Theme from "Barry
Lyndon")); O'Keeffe's Slide/An Suisín Bán/The
Star Above the Garter/The Weavers

The band's fourth outing, recorded in London in September
1972 and February 1973, sees the early influence of Derek
Bell, the Belfast harper, who joins the group at this point.
The Chieftains' professionalism, originality, and careful
selection of material make this record one of its best.
Standout tunes include "Mná na h Éireann (Women of Ireland),
which was used as the love theme of Stanley Kubrick's film,
"Barry Lyndon." Also noteworthy are "Drowsie Maggie" and
"The Morning Dew," which the band sometimes uses to introduce
each member during concerts. "Carrickfergus" and "Lord
Mayo," a delightful march, round out the best selections.
[LP, CS]

42.   <u>The Chieftains 5</u>. (1975)   Shanachie 79025

    ARTISTS: Paddy Moloney-uilleann pipes, tin whistle;
Seán Potts-tin whistle; Michael Tubridy-flute, concertina,
tin whistle; Seán Keane-fiddle; Martin Fay-fiddle; Derek
Bell-harps, oboe, timpán; Peadar Mercier-bodhrán, bones; with
Ronnie McShane-bones. Produced by Paddy Moloney.

    CONTENTS: The Timpán Reel; Tabhair dom do Lámh
(Give Me Your Hand); Three Kerry Polkas; Ceol
Bhriotánach (Breton Music); The Chieftains'
Knock on the Door; The Robbers' Glen; An Ghé
agus an Grá Geal (The Goose and Bright Love);
The Humours of Carolan; Samhradh, Samhradh
(Summertime, Summertime); Kerry Slides

Derek Bell introduces the timpán, an instrument similar to a
hammered dulcimer, and the oboe into the instrument repertoire. Rory Dall Ó Catháin's popular impromptu piece "Tabhair Dom do Lámh," "The Timpán Reel," the marvelous "Ceol
Bhriotánach," in which Bell substitutes the oboe for the
popular Breton bombarde, and the ethereal beauty of "Samh-

radh, Samhradh" are the best selections. This is the first
lp to be released stateside and coincided with the band's
first major tour of the United States in fall 1975. **[LP, CS]**

43.   The Chieftains 6:
          Bonaparte's Retreat. (1976)   Shanachie 79026

    ARTISTS: Paddy Moloney-uilleann pipes, tin whistle,
bodhrán; Seán Potts-tin whistle, bodhrán; Martin Fay-fiddle;
Seán Keane-fiddle; Michael Tubridy-flute, concertina, tin
whistle; Derek Bell- harps, oboe, tiompán; with Ronnie Mc-
Shane-bones; Kevin Conneff-bodhrán; Dolores Keane-vocals; and
James O'Connor, Jer O'Connor, Joan O'Connor, John Spillane,
Tom McCarthy, Kathleen McCarthy, Bernadette McCarthy, Marion
McCarthy, Bobbie Casey, and Mary Flaherty-dancers. Produced
by Paddy Moloney.

    CONTENTS: The Chattering Magpie: The Dunmore
Lasses, The Pigeon on the Gate, Top It Off, The
Chattering Magpie; An Chéad Mháirt den Fhomhar
(The First Tuesday of Autumn)/Green Grow the
Rushes O; Bonaparte's Retreat; Away with Ye:
Ask Me Father, Casadh an tSúgáin (The Twisting
of the Rope), Old Hag You Have Killed Me;
Caledonia: Máirséail Alasdroim, Langstrom's
Pony (also known as The Fourpenny Girl); Iníon
Nic Diarmada ((Miss MacDermott) also known as
The Princess Royal)/Máire Dhall (Blind Mary)/
John Drury; The Rights of Man; Round the House
and Mind the Dresser

Moloney's musical direction with the title cut is impressive. In "Bonaparte's Retreat" the band tells the sad tale
of the defeat of Napolean and the loss of Ireland's hope of
French help in gaining independence from England. **[LP, CS]**

44.   The Chieftains 7. (1977)   Columbia 35612

    ARTISTS: Paddy Moloney-uilleann pipes, tin whistle;
Seán Potts-tin whistle, bones; Seán Keane-fiddle, tin whistle; Martin Fay-fiddle, bones; Michael Tubridy-flute, concertina, tin whistle; Derek Bell-neo Irish harp, mediaeval
harps, tiompán, oboe; Kevin Conneff-bodhrán. Produced by
Paddy Moloney.

    CONTENTS: Away We Go Again: Tarbolton, Lucy
Campbell, Carolan's Receipt for Drinking, The
Dark Haired Lass, The Morning Star; Dochas
(Hope): Amhrán Dochais, Cáit Ní Dhuibhir;
Hedigan's Fancy; John O'Connor/The Ode to
Whiskey; Friel's Kitchen: Bímid ag ól is a'
Pógadh na mBan, An Buachaill Dreoite, Seán
Reid's Reel (also known as The West Wind);
No. 6 the Coombe: Chuimhne an Phiobaire (The
Piper Remembered), The Repeal of the Union, The
Duke of Leinster; O'Sullivan's March/An Sean
Duine; The Ace and Deuce of Pipering; The
Fairies' Lamentation and Dance; Oh! The Bree-
ches Full of Stiches

Band members share in the arrangements on this album, the first for Columbia Records. Highlights include "Hedigan´s Fancy," "The Fairies Lamentation and Dance," "Friel´s Kitchen," and "John O´Connor/The Ode to Whiskey." **[LP, CS]**

45.   The Chieftains 8. (1978)   CBS 83262

 ARTISTS: Paddy Moloney-uilleann pipes, tin whistle; Seán Potts-tin whistle; Seán Keane-fiddle; Martin Fay-fiddle, bones; Michael Tubridy-flute, concertina, tin whistle; Derek Bell-neo Irish harp, mediaeval harp, tiompán; Kevin Conneff-bodhrán. Produced by Paddy Moloney.

 CONTENTS: The Session: Elizabeth Kelly´s Delight, Fraher´s, Dinny Delaney´s Jig (also known as The Old Hag at the Kiln); Dr. John Hart; Seán Sa Cheo (Seán in a Fog); Hornpipes: An tSean Bhean Bhocht (The Poor Old Woman), The Fairies´ Hornpipe; Sea Image: includes Anach Cuan, The Rolling Wave; If I Had Maggie in the Wood; An Speic Seoigheach; The Dogs Among the Bushes: Athol Brose, The Dogs Among the Bushes; Miss Hamilton; The Job of Journeywork; The Wind that Shakes the Barley/The Reel with the Beryle

Best tunes include the captivating tone poem "Sea Image," the animated medley of jigs entitled "The Session," and "Miss Hamilton," the only surviving melody of Cornelius Lyons, a contemporary of Carolan. **[LP, CS]**

46.   The Chieftians 9:
         Boil the Breakfast Early. (1980)   Columbia PC 36401

 ARTISTS: Paddy Moloney-uilleann pipes, tin whistle; Seán Keane-fiddle; Martin Fay-fiddle, bones; Derek Bell-neo Irish harp, mediaeval harp, tiompán; Kevin Conneff-bodhrán, vocals; Matt Molloy-flute, tin whistle; with The Rathcolle Pipe Band Drum Corp; Jolyon Jackson-cello. Produced by Paddy Moloney.

 CONTENTS: Boil the Breakfast Early: Boil the Breakfast Early, Scotch Mary, The Chicago Reel; Mrs. Judge; The March from "Oscar and Malvina"; When a Man´s in Love; Bealach An Doirín (The Path through the Wood): The Home Ruler, Terry "Cuz" Teahan´s Favourite, Charlie´s Buttermilk Mary; Ag Taisteal Na Blárnan (Travelling through Blarney); Carolan´s Welcome; Up Against the Buachalawns: Larry Redican´s Reel, Up Against the Buachalawns, Johnny McGuire´s Reel, Sweeney´s Dream; Gol Na mBan San Ár: Gol na mBan san Ár (The Crying of the Women at the Slaughter), Seán Ó Duibhir a´Ghleanna (John O´Dwyer of the Glen); Chase Around the Windmill: Toss the Feathers, Ballinasloe Fair, Cailleach an Airgid (The Hag with the Money), Cuil Aodha Slide, The Pretty Girl

Vocals become part of the Chieftains sound with Kevin Conneff
providing songs and the lilting introduction to "The Chicago
Reel." Matt Molloy, formerly of The Bothy Band and Planxty,
joins the group replacing Michael Tubridy and Seán Potts.
This is the band´s current lineup. **[LP, CS]**

47.   The Chieftains 10:
           Cotton-Eyed Joe. (1981)   Shanachie 79019

    ARTISTS: Matt Molloy, Martin Fay, Derek Bell, Seán
Keane, Paddy Moloney, and Kevin Conneff. Produced by Paddy
Moloney.

    CONTENTS: The Christmas Reel; Salut à la
Compagnie; My Love is in America: Kiss Me Kate
(also known as Charming Molly´s Reel), The
Custom Gap (also known as Bobby Casey´s Reel),
The Spindle Shank Reel, My Love is in America
(also known as The Dandy Apron and also as
Jenny Hind´s Reel); Manx Music: Illiam Dhone
(Brown William), Slumber Song, Arrane Ghelby
(The Song of the Water Kilpie), Mylecharaine´s
March, Berry Dhone (Brown Berry), Eunyssagh
Vona (Mona´s Delight); Master Crowley´s Reels;
The Pride of Pimlico; An Faire (The Gold Ring);
An Durzhunel (The Turtle Dove); Sir Arthur
Shaen/Madame Cole; Garech´s Wedding;
Cotton-Eyed Joe

Texas meets the Chieftains with "Cotton-Eyed Joe." Garech
Onórach a Brún brought the Chieftains together eighteen years
prior to this recording and the band honors him with Molo-
ney´s "Garech´s Wedding." "Manx Music," a wonderful medley
of tunes introduced to the group by harper Charles Guard,
"Cotton-Eyed Joe," a tune derived from the country dance of
the same name, and an Irish tune, "The Mountain Top," are
outstanding tracks. **[LP, CS]**

48.   Celtic Wedding: Music of Brittany
           Played by Irish Musicians. (1987)   RCA 6358-1-RC

    ARTISTS: Martin Fay-fiddle, bones; Seán Keane-fiddle;
Kevin Conneff-bodhrán, vocals; Paddy Moloney-uilleann pipes,
tin whistle; Matt Molloy-flute, tin whistle; Derek Bell-
harp, tiompán, oboe, organ; with Nolwenn Monjarret-vocals;
Bernard Pichard-bombarde; Alain Guerton-bombarde; Michel
Bertae-biniou. Produced by Paddy Moloney.

    CONTENTS: Dañs Mod Koh a Vaod; A Breton Carol:
Peh Trouz ´Zou ar en Doar (What Noise on
Earth); Dañs-Tro Fisel; Marches (Tonioù-Bale a
Vro-Wened): Julian Kadoudal, Er Studier
Yaouank (The Young Student), Er Charra Bourdet
(The Bogged-Down Cart), Er Hoarierion-
Bouleù; Dañs Bro-Leon; Heuliadenn Tonioù
Briezh-Izel; Ev Chistr ´Ta, Laou!; Jabadaw;
Celtic Wedding: Boked Eured (The Brides Bou-
quet), Evit Mont D´ar Vourc´h, Evit Mont D´an
Iliz, Adoromp Holl (Let Us Pray), A Di Da Di,

Goude an Oferenn, Ton Ar C´hezeg (The Horses
Tune), Distro D´an Ti-Feurm (Back to the Farm),
Dañs Kost Er Choad (Dance from the Woodlands),
Evit Mont Ouzh Taol (Call to the Table), Son Ar
Rost (Tune for the Roast), An Abadenn-Dañs
(The Wedding Dance), An Dro (The Turn), Soubenn
Al Laezh (The Milk Soup), Ton Kenaud

With the success of The Chieftains in China (Shanachie 79050)
the band again departs the Irish shores. This time its
destination is Ireland´s close neighbor and Celtic cousin,
Brittany. Celtic Wedding, digitally recorded and sponsored
by Brittany Ferries, explores Breton music collected by Polig
Monjarret in his recent book, Toniou Breizh-Izell (Traditional Tunes from Lower Brittany). Selections include
dances, marches, and a Breton Christmas carol, "Peh Trouz
´Zou ar en Doar," which is sung by Nolween Monjarret. "Dañs-
Tro Fisel," a three part ring dance, is quite complex and is
considered one of the most difficult Breton dances. "Dañs
Bro-Leon" is lively fun with Kevin Conneff and the band
providing vocals on the chorus. The medley, "Heuliadenn
Tonioù Breizh-Izel," offers solos by each member of the group
linked by a wonderful gavotte. Conneff is excellent on "Ev
Chistr ´Ta, Laou!," a song praising cider, the national drink
of Brittany in past times. The major focus of the recording
is "Celtic Wedding," a twenty minute medley of songs and
dances depicting the traditional Breton wedding. Through
music the ceremony is described from the bride leaving her
parent´s home to the departure of the bride and groom. [LP,
CS]

49.   The Chieftains in China. (1985)   Shanachie 79050

   ARTISTS: Paddy Moloney-Uilleann pipes, tin whistle;
Seán Keane-fiddle; Martin Fay-fiddle, bones; Derek Bell-neo-
Irish harp, tiompán; Kevin Conneff-bodhrán, Chinese gong,
vocals; Matt Molloy-flute; with Chinese ensembles. Produced
by Paddy Moloney.

      CONTENTS: Full of Joy; In a Suzhow Garden
      (Slán le Máighe); If I Had Maggie in the Wood;
      The Reason for My Sorrow (´Sé Fáth mo Bhuar-
      tha); The Chieftains in China; Planxty Irwin;
      Off the Great Wall; A Tribute to O´Carolan; The
      Wind from the South (An Gaoth Aneas); China to
      Hong Kong

This delightful release was recorded live over a three week
period in Beijing, Shanghai, and Sushou. Containing the
usual in-concert fare, the band expands its performance with
a blend of Irish and Chinese musical styles. The most interesting selections are the ones performed with Chinese en-
sembles--"Full of Joy," "Planxty Irwin," and "The Wind from
the South." Each piece provides a unique mixture of Chinese
and Irish music, which are similar in harmonies. The Chinese
flavor gives a baroque mood to these selections. An interesting contrast is the introduction to "China to Hong Kong,"
a Chinese air performed on solo fiddle. It sounds very Asian
yet has a definite Celtic quality. Although at times the
band is criticized as too studied, or stodgy, this album is a

refreshing addition to its catalog. The innovative use of
both Chinese and Irish music makes it one of the best Chieftain albums in recent years. **[LP, CS, CD]**

50.   The Chieftains Live. (1977)   Shanachie 79027

   ARTISTS: Kevin Conneff-bodhrán; Michael Tubridy-
flute, concertina, tin whistle; Seán Potts-tin whistle,
bodhrán; Paddy Moloney-uilleann pipes, tin whistle; Seán
Keane-fiddle, tin whistle; Derek Bell-neo Irish harp, tiompán; Martin Fay-fiddle. Produced by Paddy Moloney.

   CONTENTS: The Morning Dew; George Brabazon;
   Kerry Slides; Carrickfergus; Carolan's Concer-
   to; The Foxhunt; Round the House and Mind the
   Dresser; Solos: Caítlin Triall, For the Sakes
   of Old Decency, Carolan's Farewell to Music,
   Banish Misfortune, The Tarbolton/The Pinch of
   Snuff, The Star of Munster/The Flogging Reel;
   Limerick's Lamentation; O'Neill's March; Ríl
   Mhor

Recorded live at Symphony Hall in Boston and at Massey Hall
in Toronto, this album captures the true spirit of the Chieftains. (This is the last of its releases on Island Records).
[LP, CS]

   NOTES: Other recordings by the Chieftains include
Barry Lyndon/Music from the Soundtrack (Warner Brothers BS
2903), for which they received the Best Film Score Oscar,
Year of the French (Shanachie 79036), Ballad of the Irish
Horse (Shanachie 79051) from the Public Broadcasting Station
(PBS) special, and The Grey Fox (DRG 9515), which was awarded
the Canadian Genie for best film score. All four of these
soundtracks presently are in print. In addition, the band
recorded an album with classical flutist James Galway, James
Galway and The Chieftains in Ireland (RCA Red Seal 5798), a
St. Patrick's Day 1987 release on green vinyl. It is also
available on digital compact disc. The band also appeared on
a PBS concert with Galway, which was first broadcast in April
1988. An album with Van Morrison, Irish Heartbeat (Mercury
834 496), was released in June 1988.

Albums by members of the band include Tin Whistles by Paddy
Moloney and Seán Potts (Claddagh CC 15), Michael Tubridy's
The Eagle's Whistle (Claddagh CC 27), Gusty Frolicks (Clad-
dagh CC 17) and Seán Keane (Shanachie 79031) from fiddler
Seán Keane, who has also recorded an album with bandmate Matt
Molloy, Contentment is Wealth (Green Linnet SIF 1058).   Mol-
loy has three solo lps, Matt Molloy (Green Linnet SIF 3008),
Heathery Breeze (Shanachie 79064), and Stony Steps (Green
Linnet SIF 3041), and the classic, Matt Molloy, Paul Brady,
Tommy Peoples (Green Linnet SIF 3018). Kevin Conneff can be
heard on James Galway's Annie's Song and Other Galway Favorites (RCA ARL1-3061) and with Christy Moore on the legendary
album Prosperous (Tara 1001).

THE CLANCY BROTHERS AND TOMMY MAKEM

The Clancy Brothers and Tommy Makem created a worldwide
audience for Irish music in the 1950s and 1960s. They helped
to form a bridge between traditional and popular music of
Ireland with their ballad singing.

Pat, Tom and Liam Clancy hail from County Tipperary in the
Irish Republic, while Tommy Makem is from County Armagh in
Ulster. They emigrated to America in order to pursue acting
careers before becoming a force in the American folk music
scene. Although the Clancy's and Makem really had no serious
intentions of becoming professional singers in the beginning,
they decided to give singing a six month trial, as it paid
more than off-Broadway roles. The partnership lasted more
than ten years and their success was phenomenal.

Makem parted company with the Clancy's in April 1969 and
performed as a solo act for years. He also collaborated with
the Canadian group Ryan's Fancy in the late 1970s and has
performed and recorded with Liam Clancy. The Clancy Brothers
(Tom, Pat, and Bobby) still actively perform at home and
abroad. In the last few years their nephew, Robbie O'Connell, has toured with the band.

Numerous albums have been recorded by the group. This listing is just the tip of the iceberg. Contents, when available, are included in the entries. At the end of the last
entry other available album titles will be given. All albums
by the Clancy Brothers and Tommy Makem will be listed here no
matter who the lead artist is. At random three albums are
critiqued--The Clancy Brothers and Tommy Makem In Person at
Carnegie Hall, The Clancy Brothers' Greatest Hits, and We've
Come a Long Way by Makem and Liam Clancy.

THE CLANCY BROTHERS

51.   The Clancy Brothers'
        Greatest Hits. (1973)   Vanguard CSD 53/54

        ARTISTS: Liam Clancy-guitar, vocals; Pat Clancy-
vocals; Tom Clancy-vocals; with Lou Killen-concertina, pen-
nywhistle, vocals; Barry Kornfeld-guitar, banjo; Don McLean-
guitar, banjo; Dick Romoff-bass; Russ Savakus-bass.

        CONTENTS: Maid of Fife-e-o; Jug of Punch;
        Gallant Forty-Twa; Whistling Gypsy; The Leaving
        of Liverpool; Mountain Dew; The Nightengale;
        Young Roddy McCaulay; Castle of Dramore; Fa-
        ther's Grave; Johnny McAdoo; The Irish Rover;
        Old Woman of Wexford; Bonnie Charlie; Jolly
        Tinker; Haul Away Joe; The Shoals of Herring;
        The Mermaid; Kelly-The Boy from Killane; Rosin
        the Bow; Whiskey is the Life of Man; MacPher-
        son's Lament; Whiskey, You're the Devil; Holy
        Ground

This album was recorded in New York City in 1973 and is
considered a classic lp. Joining the Clancys is Lou Killen,
who became a member of the band in 1971. Killen was a

renowned solo performer in his native England and known for
his abilities on concertina and for spinning a tale through
song. He was an intregal part of the English folk music
revival of the late 1950s and early 1960s before he came to
the States in 1967. Northumberland, Killen´s native county,
is known for its distinctive accent and music style. Killen
brings this to the band along with his intriguing and marvelous interpretations of folk material. Album highlights
include "The Mermaid," "Castle of Dramore," "Jug of Punch,"
and "Rosin the Bow." Twenty additional songs are also well-
performed. **[LP, CD]**

> **NOTES:** Albums featuring Lou Killen include <u>Along the
> Coaly Tyne</u> (Topic 189), <u>Gallant Lads We Are</u> (Collector Re-
> cords 1932), <u>Old Songs, Old Friends</u> (Front Hall FHR 012), <u>Sea
> Chanteys</u> (ESP 1085), <u>Sea Songs Concert-Seattle</u> (Folkways
> 37311), <u>Steady As She Goes</u> (Collector Records 1928), and
> <u>Bright Shining Morning</u> (Front Hall FHR 06), which includes
> Killen´s wife Sally.

52.   <u>Save the Land.</u>   Audio Fidelity 5255

> **CONTENTS:** Paddy on the Railway; Youth of the
> Heart; Bonnie Ship the Diamond; Men Behind the
> Wire; Sky Boat Song; Boston Burgler; Girl from
> the North County; Nightengale; Lord of the
> Dance; Country Comfort; Grey Funnel Line
> **[LP]**

THE CLANCY BROTHERS AND TOMMY MAKEM

53.   <u>The Boys Won´t Leave the
        Girls Alone.</u> (1962)   Shanachie 52015

> **ARTISTS:** Liam Clancy, Tom Clancy, Pat Clancy, Tommy
> Makem, with Bruce Langhorne, Bill Lee, Robert Morgan, John
> Stauber, Eric Weissberg.

> **CONTENTS:** Bold O´Donahue; I´ll Tell My Ma;
> Will Ye Go, Lassie, Go?; Rothsea-O; Marie´s
> Wedding; Singin´ Bird; Holy Ground; South
> Australia; As I Roved Out; McPherson´s Lament;
> The Wild Colonial Boy; Shoals of Herring; I
> Know Who is Sick; Old Woman of Wexford
> **[LP, CS]**

54.   <u>The Clancy Brothers and Tommy Makem.</u> Columbia CS 8448

> **ARTISTS:** Liam Clancy, Tom Clancy, Pat Clancy, Tommy
> Makem, with Pete Seeger, Bruce Langhorne.

> **CONTENTS:** The Moonshiner; The Whistling Gypsy;
> My Johnny Lad; The Work of the Weavers; The Old
> Orange Flute; Brennan on the Moor; Tim Fin-
> negan´s Wake; Port Lairge; Haul Away Joe; Young
> Roddy McCorley; A Jug of Punch; Reilly´s Daugh-
> ter **[LP]**

55.   The Clancy Brothers and
      Tommy Makem.   Tradition TLP 1042

      ARTISTS: Tommy Makem, Liam Clancy, Tom Clancy, Pat
Clancy, with Bruce Langhorne, Eric Darling.

      CONTENTS: Brennan on the Moor; The Work of the
      Weavers; The Stuttering Lovers; Paddy Doyle's
      Boots; The Maid of Fife-e-o; The Bard of Ar-
      magh; The Jug of Punch; Young Roddy McCorley;
      The Barnyards of Delgaty; The Castle of Dro-
      more; The Bold Tenant Farmer; Ballinderry;
      Bungle Rye; Eileen Aroon; Johnny I Hardly Knew
      Ye [LP]

56.   The First Hurrah!. (1964)   Columbia CS 8965

      CONTENTS: The Leaving of Liverpool; The Mer-
      maid; Rocky Road to Dublin; John Todd; Rosin
      the Bow; The West's Awake; Row, Bullies, Row;
      Gallant Forty-Twa; An Poc Ar Buile(The Mad
      Goat); Carrickfergus; Bonny Charlie; Kelly-
      the Boy from Killane. [LP]

57.   Freedom's Sons.   Columbia CS 9336

      CONTENTS: Outlaw Reparee; Port Lairge; I'm a
      Free Born Man; Hi for the Beggar Man; When We
      were Under the King; Freedom's Sons; Green in
      the Green; A Medley Commemorating the 50th
      Anniversary of the Uprising of 1916: Foggy
      Dew, Drums Under the Window, Easter 1916; Lord
      Nelson

This album was recorded live in Dublin in commemoration of
the Irish Rebellion of 1916. [LP, CS]

58.   In Concert.   Columbia PC 9494

      CONTENTS: Blackwater's Side; Winds of Morning;
      In This Windy Old Weather; William Bloat;
      McAlpine's Fuzilliers; Master McGrath; Cockies
      of Bungaree; Red-Haired Mary; Mic McGuire;
      Peggy Gordon; March Medley [LP, CS]

59.   In Person at Carnegie Hall.   Columbia PC 8750

      ARTISTS: Liam Clancy, Pat Clancy, Tom Clancy, Tommy
Makem, with Bruce Langhorne, Bill Lee.

      CONTENTS: Johnson's Motor Car; The Juice of
      the Barley; O'Driscoll; Reilly's Daughter;
      Patriot Game (also known as The Merry Month of
      May); Legion of the Rearguard; Oro se do Bhea-
      tha Bhaile; A Jug of Punch; Galway Bay; The
      Children's Medley: When I was Young, Shellicky
      Bookey, Up the Long Ladder, Big Ship Sailing,

Ahem! Ahem!, Wallflowers, Mary the Money,
Frosty Weather, Man of Double Deed, The Wren
Song, Some Say the Divil´s Dead, The Irish
Soldiers, Up the Ladder; The Parting Glass

The electricity between the audience and the performers is
evident throughout this record. A classic selection is
"Children´s Medley," a re-creation of Irish childhood that
allows the group to show off its multi-talents as singers and
actors. The medley includes rhymes, jokes, street songs,
taunts, and fantasies of the young. The final cut, "The
Parting Glass," ends the album on a sentimental note. **[LP,
CS]**

60.   Isn´t It Grand Boys.   Columbia CS 9277

CONTENTS: Nancy Whiskey; Galway Races; What
Would You Do If I Married a Soldier?; Eileen
Aroon; Isn´t It Grand Boys; Galway City; My Son
Ted; Westering Ho; The Cobbler; Mingulay Boat
Song; O´Donnell Abu. **[LP]**

61.   Recorded Live in Ireland.   Columbia PC 9065

CONTENTS: Wild Rover; Maid of Fire; Butcher
Boy; Wella Wa-Oa; Beggar Man; Rocks of Bawn;
Nightingale; They´re Moving Father´s Grave to
Build a Sewer; Curlew´s Song **[LP, CS]**

62.   Sing of the Sea.   Columbia PC 9658

CONTENTS: Congo River; Santy Anno; Paddy West;
Good Ship Calibar; Farewell to Callingford;
Johnny´s Gone to Hilo; Lowlands Low; Love is
Kind; Blood Red Roses; Three Score n Ten; Heave
Away My Johnny **[LP]**

THE CLANCY BROTHERS AND TOMMY MAKEM
AND THEIR FAMILIES

63.   Irish Folk Airs.   Tradition 2083

CONTENTS: Paper & Pins; I Know Where I´m
Going; As I Roved Out; The Cobbler; Whiskey
You´re a Devil; All Around the Loney O; The
Moonshiner; Me Grandfather Died; Shell Kee
Bookey/Around to the Butcher Shop/One Two
Three; The Little Beggarman; The Real Old
Mountain Dew; The Woman from Wexford; I´ll Tell
My Ma

This is the second of a two part set with the Clancys, Makem,
and their kin. Part one is titled At Home with the Clancy
Brothers and Tommy Makem and Their Families (Tradition 2060).
[LP]

MAKEM AND CLANCY

64.   <u>We've Come a Long Way</u>. (1986)   Shanachie 52013

>   **ARTISTS:** Tommy Makem-banjo, vocals; Liam Clancy-guitar, vocals, concertina; with Arty McGlynn-guitar; Eoghan O'Neill-bass; Nollaig Casey-fiddle, viola; Conor Barry-Spanish guitar; Davy Spillane-uilleann pipes, low whistles; Noel Bridgeman-drums; Ray Preston-harmonica; Donal Lunny-bouzouki, bodhráns, keyboards.   Produced by Donal Lunny.

>   **CONTENTS:** We've Come a Long Way; Frog in the Well; Roseville Fair; The Queen of Connemara; Peg Leg Jack; The Mary Ellen Carter; Fair and Tender Ladies; The Coast of Malabar; The Highwayman; Fágfaidh Mise an Baile Seo; Parcel of Rogues; Drill Ye Tarriers Drill; Golden

A must for any Tommy Makem and Liam Clancy fan, this is their first studio album in six years. (<u>Live</u>, (Shanachie 52066), was their previous release). Donal Lunny takes the helm and has recruited a very talented backup group, including Arty McGlynn on guitar and Davey Spillane with pipes and low whistle. Makem and Clancy present various songs, some sad, some jovial, and others that tell a story. They do justice to the late Canadian singer Stan Rogers' "The Mary Ellen Carter," and with the help of Bridgeman on drums "Peg Leg Jack" is quite funny. "Parcel of Rogues" does not hold a candle to the Dick Gaughan version on <u>Gaughan</u> (Topic 12TS 384) or the rendition by Steeleye Span, <u>Parcel of Rogues</u> (Shanachie 79045). **[LP, CS]**

>   **NOTES:** Other recordings by these songsters include <u>Best of the Clancy Brothers and Tommy Makem</u> (Tradition 2050), <u>Boulavogue</u> (Ember SE 8013), <u>Christmas with the Clancy Brothers</u> (Shanachie 52017), <u>The Clancy Brothers with Robbie O'Connell Live</u> (Vanguard 79445), <u>Come Fill Your Glass with Me</u> (Tradition TLP 1032), <u>Fine Boys You Are</u> (Emerald SLD 25), <u>The Girls Won't Leave the Boys Along</u> (Emerald SLD 31), <u>Hearty and Hellish</u> (Shanachie 52014), <u>Home Boys Home</u> (Columbia 9608), <u>In Ireland</u> (Columbia 9065), <u>Irish Drinking Songs</u> (Tradition 2092), <u>Irish Songs of Rebellion</u> (Tradition 2070), <u>The Lark in the Morning</u> (Tradition TLP 1004), <u>Live in Ireland</u> (CBS 62 479), <u>Live on St. Patrick's Day</u> (Audio Fidelity 6256), <u>Presenting the Clancy Brothers and Tommy Makem</u> (Tradition 1042), <u>Raise Your Glass</u> (Emerald SLD 21), <u>Rising of the Moon</u> (Tradition 1006), <u>Reunion</u> ((Ogham 5900) available on compact disc), <u>Show Me the Way</u> (Audio Fidelity 6252), <u>A Spontaneous Performance Recording</u> (Columbia 0841), and <u>Welcome to Our House</u> (Audio Fidelity 6246). Makem and Clancy have recorded <u>Makem & Clancy</u> (Shanachie 52002), <u>The Makem and Clancy Collection</u> (Shanachie 52001), <u>The Makem and Clancy Concert</u> (Blackbird 1002), <u>Makem & Clancy Live at the National Concert Hall</u> (Shanachie 52006), <u>Tommy Makem and Liam Clancy</u> (Blackbird 5001), and <u>Two for the Early Dew</u> (Shanachie 52004). Tommy Makem's recordings include <u>Songs of Tommy Makem</u> (Tradition TLP 1044), <u>Lonesome Waters</u> (Shanachie 52011), and <u>An Evening with Tommy Makem</u> (Shanachie 52008). Liam Clancy also has solo lps, such as <u>The Dutchman</u> (Shanachie 52005), and <u>Liam Clancy</u> (Vanguard 79169).

CLANNAD

Donegal is the home of Clannad, meaning family in Irish. The band consists of Máire Ní Bhraonáin, her brothers Pól and Ciarán Ó Braonáin, and their twin uncles, Noel and Pádraig Ó Dúgain. Clannad's sound mixes folk, jazz, and rock with a strong bass line and inventive, progressive arrangements. Its multi-part melodic harmonies are hauntingly wonderful, but Máire's exquisite vocals are the most prominent feature. Singing mostly in her native Irish language, Máire's crystal clear soprano soars through the songs, touching each phrase. Her confidence, control, and phrasing are exemplary. Máire with Dolores Keane, Mary Black, and Tríona Ní Dhomhnaill are the top Irish female singers currently performing.

Since Clannad's debut lp, Clannad, in 1973, the band established itself as a first rate folk group, though not a purist band. Clannad began to gradually move away from its Celtic roots into the contemporary realm with the lp Crann Ull. The band successfully reached the pop/rock audience with Macalla (1985), and now is known more as a pop group. Clannad's Donegal roots are still present in its music, but to a much lesser degree. The group's early works are electrifying, while its recent recordings are less satisfying from a folk perspective. However, every album from Clannad through Macalla will be discussed.

65.   Clannad. (1973)   Boot ITB 4016

   ARTISTS: Máire Brennan-harp, vocals; Paul Brennan-flute, bongos, guitar, vocals; Ciarán Brennan-double bass, guitar, piano, vocals; Noel Duggan-lead guitar, vocals; Pádraig Duggan-guitar, mandola, vocals; with John Wadham-drums; Grainne McMonagle-tin whistle. Produced by John Curran.

   CONTENTS: Níl Sé Ina Iá; Thíos Chois Na Trá Domh (Down by the Black Strand); Brian Boru's March; Siobhán Ní Dhuibhir; An Mhaighdean Mhara; Liza; An tOileán Úr (The New Island); Mrs. McDermott; The Pretty Maid; An Pháirc (A Field); Harvest Home; Morning Dew

An understated but impressive debut lp from one of the power-houses in Celtic music today. This is a very young Clannad, which has become progressively more polished with each outing. Just compare this album's "Nil Sé Ina Iá" with the driving concert version five years later. Other standouts include "An tOileán Úr," "An Mhaighdean Mhara," the striking "The Pretty Maid," and a subdued "Brian Boru's March", (if a march can be subdued). Even at this early stage of its career, Clannad was experimenting with its music. **[LP, CS]**

66.   Clannad 2. (1974)   Shanachie 79007

   ARTISTS: Pól Ó Braonáin-flute, bongos, guitar, vocals; Máire Ní Bhraonáin-harp, vocals; Pádraig Ó Dúgáin-guitar, mandola, vocals; Noel Ó Dúgáin-guitar, vocals; Ciarán Ó Braonáin-bass, guitar, piano, vocals.

CONTENTS: An Gabhar Bán; Eleanor Plunkett; Coinleach Ghlas an Fhómair; Rince Philib a'Cheoil; By Chance It Was; Rince Briotánach; Dheanainn Sùgradh; Gaoth Barra na dTonn; Teidhir abhail Riú; Fairly Shot of Her; Chuaigh mé 'na Rosann

The band's harmonies highlight this delightful recording. "Dheanain Súgradh" with its wild electric guitar and "Teidhir abhail Riú" are the finest ensemble songs. Máire sings three beautiful gems, "By Chance It Was," "Chuaigh Mé 'na Rosann," and "Coinleach Ghlas an Fhómair," an Ulster song of unrequited love. Clannad 2 is one of the band's finest folk recordings. [LP, CS]

67.   Clannad in Concert. (1978)   Shanachie 79030

    ARTISTS: Máire Ní Bhraonáin-harp, vocals; Ciarán Ó Braonáin-double bass, guitar, vocals; Pól Ó Braonáin-flute, whistle, guitar, bongos, vocals; Pádraig Ó Dúgáin-mandola, guitar, harmonica, bongos vocals; Noel Ó Dúgáin-guitar, harmonium. Produced by Nicky Ryan.

        CONTENTS: Ó Bhean a 'Tí, Cén Bhuairt Sin Ort (O Woman of the House, What Ails You); Fairies Hornipipe/Off to California; Nesnsaí Mhíle Grá; Maíre Bhruinneal; Planxty Burke; An Ghiobóg; Down by the Sally Gardens; Níl Se'n Lá (It's Not Yet Day)

Recorded on its Swiss tour of 1978, these live performances capture Clannad at its best. Top honors go to the Carolan harp piece, "Planxty Burke," and the jazzy tour de force, "Níl Se 'n Lá." [LP, CS, CD]

68.   Crann Ull. (1980).   Tara 3007

    ARTISTS: Máire Ní Bhraonáin, Ciarán Ó Braonáin, Pól Ó Braonáin, Noel Ó Dúgáin, Pádraig Ó Dúgáin. (no instruments noted). Produced by Nicky Ryan.

        CONTENTS: Ar a Ghabhail 'n a 'Chuain Damh; The Last Rose of Summer; Cruscin Lán; Bacach Shile Andai; Lá Coimhthioch fan dTuath (A Strange Day in the Countryside); Crann Ull; Gathering Mushrooms; Bunan Bui; Planxty Browne

Crann Ull pales in comparison to Dúlamán, lacking the latter's magical spark. It is tentative and contemporary in sound, and is more a transitional album between the traditional recordings of the band's first four titles and the pop/soft rock of its latest efforts. Quite a disappointment! However, the instrumentals, "Lá Coimhthioch fan dTuath" and "Planxty Browne," rise above the mire. [LP, CS]

69.   Dúlamán. (1976)   Shanachie 79009

    ARTISTS: Máire Ní Bhraonáin-harp, vocals; Ciarán Ó Braonáin-bass, guitar, mandolin; electric piano; glocken-

spiel, bodhrán, vocals; Pól Ó Braonáin-flute, whistle, guitar, bongos, vocals; Noel Ó Dúgáin-guitar, vocals; Pádriag Ó
Dúgáin-mandola, mandolin, guitar, vocals; with Nicky Ryan-
vocals.   Produced by Nicky Ryan.

> CONTENTS: Dúlamán; Cumha Eoghain Rua Uí Néill
> (Lament for Owen Roe); Two Sisters; Éirigh Suas
> a Stóirín (Rise Up My Love); The Galtee Hunt;
> Éirigh is Cuir Ort do Chuid Éadaigh (Arise and
> Dress Yourself); Siúil a Rún; Mo Mháire;
> dTigeas a Damhsa; Cucanandy; The Jug of Brown
> Ale

With its third album Clannad shows an enormous amount of
musical maturity and confidence. Dúlamán contains some of
the most satisfying material, including the wonderful vocal
clarity of "Siúil a Rún," "Mo Mháire," and the band's harmonies on "dTigeas a Damhsa." "Dúlamán" (meaning seaweed)
possesses very tasteful instrumentation and striking harmonies. [LP, CS]

70.   Fuaim. (1982)   Tara 3008

> ARTISTS: Máire Ní Bhraonáin-harp, vocals; Eithne Ní
Bhraonáin-keyboards, vocals; Ciarán Ó Braonáin-double bass,
guitar, synthesizer, piano, mandolin, vocals; Pól Ó
Braonáin-flute, guitar, tin whistle, vocals; Pádraig Ó
Dúgáin-mandola, mouth organ, vocals; Noel Ó Dúgáin-guitar,
vocals; with Neil Buckley-clarinet, soprano and alto saxophones; Noel Bridgeman-percussion; Pat O'Farrell-electric
guitar.   Produced by Nicky Ryan.

> CONTENTS: Na Buachaillí Álainn; Mheall sí lena
> Glórthaí Mé; Bruach na Carriage Báine; Lá Breá
> fán dTuath; An tÚll; Strayed Away; Ní Lá na
> Gaoithe Lá na Scoilb?; Lish Young Buy-a-
> Broom; Mhorag ´s na Horo Gheallaidh; The Green
> Fields of Gaothdobhair; Buaireadh An Phósta

Almost entirely written by Ciaran and Pól Ó Braonáin, Fuaim
contains one traditional piece, "Bruach na Carriage Báine," a
fair to middling tune. [LP, CS]

71.   Legend - Music from the T.V. Series
       Robin of Sherwood. (1984)   Tara 3012

> ARTISTS: Maire Brennan-harp, lead vocal; Paul Bren-
nan-guitar, flute, tin whistle, keyboards, vocals; Ciaran
Brennan-double bass, synthesizers, guitar, vocals; Pat Dug-
gan-mandola, guitar, vocals; Noel Duggan-guitar, vocals; with
James Delaney-keyboards; Paul Moran-drums; Pat Farrell-electric guitar; Frank Ricotti-percussionist.   Produced by Tony
Clarke.

> CONTENTS: Robin (the Hooded Man); Now is Hue;
> Herne; Together We; Darkmere; Strangeland;
> Scarlet Inside; Lady Marian; Battles; Ancient
> Forest

Tony Clarke, well-known for his work with the Moody Blues,
slickly produced this TV soundtrack to "Robin of Sherwood."
This is the first Clannad lp to be released on a major American label, (RCA AFL1-5084), in addition to its Irish release
on Tara Records. **[LP, CS]**

72.   <u>Macalla</u>. (1985)   RCA NFL1-8063

    ARTISTS: Máire Ní Bhraonáin, Pól Ó Braonáin, Ciarán Ó
Braonáin, Pádraig Ó Dúgáin, Noel Ó Dúgáin; with Bono (Paul
Hewson)-vocals; Mel Collins-sax; Anton Drennan-electric
guitar; Danny Cummins-percussion; Steve Nye-keyboards; James
Delaney-keyboards, synthesizers; Paul Moran-drums. Produced
by Steve Nye. (No instruments listed for Clannad).

    CONTENTS: Caislean Óir; The Wild Cry; Closer
to Your Heart; In a Lifetime; Almost Seems (Too
Late to Turn); Indoor; Buachaill on Eirne;
Blackstairs; Journey's End; Northern Skyline

The most contemporary sound from the band to date. <u>Macalla</u>
or echo is marketed for the pop audience and even features a
duet with Máire and guest aritst Bono Hewson of Ireland's top
rock band U2. "In a Lifetime" is one of the best "pop" tunes
on the record. This is the band's most satisfying contemporary lp. **[LP, CS, CD]**

73.   <u>Magical Ring</u>. (1983)   Tara 3010

    ARTISTS: Pádriag Ó Dúgaín; Máire Ní Bhraonáin; Pól Ó
Braonáin; Noel Ó Dúgáin; Ciarán Ó Braonáin; with James Delaney. (No instruments are stated).

    CONTENTS: Theme from "Harry's Game"; Tower
Hill; Seachrán Charn tSiall; Passing Time;
Coinléoch Glas an Fhómhair; I See Red; Tá 'Mé
Mo Shiú; Newgrange; The Fairy Queen; Thíos Fá'n
Chósta

<u>Magical Ring</u> contains only four traditional tunes, and the
overall mood is very eerie due to the heavy use of synthesizers. Of the folk tunes included only "Coinleach Glas an
Fhómhair," a nice ballad that was originally recorded on the
group's second lp, and the lovely instrumental "The Fairy
Queen" attempt to recapture Clannad's earlier strength in
traditional work. The best contemporary selection is the
final cut, "Thiás Fa'n Chósta," a driving song reminiscent of
"Nil O Sín La" from the band's live album. "Harry's Game"
reached #16 on the British pop charts and has been used as
U-2's opening theme song for its concerts. **[LP, CS]**

    NOTES: Celtic Records tried to cash in on Clannad's
success with a live lp, <u>Ring of Gold</u> (CM 304). No origin for
these in-concert recordings is given. Clannad released its
tenth recording, <u>Sirius</u> (RCA 6846-1-R), in 1988. It has not
been as well-received as its predecessor, <u>Macalla</u>.

BRIAN CONWAY & TONY DEMARCO

74. The Apple in Winter: Irish
     Music in New York. (1981)   Green Linnet SIF 1035

   ARTISTS: Brian Conway-fiddle; Tony DeMarco-fiddle;
with Caesar Pacifici-guitar, bones. Produced by Tony De
Marco and Brian Conway.

> **CONTENTS:** O´Rourke´s/Larry Redican´s; The Bush
> on the Hill/Dave Collins´; Miss Ramsay´s/Miss
> Lyall´s/The Copper Plate; The Poppy Leaf/The
> Flowers of Spring/Jim Coleman´s; The Inter-
> national/Martin Wynne´s; The Girls of Bain-
> bridge/Michael Coleman´s/Apples in Winter;
> Dr. Gilbert´s/Over the Moor to Peggy; Lad´s
> Favorite/Leinster Buttermilk/Tim Fitzpatrick´s;
> Hurry the Jug; Tell Her I Am/Paddy Reynolds´
> Favorite; The White Mountain/Connemara Stock-
> ing; Fly by Night/The Champion/The High Level;
> Paddy O´Brien´s/Ten Penny Bit

Brian Conway and Tony DeMarco play a spirited collection of
dance tunes, accompanied nicely on guitar by Caesar Pacifici.
Conway and DeMarco successfully have blended the predominate
Sligo fiddling style with the more modern and complex New
York style, first made popular by New York City Irish fiddlers in the late 30s and 40s. DeMarco is more daring and
exuberant than Conway´s quieter, more precise delivery, but
the album´s strength is the winning combination of styles.
Many of the tunes were learned from the recordings and performances of musical masters--Michael Coleman, Lad O´Beirne,
Martin Wynne, Andy McGann, and others. Every selection is
excellently performed, including "Dr. Gilbert´s/Over the Moor
to Maggie," "Miss Ramsay´s/Miss Lyall´s," "The Girls of Bain-
bridge/Michael Coleman´s/Apples in Winter," and "The White
Mountain/Connemara´s Stocking." Pacifici adds a solo pefor-
mance on guitar with the set dance, "Hurry the Jug," which
he learned from a tape of Larry Radican. It´s a lovely tune
and a pleasant change of pace. [LP]

JACKIE DALY, SÉAMUS AND MANUS MCGUIRE

75. Buttons & Bows. (1984)   Green Linnet SIF 1051

   ARTISTS: Jackie Daly-Eb accordion, C# accordion,
concertina; Séamus McGuire-fiddle, viola; Manus McGuire-fiddle; with Charlie Lennon-piano; Garry O´Briain-mandocello.
Produced by Jackie Daly, Séamus McGuire, Manus McGuire, and
Philip Begley.

> **CONTENTS:** Cúl Aodh Jig/The Blue Angel;
> Esther´s Reel/Trip to Kinvara; The Old Resting
> Chair; Crowley´s Reels; The Norwegian Waltz/
> Liza Lynn; The Dionne Reel; Waltz from Orsa;
> Barn Dances; My Love is an Arbutus (also known
> as Coola Shore); Waltz Clog; La Bastringue; The
> Bog Carrot/Kevin Burke´s/Charlie Harris´

Buttons and bows (accordion and fiddles) combine so well
together on this album that it is somewhat difficult to
differentiate between the instruments. Jackie Daly, late of
De Danann and Reel Union, brings his multi-talents on accordion and concertina, in addition to his ability as an inter-
preter of traditional music. The McGuire brothers of Sligo
divide the bowing responsiblities. Manus plays impeccable
melody, while Séamus provides elegant harmonies on both
fiddle and viola. The talented accompaniment of Garry
O'Briain on mandocello and Charlie Lennon with piano further
enhances this excellent recording. Uncommon selections from
both sides of the Atlantic (Ireland, Shetland Islands, Sweden
and Canada) make up the contents. It is interesting to note
the difference in styles from the various countries. Daly
constructed an accordion to reproduce the typical North
American accordion sound for the Canadian piece "Waltz Clog"
and for a spirited tribute to French Canadian accordionist
Phillippe Bruneau entitled "La Bastingue."   Tom Anderson,
the master fiddler from the Shetland Islands, composed a
beautiful tribute to his grandfather, "The Old Resting
Chair," which is eloquently performed by the trio. The
fullness and vitality of the overall sound and the variety of
the contents sets <u>Buttons & Bows</u> high above other contemporary fiddle albums. **[LP, CS]**

     NOTES: Jackie Daly and the McGuire brothers now
record under the name Buttons and Bows. In 1987 they
released <u>The First Month of Summer</u> (Green Linnet SIF 1079).
The McGuires recorded <u>Humours of Lissadill</u> (Folk Legacy 78)
and <u>Carousel</u> (Gael-Linn CEF 105) with Dáithí Sproule. Jackie
Daly, in addition to his work with the aforementioned bands
performs on <u>Music from Sliabh Luachra, Volume 6</u> (Topic 358).
He has recorded an album with Seamus Creagh, (Gael Linn 057)
and <u>Eavesdropper</u> with Kevin Burke (Green Linnet SIF 3002).
Daly currently performs with Patrick Street.

DE DANANN

De Danann is an Irish band that formed in 1975 in Spiddal, a
small town in the Irish speaking part of Connemara in west
Galway. The group takes its name from Tuatha De Danann, or
the people of the goddess Danann in Irish mythology. De
Danann is one of the most successful traditional bands on
both sides of the Atlantic. Ironically, one of its first
hits was "Hey Jude," a very untraditional song given the
Celtic treatment. Overall, De Danann arranges its music in
the traditional mode with a stamp of originality.

De Danann has been called a supergroup, having had in its
membership some of the top musicians in Irish music. The
founding members, Alec Finn, Frankie Gavin, and Johnny McDonagh, are still active in the band. Others who have played a
part in De Danann include multi-instrumentalists Johnny
Moynihan, Charlie Piggot, and Andy Irvine, accordionists
Jackie Daly and Martin O'Connor, and singers Dolores Keane,
Maura O'Connell, and Mary Black.

The foundation of De Danann's sound is in the complex melodies of the infectious dance tunes. The music usually cen-
ters around the blazing fiddle of Gavin with lush accompani-

ment on bouzouki, banjo, mandolin, guitar, and melodeon, plus
the rhythmic bodhrán. The band also has had several powerful
vocalists. De Danann is a first rate, consistently solid
band.

76.   Anthem.   (1985)   Dara 013

  ARTISTS: Frankie Gavin-fiddle, flute, viola, piano;
Alec Finn-bouzouki, guitar; Martin O'Connor-accordion; Johnny
McDonagh-bodhrán; Mary Bergin-whistle; Jackie Daly-accordion;
Mary Black-vocals; Dolores Keane-vocals; Maura O'Connell-vo-
cals. Produced by John Dunford, Alec Finn, and Frankie
Gavin.

  CONTENTS: The Wren's Nest; Let It Be; Johnston's Hornpipe; Connie from Constantinople;
Johnny I Hardly Knew Ye; Ríl an Spidéal; Anthem
for Ireland; Jimmy Burnes and Dinkies; Diglake
Fields; Duo in G; Paddy's Lamentation

For this recording, singers Dolores Keane and Maura O'Connell
join De Danann's regular vocalist, Mary Black, in providing
some of the best selections on the album. Black's "Johnny I
Hardly Knew Ye" is breathtaking, and Keane's "Anthem for
Ireland" is heartfelt. "Let It Be" is very low keyed and not
as successful as the band's earlier rendition of the Beatles'
"Hey Jude." Black again scores with her solo, "Paddy's
Lamentation." The remaining tracks contain several energetic
tunes that include "Jimmy Burnes and Dinkies," "Duo in G,"
and Gavin's composition, "The Wren's Nest." **[LP, CS]**

  NOTES: Maura O'Connell has two solo lps, Just in Time
(Polydor 831 1844), and Western Highway (Raglan RGLP 9).

77.   The Best of De Danann.   (1984)   Shanachie 79047

  ARTISTS: Frankie Gavin-fiddle, tin whistle; Alec
Finn-bouzouki, guitar, steel guitar; Charlie Piggott-banjo,
melodian, mandolin, tin whistle; Johnny "Ringo" McDonagh-
bodhrán, bones; Jackie Daly-accordion; Dolores Keane-vocals;
Johnny Moynihan-vocals, harmonica, tin whistle; Maura O'Connell-vocals.

  CONTENTS: Mulvihill's Reel/The Dawn; The Banks
of Red Roses; Coleraine Jig/Derrane's/John
Stenson's/Moher Reel; Rambling Irishman; Johnny
Leary's Polka/O'Keefe's Polka; Johnny I Do Miss
You; Maggie; The Flowers of Spring/Jackie
Small's Jig; The Mountain Streams; Conlon's
Jig/Padraig O'Keefe's/Head of Cabbage/Boy of
Malin; My Irish Molly-O; The Banks of the
Quay/Curcaharan Cross; Carolan's Delight

This greatest hits compilation covers De Danann's first four
albums--De Danann, Selected Jigs, Reels and Songs, Mist
Covered Mountain, and Star Spangled Molly. The band's personnel has remained fairly constant, and its high caliber
performances consistently create fine recordings. **[LP, CS,
CD]**

78.   <u>De Danann</u>. (1975)   Boot 4018

>   **ARTISTS:** Dolores Keane-vocals; Frankie Gavin-fiddle;
> Charlie Piggott-melodeon, banjo, whistle, bouzouki; Alec
> Finn-bouzouki; Johnny "Ringo" McDonagh-bodhrán. Produced by
> Donal Lunny.

>   **CONTENTS:** Tripping Up the Stairs/A Trip to
>   Athlone; The Sunny Banks/Farewell to Erin; The
>   Mountain Streams; Cathleen Hehir's; Eighteen
>   Years Old; The Green Fields of Rossbeigh/Toss
>   the Feathers; The Duke of Leinster/Tar Bolton;
>   The Blackbird/The Jolly Clamdiggers; Rambling
>   Irishman; The Gold Ring; The Shores of Lough
>   Bran; Glenbeigh Hornpipe/Mountain Lark/The
>   Musical Priest

De Danann's debut album, originally released on Polydor, is a
delight! The band possesses a graceful and rhythmic sound,
featuring regional styles of Galway and Kerry. De Danann
utilizes its own innovated sound, characterized by duets,
solos, and ensemble arrrangements. Especially enjoyable are
the marvelous bouzouki duets and bouzouki and banjo duets by
Finn and Piggott. One outstanding example is "The Blackbird." Gavin, at this time one of a few young, promising
musicians, performs exceptionally on fiddle throughout the
album. His playing is especially fine on "The Gold Ring."
Vocally, Dolores Keane, a member of the prominent Keane
family of Galway, furnishes four stunning songs. Both "The
Mountain Streams," which she learned from Paddy Tunney, and
"The Shores of Lough Bran" are excellent. [LP, CS]

79.   <u>The Mist Covered Mountain</u>. (1980)   Shanachie 79005

>   **ARTISTS:** Frankie Gavin-fiddle, whistle, viola; Alec
> Finn-steel guitar, bouzouki, mandocello; Charlie Piggott-
> steel guitar, banjo, mandolin; Johnny "Ringo" McDonagh-bodh-
> rán, bones; Jackie Daly-acordion; with Seán Ó Conaire-vocals;
> Tom "Pháidín Tom" Ó Coisdealbha-vocals. Produced by De
> Danann.

>   **CONTENTS:** Mac's Fancy/The Mist Covered Moun-
>   tain; Cameronian Reel/Doon Reel; Séamaisín;
>   Mulvihill's Reel/The Dawn; The Banks of the
>   Nile; Johnny Leary's Polka/O'Keefe's Polka/
>   Johnny I Do Miss You; Mister O'Connor; Henry
>   Joy; The Cottage in the Grove/Seán Ryan's
>   Reel; Máire Mhór; Langstrom's Pony/The Tap
>   Room/Lord Ramsey's Reel

On their third outing De Danann is joined by Jackie Daly, a
premier accordionist from County Cork. He replaces Johnny
Moynihan. Daly brings depth to the group's instrumental
harmonies, especially with the lyrical "Mister O'Connor."
Two guest Irish singers, Seán Ó Conaire of Connemara and the
late Tom Pháidín Tom, offer two songs apiece. The latter, 85
years old at the time, died a few months after recording
these selections. The best of their songs are Tom's "Henry
Joy" and "Séamaisín" by Ó Conaire. Instrumentally, De Danann
perform several standout tunes--the high spirited reels

"Cameronian Reel/Doon Reel," "The Cottage in the Grove/Seán
Ryan's Reel" with Charlie Piggott's fine banjo, and the set
"Johnny Leary's Polka/O'Keefee's Polka/Johnny I Do Miss You."
[LP, CS]

80.   Selected Jigs, Reels
      and Songs. (1978)   Shanachie 79001

      ARTISTS: Frankie Gavin-fiddle, flute and whistle;
Johnny Moynihan-bouzouki, mandolin, whistle, harmonica,
vocals; Charlie Piggott-banjo, mandolin, whistle, bouzouki,
melodeon; Alec Finn-bouzouki; Johnny "Ringo" McDonagh-bones,
bodhrán. Produced by Carsten Linde, Nicky Ryan, and De
Danann.

           CONTENTS: Tom Billy's/Ryan's Jig/The Sandmount
           Reel/The Clogher Reel; Love Will Ye Marry
           Me/Byrne's Hornpipe; The Broken Pledge/Jenny's
           Welcome to Charlie; The Banks of the Quay/Cru-
           caharan Cross; The Flower of Sweet Strabane;
           The Flowers of Spring/Jackie Small's Jig; The
           Log Cabin/Bean a' Ti Ar Lar; Carolan's Draught;
           The Banks of Red Roses; Over the Bog Road; The
           Hags Purse/The Collier's Jig; Barbara Allen;
           Dear Irish Boy/Johnny Leary's Polkas

The second De Danann album continues the spirited spontaneity
of this Irish band. The groups is joined by Johnny Moynihan,
late of Planxty and Sweeney's Men, who has been credited with
the introduction of the Greek bouzouki into Irish music in
the mid-1960's. (He left the band after this recording's
release and was replaced by Tim Lyons). As with its debut
lp, De Danann, this album offers the excellent counterpoint
of the bouzouki by Finn, Gavin's fiddle versatility, the
vitality and multi-instrumental talents of Piggott, and the
brilliant bodhrán by McDonagh. The instrumentals and overall
sound are enhanced by the addition of Moynihan, whose vocals
are engaging, especially the unaccompanied "The Flower of
Sweet Strabane" and "Barbara Allen." De Danann's strength is
in its tightly arranged instrumentals and the ensemble sets.
"Tom Bill's Jig/Ryan's Jig/The Sandmount Reel/The Clogher
Reel" is the best example. A three-part whistle selection,
"The Banks of the Quay/Crucaharan Cross," was collected by
Piggott's grandfather in the early 1900's and is also
well-performed. [LP, CS]

81.   Song for Ireland. (1983)   Sugar Hill SH 1130

      ARTISTS: Frankie Gavin-fiddle, flute, piano, viola,
tin whistle; Alec Finn-bouzouki, guitars; Johnny (Ringo)
McDonagh-bodhrán, bones; Martin O'Connor-melodeon; Brendan
Reagan-guitar, mandolin; Mary Black-vocals; with Jackie
Daly-accordion; Maura O'Connell-operatic vocals. Produced by
Nick Bicât and De Danann.

           CONTENTS: The Arrival of the Queen of Sheeba
           (in Galway); Hard Times; Mulqueen's Reels; The
           Turkey in the Straw; Live Not Where I Love; The
           Hearty Boys of Ballymoate; Song for Ireland;

> The Bells of St. Louis; The Chicken Reel;
> Charlie Harris' Reels; Jenny Rocking the Crad-
> le; Barney from Killarney.

De Danann produces another high quality recording with this
lively album of exhilarating dance tunes and interesting
songs. The highlight is Mary Black, whose crystal clear
vocals grace three selections. "Hard Times" and "Live Not
Where I Love' are well-performed songs, but "Song for Ireland" is an outstanding example of her vocal gifts. New
members of the group include Brendan Reagan on banjo and
Martin O'Connor on box (accordion, that is). **[LP, CS]**

82.   The Star Spangled Molly. (1981)   Shanachie 79018

   ARTISTS: Jackie Daly-accordion; Alec Finn-bouzouki,
guitar, tenor guitar; Frankie Gavin-fiddle, flute, vocals;
Johnny "Ringo" McDonagh-bodhrán, bones; Charlie Piggot-banjo;
Maura O'Connell-vocals. Produced by De Danann and Nicky
Ryan.

   > **CONTENTS:** Coleraine Jig/Derrane's/John Sten-
   > son's/Moher Reel/Maggie; Kitty's Wedding/The
   > Rambler; New Irish Barn Dance; Come Back Again
   > to Me, Mavourneen; Conlon's Jig/Padraig O'
   > Keefe's/Head O' Cabbage/Boys of Malin; The
   > Cuckoo's Nest; My Irish Molly-O; Hey Jude;
   > Morrison's/The Tailor's Thimble/Wellington's;
   > I'm Leaving Tipperary

Vocals by singer Maura O'Connell are a major attraction.
Selections are predominately from the glory days of the
1920's, when Irish American music was in its prime. High-
lights include "Maggie," "Hey Jude," "Kitty's Wedding/The
Rambler," "Conlon's Jig/Padriag O'Keefe's/Head O' Cabbage/
Boys of Malin," and "My Irish Molly-O." **[LP, CS]**

   NOTES: De Danann scored the soundtrack to "The Irish
R. M." (Release RRL 8012), a PBS production and in 1987
released Ballroom (Green Linnet SIF 3040), featuring the
vocals of Dolores Keane.

SEAMUS EGAN

83.   Traditional Music
       of Ireland. (1985)   Shanachie 29020

   ARTISTS: Seamus Egan-flute, tres, banjo, mandolin,
whistle, pipes; with Siobhan Egan-fiddle; Rory Ann Egan-
accordion; Mick Moloney-guitar; Lori Cole-piano; Jimmy
Keane-electronics; Rosalyn Briley-harp. Produced by Mick
Moloney.

   > **CONTENTS:** The Maids of Galway; The Munster
   > Cloak; The Convenience Reel/Gan Ainm/Hills of
   > Offaly/Guns of the Magnificent Seven; Bach
   > Gavottes; Lock the Door/Get Up Old Woman and
   > Shake Yourself/What Ails You?; Waltz from
   > Transtrand; Castle Ceili's/Pay the Girl Her

Fourpence/Miko Russell's; McDermott's Fancy/
Swans Among the Rushes/Chicago/The Swallow's
Nest; Baltimore Salute/The Lansdowne Lass/
Jackie Coleman's; The Ebb Tide/The Chorus Reel;
Aggie's Waltz; Grandmom's

It is amazing to listen to this solid and highly professional
album, and even more astonishing to realize that the princi-
ple musician, Seamus Egan, is only sixteen years old! Al-
ready an all-Ireland champ on three instruments, Egan cap-
tivates his listening audience with his talents on flute,
whistle, banjo, mandolin, tres, and pipes. His choice of
material reflects a variety of sources, (books, recordings
and performces from other artists), and music types, including reels, jigs, a lullaby, and even Bach gavottes. Standout
tunes include Egan's marvelous whistle solo, "Baltimore
Salute/The Lansdowne Lass/Jackie Coleman's" and "The Maids of
Galway," a reel medley with Egan on flute and Mick Moloney
accompanying on guitar. Egan never loses his edge on this
well-executed tune. In addition to Moloney, Egan is accom
panied by his talented sisters, Siobhan and Rory Ann. This
is an impressive debut record from a young man, who is not a
flash in the pan. The future looks bright for this multi-
talented prodigy. Kudos to Mick Moloney for the excellent
production. **[LP, CS]**

NOTES: Seamus Egan also appears on The Invasion
(Green Linnet SIF 1074) accompanying Jerry O'Sullivan.

SEAMUS ENNIS

84.   The Best of Irish Piping. (1984)   Tara 1002/9

ARTISTS: Seamus Ennis-uilleann pipes.

CONTENTS: [The Pure Drop]-The Pure Drop/The
Flax in Bloom; The Fairy Boy; The Groves Horn-
pipe/Dwyer's Hornpipe; O'Sullivan the Great;
When Sick, Is It Tea You Want/The Humours of
Drinagh; By the River of Gems/The Rocky Road
to ublin; Ask My Father/Pat Ward's Jig; Valen-
cia Harbour; The Standing Abbey/The Stack of
Barley; The Lietrim Thrush/Miss Johnson; The
Return to Fingal; Chase Me Charlie/The Dingle
Regatta; White Connor's Daughter Nora; Slieve
Russell/Sixpenny Money; Stay for Another While/
I Have No Money/The Cushogue; The Brown Thorn.
[The Fox Chase]-Music at the Gate/The Pigeon on
the Gate; The Blooming Meadows/Kitty's Rambles;
Ned of the Hill; Smash the Windows/The Dark
Girl in Blue; The Derry Hornpipe/The Cuckoo's
Nest; The Trip O'er the Mountain; The Merry
Sisters/Music in the Forge/Castle Kelly; Johnny
Cope; The Rainy Day/A Fair Wind; The Fox Chase;
The Braes of Busby/Colonel Frazer; The Kid on
the Mountain.

Compiled in 1984 from two older out of print Tara recordings,
The Pure Drop and The Fox Chase, this cassette is billed as
the best of Seamus Ennis. Alas, it falls short of its

title. This particular collection is tedious and presents a
static impression of Ennis, one of Ireland's most renown
pipers. With a little variation this collection could have
been representative of this excellent musician. **[CS ONLY]**

SEAMUS ENNIS

85.   Forty Years of Piping.   Green Linnet SIF 1000

   ARTISTS: Seamus Ennis-uilleann pipes, tin whistle,
vocals.

   CONTENTS: The Merry Blacksmith/The Rainy
   Day/The Silver Spear; "First You Must Learn the
   Grip"; The Bucks of Oranmore; The Bucks of
   Ornamore/The Sligo Maid's Lament; The Pirates
   are Dug and the Frost is All Over; The Fox
   Chase; If All the Young Maidens were Blackbirds
   and Thrushes; The Copper Plate; The Silver
   Spear/The Dublin Reel/Miss Monahan; Salamanca/
   Duke Gordon; Don Niperi Septo; Donegal Reel;
   Paudeen O'Rafferty/The Friar's Jig; Speed the
   Plough/The Merry Blacksmith/The Forge Music;
   The Lark's March; Sixpenny Money/When the Cock
   Crows It is Day; Piper of the Embers/Down the
   Back Lane/Sixpenny Money; I'll Mend Your Pots
   and Kettles O; The Broken Pledge; Paddy Kil-
   loran's Reel; Gentle Philip Fahy

Forty Years of Piping, covering from the 1930s through the
mid-1970s, is a compiliation of old, rare recordings, repro-
cessed and edited by Green Linnet. It also includes newer
performances the label recorded. Collected by American folk
singer and piper, Patrick Sky, this two record set gives a
broader view of Seamus Ennis and his valuable contributions
to Irish piping and Irish music than The Best of Irish Piping, (Tara 1002/9). In addition to pipe tunes, Ennis contributes stories, songs and tin whistle pieces. Some of the
best selections are "The Bucks of Oranmore/The Sligo Maid's
Lament," "Don Niperi Septo," "The Pirates are Dug and the
Frost is All Over," and "Sixpenny Money/When the Cock Crows
It is Day." This lp is a classic musical biography of an
important figure in traditional Irish music. **[LP]**

JOHN FAULKNER

86.   Kind Providence. (1986)   Green Linnet SIF 1064

   ARTISTS: John Faulkner-guitars, bouzouki, fiddles,
hurdy gurdys, drones, vocals. Produced by John Faulkner.

   CONTENTS: Sweet Thames Flow Softly; The Whale-
   catchers/The Drunken Lady; Planxty Gan Ainm;
   The Wild Rover; Johnny Coughlin; McCaffery; The
   Banks of Newfoundland; The Forger's Farewell;
   The Road to Cashel/Jackie Daly's; Newry Town

Kind Providence is John Faulkner's first solo album in an
illustrious career spaning over 25 years. Most recently
known for his work with his wife, Galway singer Dolores
Keane, and the bands they founded (Reel Union and Kinvara),
Faulkner was influenced early by the acclaimed performer Ewan
MacColl during the 1960s and early 1970s in London as a
member of MacColl's Critics Group. This album is indeed a
triumph and a completely solo effort. Faulkner plays all the
instruments, performs both lead and harmony vocals, and also
serves as the record's producer. He impeccably performs the
selections collected from England, Ireland, and Canada.
Faulkner is a brilliant instrumentalist, which is evident
throughout the album. His use of drones and hurdy gurdys is
very interesting and eerie, especially on "The Wild Rover."
He enhances the emigration song, "Johnny Coughlin," with the
melodic accompaniment of the bouzouki and his vocal harmonies. The fiddle is at its best on the reel set, "The Road
to Cashel," a Charlie Lennon composition, and "Jackie
Daly's," which Faulkner learned from Daly, an excellent
accordion player. The remaining selections prove John Faulkner to be a very talented storyteller and musician.   [LP,
CS]

THE FLYING CLOUD

87.   Traditional Music from Ireland,
      England and Scotland. (1978)   Adelphi AD 1029

      ARTISTS: Brian Brooks-vocals, mandolin, bouzouki,
guitar, whistles, recorder; Tony DeMarco-fiddle; Dan Milner-
vocals, bodhrán, organ; Caesar Pacifici-guitars, tenor banjo,
bones. Produced by John Townley and Christine Townley.

      CONTENTS: Brave Old Donnelly; Tibbie Dunbar;
      The American Stranger; McNamara's/Fitzgerald's;
      Dunlavin Green; Charlie Piggott's/Rattlin'
      Roarin' Willie/An Phis Fhliuch; Farewell to
      Whiskey/A Lady Fair/Tralee Gaol; The Galtee/The
      Duke of Leinster; Jack Orion (includes Farewell
      to Ireland and Master Roger's)

A first rate English/American band based in New York whose
only lp is still available after more than nine years, Flying
Cloud is a competent group with four fine performers. In
this collection of songs and dances, each member performs
well. Highlights include "Dunlavin Green," "The American
Stranger," and "Jack Orion," in which Tony DeMarco flies
through the break on fiddle to the tune of "Farewell to
Ireland." A pleasant record. [LP]

      NOTES: Tony DeMarco teamed up with Brian Conway to
record The Apple in Winter: Irish Music in New York (Green
Linnet SIF 1035). Caesar Pacifici was a guest artist on this
album, too.

FINBAR FUREY

88.   The Irish Pipes of Finbar Furey.   Nonesuch H-72048

ARTISTS: Finbar Furey-uilleann pipes, tin whistle; with Eddie Furey-guitar.

CONTENTS: Rakish Paddy; The Hag with the Money; Castle Terrance; Madame Bonaparte; The Young Girl Milking Her Cow; Fin's Favourite; Peter Byrne's Fancy; O'Rourke's Reel; Roy's Hands; Planxty Davy; The Bonny Bunch of Roses; Eddie's Fancy; The Silver Spear

Eerie at times, while rousing and jovial in other instances, the uilleann pipes is a fascinating instrument that can be fully appreciated only in person. However, many recordings of the pipes give the listener a glimpse of the instrument's complexity and versatility. This recording is a fine example of this.

Finbar Furey, only twenty-one when the lp was recorded, offers a variety of dance tunes and tempos from jigs to hornpipes. Most selections are unaccompanied and well-performed. Four tin whistle tunes add excellent contrast to the pipes and to the appeal of this album. Eddie Furey, Finbar's brother, accompanies him on guitar. [LP]

THE FUREY BROTHERS AND DAVEY ARTHUR

89.   The Sound of the Fureys &
      Davey Arthur.   Polydor 2490160

ARTISTS: The Furey Brothers and Davey Arthur perform on various instruments, including guitar, mandolin, uilleann pipes, banjo, whistle and vocals.

CONTENTS: The Green Fields of France; Gypsy Davey; The Reason I Left Mullingar; Clare to Here; Selection of Reels: Ask Me Father/Finbar Dwyer's/The Old Oak Tree/Lark on the Strand; Her Father Didn't Like Me Anyway; Shipyard Slips; The Leaving of Nancy; O'Carolan's Tribute; The Rooster; Night Ferry; Lament; Beer, Beer, Beer; Lonesome Boatman

A collection of mostly pleasant songs, backed by some tasty accompaniment, dominates the contents of this album, a greatest hits compilation taken from various records dated 1976-1981. No information on the band or its music is included, but their sound is similar in style to the Wolfe Tones or Clancy Brothers. Eric Bogle's "Green Fields of France" and "Clare to Here," written by Ralph McTell, are the best of the lot. [LP]

NOTES: The Furey Brothers have recorded extensively, especially with Davey Arthur, and many of their albums are still available. Examples include Emigrant (Polydor 2904009), Morning on a Distant Shore (Polydor 290410), The Sound of the Fureys (Polydor 2491060), In Concert--Live (Ritz 25), When You were Sweet Sixteen (Ritz 04), and Steal Away (Ritz 05). Finbar and Eddie have also recorded Finbar and Eddie Furey (Transatlantic TRA 3006), The Dawning of the Day (Dawn 3037), I Know Where I'm Going (Isle 3006), and Lonesome

Boatman (Transatlantic TRA 191). Finbar Furey recorded an
album with Bob Stewart, Tomorrow We Part (Crescent Records
ARS 110), which presents the combination of the pipes with
the psaltery.

DICK GAUGHAN AND ANDY IRVINE

90.   Parallel Lines. (1983)   Green Linnet SIF 3201

    ARTISTS: Dick Gaughan-acoustic guitar, electric
guitar, bass, vocals; Andy Irvine-bouzouki, mandola, mandolin, hurdy gurdy, harmonica, vocals; with Martin Buschmann-
saxophone; Nollaigh Ni Cathasaigh-fiddle; Judith Jaenic-
ke-flute; Bob Lenox-Fender Rhodes piano. Produced by Andy
Irvine and Dick Gaughan.

        CONTENTS: The Creggan White Hare; The Lads O'
        the Fair/Leith Docks; At Twenty-One; My Back
        Pages/Afterthoughts; The Dodgers Song; Captain
        Thunderbolt (also known as The Shannonside and
        also as Lough Allen Side); Captain Colston;
        Floo'ers O' the Forest

What a feast of songs from two renown Celtic performers!
Dick Gaughan, one of Scotland's top singer/songwriters, known
for his work with Five Hand Reel and Boys of the Lough, is
joined by Ireland's Andy Irvine, an excellent singer, instrumentalist, and a founding member of the seminal groups
Sweeney's Men and Planxty. This duo has created a superb
album, showcasing their infinite instrumental and vocal
talents. Recorded in West Germany, Parallel Lines presents a
mixture of traditional and contemporary songs arranged by the
duo. Vocally the pair have distinctive singing styles.
Irvine's versions of the humorous "The Creggan White Hair"
and the exciting pirate tale "Captain Colston" are two of his
best contributions. The uniqueness of Gaughan's voice and
style is striking. His lilting cadence gives "Floo'ers O'
the Forest," "The Lads of the Fair," and Bob Dylan's "My Back
Pages" a haunting quality. Instrumentally, the interaction
between Gaughan and Irvine on various instruments enhances
every selection. Their high caliber performances make this
album an important addition to any collection. **[LP]**

    NOTES: Solo recordings by Dick Gaughan include Hand-
full of Earth (Advent 3602), A Different Kind of Love Song
(Advent 3604), Gaughan (Shanachie 79057), Coppers & Brass
(Topic 315), No More Forever (Trailer Leader 2072), and Kist
O' Gold (Trailer Leader 2103). As a member of Five Hand
Reel, Gaughan recorded Five Hand Reel (Black Crow CRO 211)
and For A'That (Black Crow CRO 212), which were re-issued in
1987. Andy Irvine has one solo 1p, Rainy Sundays... Windy
Dreams (Tara 3002). He has recorded with Paul Brady, Andy
Irvine and Paul Brady (Green Linnet SIF 3006), and was a
member of Sweeney's Men, Sweeney's Men (Transatlantic TRASAM
37) and Tracks of Sweeney (Transatlantic TRASAM 40). Irvine
was also a founding member of Planxty, and he currently
records and performs with Patrick Street.

FRANKIE GAVIN

91.   Up and Away. (1983)   Gael-Linn CEF 103

ARTISTS: Frankie Gavin-concert flute, fiddle, tin
whistle, accordion; with Charlie Lennon-piano; Johnny "Ringo"
McDonagh-bodhrán. Produced by Frankie Gavin, Charlie Lennon,
and Jackie Small.

CONTENTS: Seit Eddie Moloney (Eddie Moloney's
Set); The Moving Pint/Dog Big and Dog Little;
Buck from the Mountain/McPartlin's Style;
Col. Rogers/Happy Days of Youth; Up Leitrim;
Early Breakfast/Scotch Mary; Bocannaí Uaráin
Mhóir (The Bucks of Oranmore); My Love is But a
Lassie/Dark Girl Dressed in Blue; Kilty Town/
McFadden's Favourite; McLaughlin's Flings; Five
Mile Chase/The Glass of Beer/Richard Dwyer's;
Frankie Gavin's Irish Orchestra: Mike Flana-
gan's/Doirí an Choláiste (The College Grove)/
Leitrim Thrush

Best known for his exuberant fiddling with De Danann, Frankie
Gavin proves to be excellent with the flute on this delightful album. Up and away aptly describes the style and quality
of the music. Gavin shines in his performances and arrangements. All selections are traditional and arranged by Gavin
except "The Moving Pint/Dog Big and Dog Little" and "Kilty
Town," which are original compositions by Charlie Lennon,
Gavin's piano accompanist. Top honors go to several selections. "The Moving Pint/Dog Big and Dog Little" which utilizes overtracking for fiddle and flute, and Ringo McDonagh's
raucous bodhrán beat on "Up Leitrim" and "Five Mile Chase"
are three of the best tunes. "McLaughlin's Flings" and
"Kilty Town/McFadden's Favourite" round out the finest cuts.
[LP]

FRANKIE GAVIN AND ALEC FINN

92.   Traditional Music of Ireland:
       Fiddle and Bouzouki. (1977)   Shanachie 29008

ARTISTS: Frankie Gavin-fiddle, whistle; Alec Finn-
bouzouki. Produced by Richard Nevins and Daniel Michael
Collins.

CONTENTS: Martin Wynne's/Austin Tierney's; Cup
of Tea; Peacock's Feather; Drowsy Maggie/Star
of Munster; Charles O'Connor; Jackson's; Pigeon
on the Gate; Ryan's; Bunch of Green Rushes/Sean
Frank; Murphy's; The Congress Reel; Concert
Reel

Frankie Gavin and Alec Finn, two founding members of the
energetic band De Danann, recorded this informal session in
Greenwich Village during an American tour. Do not under-
estimate the quality of this album due to its informal
birth. The music flows from this duo in a relaxed yet vibrant manner. The tempo is upbeat, mostly reels, with even a
planxty from Carolan, "Charles O'Connor." Finn's bouzouki

is perfect accompaniment for Gavin's masterful fiddle. Finn
has retained the Greek tuning, which provides excellent
counterpoint to traditional Irish music.
[LP, CS]

GENERAL HUMBERT

93.   General Humbert II. (1983)   Shanachie 79032

> ARTISTS: Shay Kavanagh-guitar,bouzouki; Mary Black-
> vocals, bodhrán; John Donegan-mandolin, harmonium; Vincent
> Kilduff-uilleann pipes, tin whistle, flute; with Kevin Glackin-fiddle; Arthur Keating-French horn. Produced by Nicky
> Ryan.

> CONTENTS: Amhrán Phéter Báille; Dans Klemm/An
> Dro; St. Helena; Old Joe's/Old Tipperary/Jig of
> Slurs; Duilleoga; Reverb in the Cans/The Crooked Road/Lucy Campbell; Mo Ghile Mear; Mrs.
> Kelly's Chickens/The Trip Over the Mountains;
> Mrs. Delaney/Carolan's Cup/Conor O'Reilly; Fare
> Thee Well, My Own True Love

The second recording and first American release by this Irish
band is quite an accomplishment. Formed in 1976, General
Humbert consists of three musicians performing on keyboards,
stringed and wind instruments, and a wonderful vocalist, Mary
Black. Her exquisite singing highlights this album. Black's
vocal clarity and strength is prominent throughout, but
especially on "St. Helena," "Amhrán Phéter Báille," and
"Duilleoga." As she wraps her voice around the lyrics, each
line comes alive. The accompanying five instrumentals are
well-performed with the jig set "Old Joe's/Old Tipperary/Jig
of Slurs" a fine example. The use of harmonium gives "Mo
Ghile Mear" a reverential feeling that contrasts with the
version by Relativity (Green Linnet SIF 1059). [LP, CS]

> NOTES: General Humbert's first album, General Humbert
> on Celtic Records is currently out of print. Mary Black can
> be heard on two De Danann albums, Song for Ireland (Sugar
> Hill SH 1130), and Anthem (Dara 013). She also has recorded
> several solo albums, Mary Black (Dara 002), Without the
> Fanfare (Dara 013), Collected (Dara 011), and a live lp, By
> the Time It Gets Dark (Dara 027), which is produced by her
> husband, Declan Sinnott. In addition, an album with her
> family, The Black Family (Dara 023), recently was released.

PADDY GLACKIN

94.   Glackin. (1977)   Gael-Linn CEF 060

> ARTISTS: Paddy Glackin-fiddle; with Micheál Ó Súil-
> leabháin, Séamus Glackin, Tomás Glackin and Caoimhín Glackin.
> Produced by Tony MacMahon.

> CONTENTS: Cor Pheait Uí Thuathaigh (Pat Tuo-
> hey's Reel)/Sean tSráid an Chubhthaigh (Old
> Cuffe Street); Seán Ó Duibhir an Ghleanna;
> Stócaigh Mhalainne (The Boys of Malin)/An

Bóthar Ard go Linton (The High Road to Linton);
Diúic Laighean (The Duke of Leinster)/Drúcht na
Maidne (The Morning Dew); An Giorria San Arbhar
(The Hare in the Corn)/Port Phádriag Uí Chaoimh
(Pádriag O'Keefe's Jig); Cúlú Bonaparte (Bona-
parte's Retreat); Coir Mhic Pháidín (McFadden's
Reels); Slipéid Inúne Patterson (Miss Patter-
son's Slipper); Cuir Buaic Leis (Top It Off)/Na
Bruacha Grianmhara (The Sunny Banks); An Cupán
Sughtromáin (The Cup of (Overdrawn) Tea)/Cor
Sheáin Uí Dhochartaigh (John Doherty's Reel);
Altraigh na deá-mhná (Cherish the Ladies); An
Snaoisín Tobac (The Pinch of Snuff)/An tÉirean-
nach Fiánta (The Wild Irishman); Cor Julia
Delaney (Julia Delaney's Reel)/Gliondàr Máthar
(Mother's Delight); Rí na bPíobaí (The King of
the Pipes)/Port Arthur Darley (Arthur Darley's
Jig); Na Cosáin Ghairbhéil (The Gravel Walks);
Cathaoir Rua (Red-Haired Charles)/Seilg na
Bóinne (The Boyne Hunt); Port Singil (Single
Jig)

Paddy Glackin, formerly of the Bothy Band, gives a brauvera
fiddle performance. Backed by Seámus, Tomás, and Caoimhín
Glackin, and Micheál O Suilleabháin, Glackin plays many first
class fiddle standards. Highlights include "Slipeid Iníne
Patterson," his solo fiddle on "Rí na bPíobaí/Port Arthur
Darley," and "An Giorria San Arbhan/Port Phadraig Uí
Chaoimh." "Na Cosáin Ghairbheil" is performed well by all
four Glackins, and O Suilleabháin's harsichord provides a
baroque mood to "Seán Ó Duibhir an Gleanna." The album is
excellent and played with gusto. **[LP]**

NOTES: Paddy Glackin has recorded <u>Hidden Ground</u> (Tara
2009) with Jolyon Jackson, a mixture of fiddle and keyboards,
<u>Flags of Dublin</u> (Topic 12TS 383) with Mick Gavin and Michael
O Brien, and <u>Paddy and Paddy</u> (Tara 2007) with Paddy Keenan.

CHARLES GUARD

95. <u>Avenging and Bright</u>. (1978)   Shanachie 79014

ARTISTS: Charles Guard-harps; with Michael Kneale-
fiddle; Bob Carswell-tin whistle.

CONTENTS: Muiris Ó Conchubhair (Maurice O'Con-
nor); Scottish Selection: Heman Dubh/Tha mi
sgith/The Peat Fire Flame; Tra Va Ruggit Creest
(When Christ was Born); Burn's March; Craobh
nan Teud (Lament for the Lost Harp-Key); Manx
Dances: Tom the Tailor/The Fairies' Reel; Yn
Eeanleyder as Y Lhondoo (The Fowler and the
Blackbird); Tabhair Dom Do Lámh (Give Me Your
Hand); Mrs. Poer (also known as Carolan's
`Concerto'); Moore's Irish Melodies: Silent O
Moyle/Avenging and Bright; Ny Kiree fo Niaghtey
(The Sheep Under the Snow); Brian Boru's March;
Cumha an Chláirseora (The Harper's Lament);
Arrane Ghelbee (The Song of the Water Kilpie);
The Haughs o'Cromdale

Manx harper Charles Guard is well-known and admired throughout the British Isles and Ireland. On this album he performs
tunes from the traditions of Ireland, Scotland, the Isle of
Man, and the Isle of Skye. Additionally, there are two
lovely Thomas Moore melodies and a striking original composition by the harpist, "Cumha an Chláirseora." Guard, who
is accompanied on only a few cuts by the fiddle and whistle,
plays a contemporary re-creation of the wire-strung harp,
noted for its bell-like tonal quality, and a gut-strung,
neo-Celtic harp. Every selection is expertly performed and
does justice to the traditions represented. Guard plays
delicately and dramatically depending on the tune. The
album's best tracks include "Arrane Ghelbee," the lyrical
version of "Brian Boru's March," which is a nice contrast to
more orchestrated renditions, and "The Haughs O'Cromdale," in
which Guard performs it as a strathspey, an air, and finally
a reel. The Manx tunes are enchanting, especially "Tom the
Tailor/The Fairies Reel." Charles Guard is a skillful,
imaginative, and outstanding harper. [LP]

MICK HANLY

96.   As I Went Over
       Blackwater. (1982)   Green Linnet SIF 3007

     ARTISTS: Mick Hanly-guitar, vocals; with Donal Lun-
ny-bouzouki, synthesizer, harmony vocals; Andy Irvine-har-
monicas, hurdy gurdy, mandolin, harmony vocals; Matt Molloy-flute; Noel Hill-concertina; Paddy Glackin-fiddle; Declan
Sinnott-electric guitar; Sean Hanly-bodhrán. Produced by
Donal Lunny.

        CONTENTS: Jack Haggerty; The Guerriere and the
        Constitution; Every Circumstance; The Dewey
        Dens of Yarrow; Miss Bailey (also known as
        Unfortunate Miss Bailey)/Jessica's Polka; I
        Wish My Love was a Red Red Rose; Off to Cali-
        fornia/The Plains of Boyle; The Scourge of the
        Nation; As I Went Over Blackwater

As I Went over Blackwater is a delightful album. Mick
Hanly, a storyteller and humorist, presents a wide range of
material reflecting both his serious and satirical sides.
Hanly is backed by the creme de la creme of Irish traditional
musicians, and performs songs mainly collected from printed
sources. He also wrote several accompanying tunes to the
printed lyrics, in addition to composing a polka for his
daughter, Jessica. Whether original or traditional, Hanly's
interpretations are top-notched. One of the finest is "The
Dewey Dens of Yarrow," a sorrowful ballad of lost love, which
is accompanied perfectly on flute by Matt Molloy. (A shorter
version of this song can be found on Celtic Folkweave (Poly
dor 2908 013), an album which Hanly recorded with Mícheál Ó
Domhnaill). Hanly learned the title cut from his grandmother
and includes a splendid electric slide guitar background.
For humor, "Miss Bailey," and "Every Circumstance," stand out
as the best examples. [LP]

MICK HANLY

97.   A Kiss in the Morning
      Early. (1982)   Green Linnet SIF 3017

    ARTISTS: Mick Hanly-guitar, vocals; with Paddy Glack-
in-fiddle; Tríona Ní Dhomhnaill-harpsichord; Donal Lunny-
bouzouki; Rick Epping-concertina, harmonica; Peter Brown-
pipes; Matt Molloy-flute. Produced by Donal Lunny and
Mícheál Ó Domhnaill.

    CONTENTS: Farewell, Dearest Nancy; The Mer-
chant's Daughter; My Johnny Was a Shoemaker;
Song of Repentance; Rosemary Fair; A Kiss in
the Morning Early; An tSean Bhean Bhocht; The
Verdant Braes of Screen; The Cod Liver Oil; The
Reluctant Pirate

Another fine album by this multitalented singer and guitarist. Originally issued in 1976 on Mulligan Records, A Kiss
in the Morning remains refreshing and electrifying after more
than ten years. Hanly collected his material from More Irish
Street Ballads (Three Candles Press) by Colm O Lochlain
except for "The Reluctant Pirate." Top honors go to "My
Johnny Was a Shoemaker," "A Kiss in the Morning," "Cod Liver
Oil," and "The Reluctant Pirate." **[LP]**

    NOTES: In addition to his work on Celtic Folkweave,
Mick Hanly also performed for a time with Moving Hearts.

NOEL HILL AND TONY LINNANE

98.   Noel Hill and Tony Linnane. (1979)   Tara 2006

    ARTISTS: Noel Hill-concertinas; Tony Linnane-fiddle;
with Matt Molloy-flute; Alec Finn-bouzouki, mandocello;
Mícheál Ó Domhnaill-church harmonium. Produced by Mícheál Ó
Domhnaill.

    CONTENTS: Humours of Ballyconnell/Drunken
Landlady/Ryan's Reel; Geese in the Bog; Joe
Cooley's Hornpipe/Miss Monaghan; Skylark/Fox-
hunter; Reevey's Reel/Golden Keyboard; Kil-
loran's Reel/Mountain Reel; Anderson's Reel/
Carthy's/Sweeney's Dream; Johnny Cope; Scotsman
Over the Border/Tom Billy's Jig; A Pigeon on
the Gate; Daniel O'Connell: The Home Ruler/
Kitty's Wedding; Lady Anne Montgomery/Cooley's
Reel

Noel Hill and Tony Linnane were teenagers when this inspiring
album was recorded in late 1978. Their vitality and prowess
on concertina and fiddle is exceptional throughout this good
collection of traditional Irish instrumentals. Produced by
Mícheál Ó Domhnaill, this record also features the talents of
Alec Finn of De Danann on bouzouki and mandocello, and Matt
Molloy from the Bothy Band on flute. In addition to duets
and ensemble pieces, both Hill and Linnane perform solo.
Hill's concertina tune, "Johnny Cope," on which Ó Domhnaill
has added the harmonium to resemble a chanter is the best.

Two reel sets, "Humours of Ballyconnell/Drunken Landlady/ Ryan's Reel" and "Anderson's Reel/Carthy's Reel/ Sweeney's Dream," present the duo and their guest artists the finest performances. [LP]

TONY HILL AND TONY MACMAHON

99.   I gCnoc na Graí. (1985)   Gael-Linn CEF 114

ARTISTS: Noel Hill-concertina; Tony MacMahon-accordion. Produced by Noel Hill.

CONTENTS: The Humours of Castlefin; The Ash Plant; Port na bPúcaí; Young Tom Ennis; The Pure Drop; The New Custom House; An Fáinne Óir; Cooley's Jig; The Old Concertina Reel; A hAon sa Dó na Píobaireachta (The Ace and Deuce of Piping); The Green Groves of Erin; Paul Halfpenny; The New-Mown Meadow; The Trip to Athlone; Aisling Gheal

Recorded in Dan Connell's pub in Knocknagree on the border of Co. Cork and Co. Kerry, I gCnoc na Graí combines the talents of Noel Hill on concertina and Tony MacMahon with accordion. Both deliver an unrestrained, exciting collection of tunes accompanied by Clare dancers, whose footwork is featured prominently on many selections. This is a nonstop dance party with not a still foot (dancers and spectators alike) in the house. Hill and MacMahon roar through twelve wonderfully performed traditional dances (jigs, reels, double jigs, etc.). "The Humours of Castlefin," "An Fáinn Óir," "Cooley's Jig," and "Trip to Athlone" are excellent examples of the overall high quality. Two airs, "Aisling Gheal" and the exquisite "Port na bPúcaí," complete the selections. [LP]

HOW TO CHANGE A FLAT TIRE

100.   A Point of Departure.* (1977)   Front Hall FHR 09

ARTISTS: Jim Cowdery-guitar, mandolin, banjo, recorders; Bo Hinrichs-flute, fife, whistle; Dean Kuth-bodhrán, spoons, bones, concertina, mandolin; Jim Martin-banjo, guitar, mandolin; Ginny Phelps-guitar, wooden spoons, vocals.

CONTENTS: The Little Purse of Money; Jug of Punch; Jenny's Welcome to Charlie; The Blackthorne Tree; Eilis Ni Cheallaigh; Roger the Weaver; The Battering Ram; The Seal-Woman's Croon; Bumper Squire Jones; Padriac O'Keefe's; The Hag with the Money; Boring the Leather; Banish Misfortune; The Weavers; John McCanaty's Courtship; Paddy Fahy's; Chicago; Jenny's Wedding; Kiss the Maid Behind the Barrel; The Battle of Clontarf; Lord King

A fine debut album from this East Coast American group, which originally formed in 1975 at the California Institute of the Arts. How to Change a Flat Tire specializes in instrumentals with vocals by Ginny Phelps. [LP]

HOW TO CHANGE A FLAT TIRE

101.   Traditional Music of Ireland
       and Shetland. (1978)   Front Hall FHR 018

   ARTISTS: Maggie Holzberg-fiddle; Dean Kuth-concer-
tina, bodhrán, spoons, bones; Jim Martin-mandolin, guitar,
banjo; Jim Cowdery-recorder, mandolin, whistle. Produced by
Bill Spence and How to Change a Flat Tire.

    CONTENT: Langstrom's Pony/The Ballykeal Jig/
    The Pipe on the Hob; Sister Jean/Kiss Her and
    Clap Her/Gibbie Grey's/Andrew Polson's; Fare-
    well to Williamstown/Peter's Jig/Martin's New
    Haircut; Paddy Fahy's/Green Grow the Rushes;
    Farewell to Peggy/Richard Dwyer's/Jack in the
    Fog; The Gummaho/Martin Talty's; A Pinch of
    Snuff/The Yorkshire Lasses; Father Burke/The
    Whinny Hills of Leitrim/Elizabeth Kelley's
    Delight; Foxy Mary/Art O'Keefe's/The Scartaglen
    Jig; Da Muckle Reel o' Finnigirt; Jeannie Choke
    da Bairn/Wha'll Dance Wi' Wattie?/Square da
    Mizzen/Da Black Hat; Paddy McFadden/Behind the
    Bush in Parkhanna/The Highlander/Tom Barrett's

Their second album contains instrumentals from the Shetland
Islands and Ireland, and is a stonger record that its predecessor. The addition of talented fiddler Maggie Holzberg is
quite an asset. Highlights include "Farewell to Peggy" and
"Da Muckle Reel o' Finnigirt." **[LP]**

THE IRISH TRADITION

102.   The Corner House. (1978)   Green Linnet SIF 1016

   ARTISTS: Brendan Mulvihill-fiddle; Billy McComiskey-
accordion, concertina, harmonium; Andy O'Brien-vocals, guitar; with Mick Moloney-harmony vocals, bouzouki, mandolin,
tenor banjo, mandola. Produced by Mick Moloney.

    CONTENTS: Smash the Windows/Fred Finn's;
    Windmills; In and Out the Harbor (also known as
    Peggy on the Settle); The Maid at the Spinning
    Wheel/The Collier's Jig (also known as Do You
    Want Any More); The Hiring Fair; The Corner
    House/My Maryann; Loftus Jones; The Spike
    Island Lassies/The Humours of Tulla; The Dark
    Eyed Sailor; Molly on the Shore/The Tempest;
    England's Motorway; The Congress Reel/Down the
    Broom/The Star of Munster

The Irish Tradition, three musicians based in the Washington,
D.C. area, is a well-balanced ensemble with great depth of
talent and a varied repertoire. Corner House, the band's
first major release, is impressive. Producer Mick Moloney
assists with stringed accompaniment and harmony vocals, and
the overall performance of the artists is solid and enthu-
siastic.

Fiddler Brendan Mulvihill won his first All-Ireland Championship at eighteen, and his controversial stutter-roll ornamentation is in evidence on the album. Mulvihill's solo, "In
and Out of the Harbor," is a good example of his talents.
This West Limerick tune has been handed down for three generations in his family. American born Billy McComisky has
played button accordion since the age of six. He is a competent and inspired accompanist and solo artist. McComisky
utilizes an unusual and original bass line, which is best
illustrated on "The Spike Island Lasses/The Humours of
Tulla." Andy O'Brien rounds out the trio with four songs, of
which "England's Motorway" is the most impressive. The
Corner House should expand the audience of this underrated
band. [LP, CS]

THE IRISH TRADITION

103.   The Times We've Had. (1985)   Green Linnet SIF 1063

ARTISTS: Brendan Mulvihill; Billy McComiskey; Andy
O'Brien; with Myron Bretholz-bodhrán. Produced by Mick Moloney.

CONTENTS: Paddy Fahy's/Paddy O'Brien's; The
Shipyard Apprentice; The Quilty/Sault's;
Michael O'Connor; Paddy's Lamentation; Festus
Burke; The Yellow Tinker/The Sally Gardens; A
Lady Fair; Happy Days/Flight of the Wild Geese;
The Wild Rover; Lad O'Beirne's/The Small Hills
of Offaly

Still as exciting as its New York debut more than ten years
ago, the Irish Tradition is a refreshing joy. Their musicianship is excellent (both McComiskey and Mulvihill are
All-Ireland Champions), and their selection of material
provides each member and the trio as a whole with a vehicle
to showcase this talent. The Times We've Had, the band's
second album on Green Linnet, is an excellent follow-up to
its debut lp, The Corner House, (Green Linnet SIf 1016). The
dance sets, which are the group's trademark, highlight this
record, but the solo pieces also are very good. "Michael
O'Connor," a beautiful Carolan composition, is performed on
fiddle by Mulvihill. Irish baroque fiddle? Yes, and it is a
wonderful departure from the usual harp! McComiskey simply
shines with the solo accordion reels, "The Yellow Tinker/The
Sally Gardens," and O'Brien performs four stunning songs, of
which "Paddy's Lamentation," a song of conscripting Irish
immigrants into the Union army during the American Civil War,
is one of his best. The Irish Tradition's dynamism and
talent should not be missed. [LP, CS]

NOTES: Solo albums by two members of the Irish Tradi-
tion are Makin' the Rounds by Billy McComiskey (Green Linnet
SIF 1034) and Brendan Mulvihill's Flax in Bloom (Green Linnet
SIF 1020).

ANDY IRVINE

104.   Rainy Sundays...
       ...Windy Dreams. (1980)   Tara 3002

ARTISTS: Andy Irvine-hurdy gurdy, mandola, harmonica, Flyde bouzouki, mandolin, vocals; with Donal Lunny-harmonium, pan flute, bouzouki, guitar, 10-string bouzouki, percussion, bore and snore, vocals. Liam O'Flynn-uilleann pipes; Frankie Gavin-fiddle, viola, flute; Paul Brady-guitar, piano; Rick Epping-harmonica, Jews harp, accordion; Lucienne Purcell-vocals; John Wadham-bongo, congas; Paul Barrett- Fender Rhodes, Polymoog; Garvan Gallagher-El. bass; Keith Donald-soprano sax. Produced by Donal Lunny.

> **CONTENTS:** The Emigrants: Come to the Land of Sweet Liberty, Farewell to Old Ireland, Edward Connors; Longford Weaver; Christmas Eve; Farewell to Ballymoney; Romanian Song (Blood and Gold); Paidushko Horo; King Bore and the Sandman; Rainy Sundays

Andy Irvine has long been an important figure in the Irish folk music renaissance. He was a founding member of Sweeney's Men and the legendary Planxty, and has an active solo career. Irvine is in demand as an accompanist, and currently is a member of Patrick Street. For this album he is accompanied by former Planxties, Donal Lunny, Paul Brady, and Liam O'Flynn, in addition to Frankie Gavin of De Danann. This warm, personable lp combines traditional pieces with Irvine's original compositions and his Eastern European influences. The delightful "Romanian Song" and the accompanying dance, "Paidushko Horo," are performed in 5/16 time or Paidushko rhythm and provide a contrast with the other selections. Luciene Purcell has a wonderful Balkan sound to her voice, making this one of the many album highlights. Irvine performs a trio of songs on the Irish emigrant--"Come to the Land of Sweet Liberty," "Farewell to Old Ireland," and "Edward Connors,"--which portray the sadness and bitterness of leaving home for the unknown in American and Canada. Another excellent selection is the reel "Christmas Eve," which stars Frankie Gavin on fiddle and Rick Epping with Jew's harp. **[LP, CS]**

NOTES: Andy Irvine also appears on The Gathering (Greenhays GR 705).

ANDY IRVINE/PAUL BRADY

105.   Andy Irvine and
       Paul Brady. (1981)   Green Linnet SIF 3006

ARTISTS: Andy Irvine-bouzouki, mandolin, hurdy gurdy, harmonica, mandola, guitar, vocals; Paul Brady-guitar, mandolin, bouzouki, whistle, cittern, harmonium, vocals, backing vocals; with Donal Lunny-bouzouki, bodhrán, guitar, backing vocals; Kevin Burke-fiddle. Produced by Donal Lunny.

> **CONTENTS:** Plains of Kildare; Lough Erne Shore; Fred Finn's Reel/Sailing into Walpole's Marsh; Bonny Woodhall; Arthur McBride and the Sergeant; The Jolly Soldier; The Blarney Pilgrim; Autumn Gold; Mary and the Soldier (also known as The Gallant Soldier); The Streets of Derry

(also known as The Dreary Gallows); Martinmas
Time; The Little Stack of Wheat

This exceptional album, originally released in 1976, contains
flawless vocals and striking instrumentation. Andy Irvine
and Paul Brady, both from Planxty, give a commanding performance on each selection. Top honors include the anti-recrui-
ting song "Arthur McBride and the Sergeant," which is sung by
Brady, Irvine's wistful original composition, "Autumn Gold,"
the powerful instrumental "Fred Finn's Reel/Sailing into Walpole's Marsh," the wonderfully humorous "Martinmas Time," and
the Ulster love song "Lough Erne Shore." The latter is
eerily accompanied by the hurdy gurdy. [LP]

THE JOHNSTONS

106.   The Johnstons
            Anthology. (1978)   Transatlanic MTRA 2012

   ARTISTS: Luci Johnston, Adrienne Johnston, Mike
Johnston, Paul Brady, Mick Moloney, Chris McCloud. (An
educated guess from the sketchy liner notes). Compiled by
John Briley.

        CONTENTS: Bitter Green, The Barleycorn; If I
        Sang My Song; Colours of the Dawn; The Story of
        Isaac; My House; Give a Damn; Both Sides Now;
        O'Carolan's Concerto; If I Could; The Wind in
        My Hands; The Flower of Northumberland; Con-
        tinental Trailways Bus; The Tunnel Tigers

The Johnstons were one of the first Irish bands to combine
traditional material with contemporary songs. Long over-
looked during their lifetime, the Johnstons helped bridge the
gap between the pub songs of the popular Clancy Brothers and
similar bands, and the more contemporary sound begining to be
heard in Britain and America. There is little argument that
the band was important to the beginnings of the resurgence of
Irish music in the seventies. The Johnstons also introduced
two musicians, Paul Brady and Mick Moloney, who are prominent
today.

The band was known for its refreshing harmonies and mixture
of rock, pop, and folk. This album is a collection of songs
taken from the Johnstons' albums and singles, most of which
unfortunately have been deleted from Transatlantic's cata-
logue. The liner notes give a little history of the band and
note on which album or single the tunes appeared, but there
is no mention of the albums' titles, just the record
numbers. Very curious. The Johnstons had seven albums,
including Give a Damn and Colours of the Dawn, but little
else is given by way of a discography. The contents are a
mixed bag, from a Carolan instrumental to Joni Mitchell and
Gordon Lightfoot material. Some of the best songs on this
anthology include "Barleycorn," "Colours of the Dawn," "The
Flower of Northumberland," and the wonderful harmonies of
"The Tunnel Tigers." [LP]

DOLORES KEANE

107.   <u>There Was a Maid</u>. (1978)   Claddagh CC 23

    ARTISTS: Dolores Keane-vocals, wooden flute; with
Peadar Mercier-bodhrán; Martin Byrnes-fiddle; and Reel Union
(no individual artists or instruments mentioned).

        CONTENTS: The Generous Lover; The Bantry
        Girl´s Lament; Tá mo Cleamhneas Deanta (My
        Match is Made); Lord Gordon´s Reel/The Laurel
        Bush; Johnny and Molly; The Shaskeen Reel;
        Lament for Owen Roe O´Neill; Seven Yellow
        Gypsies; Tommy Coen´s Reel; There Was a Maid in
        Her Father´s Garden; The Carroroe Jig/Whelan´s
        Jig; The Bonny Bunch of Roses O

The Keane family of County Galway has been prominent in
traditional music for generations. Their talents as vocalists and instrumentalists are well-documented on a 1985
recording, <u>Muintir Chatháin</u> (Gael Linn CEF 107). <u>There Was a
Maid</u>, Dolores Keane´s first album, pays tribute to her family
and the musicians who visited the Keane home in Caherlistrane. This is a simple, unadorned album, which spotlights
Dolores Keane´s strong yet smooth vocal style. Her voice
flows easily through the difficult traditional ornamentations. "Tá mo Cleamhneas Deanta," a song of arranged
marriages and "The Bonny Bunch of Roses O," are two of the
best examples of her excellent delivery. Joined by former
Chieftain, Peadar Mercier, and Reel Union, which includes
Keane´s husband, John Faulkner, Keane performs a variety of
songs. An outstanding selection is the unaccompanied, "There
Was a Maid in Her Father´s Garden," a popular old song with
many variations. This particular version Keane learned as a
child from her grandmother. The band provides spirited
accompaniment on "Seven Yellow Gypsies," and slow, lamenting
backup on fiddle and pipes for "The Bantry Girl´s Lament."
Reel Union and Keane also perform three dance sets with "The
Laurel Bush" the standout selection. **[LP]**

DOLORES KEANE & JOHN FAULKNER

108.   <u>Broken Hearted
I´ll Wander</u>. (1979)   Green Linnet SIF 3004

    ARTISTS: Dolores Keane-vocals, concertina, flute,
hurdy gurdy drones, bodhrán, whistle; John Faulkner-bouzouki,
guitar, hurdy gurdy drones, vocals; with Kieran Crehan-fid-
dle; Éamonn Curran-whistle, chanter, drones, pipes. Produced
by P. J. Curtis.

        CONTENTS: The Ploughboy; Month of January;
        Will Ye Go to Flanders; Tommy Peoples/Mary
        Shore; Johnny Lovely Johnny; Mouth Music/Eddie
        Curran´s Favourite; The Low Low Lands of Hol-
        land; Kyle Brack Rambler/Miss McGuinness/Speed
        the Plough; Allan Tyne of Harrow; The Home
        Ruler/Cross the Fence; The Bonny Light Horseman

This is the first of three collaborations with Green Linnet
Records by the husband and wife team, Dolores Keane and John
Faulkner. Joined by fiddler Kieran Crehan and Éamonn Curran
on pipes, the foursome produces an excellent collection of
songs and tunes. Keane and Faulkner alternate lead vocals.
Keane is simply wonderful on "The Low Low Lands of Holland"
and "The Month of January," a song she learned from Cathal
McConnell and Len Graham. Her performances are clear and
strong, plus well-arranged. Faulkner vocally creates some
treasures. "Allan Tyne of Harrow," a tale of a highwayman
Faulkner learned from Ewan MacColl, and "The Bonny Light
Horseman," are his best songs. He is joined by Keane for the
rapid fire "Mouth Music" (Pórta Béal), a Scottish tradition
in which the singers imitate the instruments (the pipes, for
example) with their voices. A most fascinating sound. [LP]

   NOTES: This album was originally released on Mulligan
(LUN 033) and reissued by Green Linnet.

DOLORES KEANE & JOHN FAULKNER

109.   Farewell to Éirinn: Music and
       Songs of Emigration from
       Ireland to America. (1981)   Green Linnet SIF 3003

   ARTISTS: Dolores Keane-vocals, flute, bodhrán, concertina; John Faulkner-guitar, bouzouki, fiddle, hurdy gurdy,
vocals; with Éamonn Curran-uilleann pipes, tin whistle.
Produced by Dolores Keane, John Faulkner, Seamus O'Neill and
Carsten Linde.

       CONTENTS: Farewell to Ireland (Air)/Paddy's
       Green Shamrock Shore; Edward Conners; The
       Kilnamartyr Emigrant; Staten Island/The Green-
       fields of America (Reel); Sliabh Gallion Braes;
       Cragie Hills; The Farmer Michael Hayes; The
       Maid of Mount Cisco/Farewell to Connaught;
       Farewell to Ireland (Reel); The Greenfields of
       America

Keane, Faulkner, and Curran present a fine recording of songs
on Irish emigration to America, exemplifying the sorrow,
fear, and hopes of the emigrants. Both Keane and Faulkner
offer strong vocals, in addition to excellent instrumentals
and accompaniment. Curran is very good on both pipes and
whistle. Highlighting the lp are the sparkling vocal harmonies of "Sliab Gallion Braes," and Faulkner's three solos
("Edward Conners," "The Green Fields of America," and "Farmer
Michael Hayes"). Curran on pipes with "The Staten Island/The
Green Fields of America" and Keane's "Cragie Hills" also
standout.

Farewell to Eirinn is a tribute to the nearly two million
people, who were forced to leave Ireland between 1845 to
1855. This figure represents a quarter of the Irish popula-
tion at that time. This is a sad commentary on Anglo Irish
relations and one of the most tragic times in Irish history.
[LP]

DOLORES KEANE AND JOHN FAULKNER

110. <u>Sail Óg Rua</u>. (1984)   Green Linnet SIF 3033

    ARTISTS: Dolores Keane-vocals, bodhrán; John Faulk-
ner-vocals, fiddle, bouzouki, guitar; with Sarah Keane-
vocals; Éamonn Curran-uilleann pipes; Jackie Daly-button
accordion; Seán Keane-flute; James Kelly-fiddle; Martin
O´Connor-button accordion; Jackie Small-fiddle; Paul Barrett-
Fairlight Computer Musical Instrument (CMI). Produced by
Dolores Keane and John Faulkner.

        CONTENTS: Jimmy Mo Mhíle Stór; The Wee Weaver;
        Eddie Kelly´s Set; Moll Dubh an Ghleanna;
        Carolan´s Cup; Thuas ag Gort an Chornáin; Green
        Grow the Laurels; Galtee Ranger/Denis Murphy´s/
        The Doon Reel; Sail Óg Rua; Galway Bay

Dolores Keane and John Faulkner are outstanding proponents of
Irish folk music, and <u>Sail Óg Rua</u>, showcases their talents.
Joined by musicians, with whom they have performed and toured
under the names Kinvara and Reel Union over the past few
years, Keane, Faulkner, and this ensemble creates a most
interesting collection of lively, well-blended dance tunes,
such as "Eddie Kelly´s Set," and lovely songs, of which
"Jimmy Mo Mhíle Stór," is one of the best examples. Keane
possesses a husky, yet rich voice, which easily performs the
ornamentations so prevalent in the Galway singing tradition.
An intriguing selection is the slow air, "Sail Óg Rua," a
duet with Keane and her aunt, Sarah Keane, whose thinner,
higher voice contrasts with Dolores´ robust vocals. Faulk-
ner´s stringed accompaniment is at its best with "Green Grows
the Laurels," which also features his vocal harmonies on the
chorus, in addition to his bouzouki background. Keane and
Faulkner employ vocal overdubbing and the accompaniment of
Paul Barrett on the Fairlight Computer Musical Instrument to
create depth to their duet on "The Wee Weaver." The Fairlight CMI gives an almost religious atmosphere to this particular selection. **[LP, CS]**

JAMES KEANE

111. <u>Roll Away the Reel World</u>. (1980) Green Linnet SIF 1026

    ARTISTS: James Keane-accordion; with Seán Keane-
fiddle; Mick Moloney-guitar, tenor banjo. Produced by Mick
Moloney.

        CONTENTS: Crossing the Shannon/Lad O´Beirne´s/
        The Rough Road; The Blooming Meadows/Paudeen
        Rafferty; Maud Miller/The Sailor´s Return/
        Paddy Murphy´s Wife; Master Crowley´s/Crowley´s
        #2; The Bride´s Favourite/Tony Rowe´s/Walsh´s
        Jig/Nora Crionna; Reel of Mullinavat/The Con-
        naught Heifer/Boys of Ballinahinch; Father
        Kelly´s/Green Fields of America (Reel); The
        Four Courts/The Cuckoo; The Tempest/Sean Frank;
        The Kesh/Morrison´s/Donnybrook Fair; Gorman´s/
        Jennie´s Wedding/The Dark Haired Lass; The
        Echo; Father Ahearn´s/O´Mahoney´s

James Keane, known for his work with the Canadian band Ryan's
Fancy, is aptly captured on record with <u>Roll Away the Reel
World</u>, a title based on a quotation by James Joyce. Keane is
accompanied by his brother Seán, a member of the Chieftains,
and Mick Moloney, who also serves as the producer. Nothing
is sedate on this recording. Keane performs mostly reels and
is joined by his brother on "Reel of Mullinavat/The Connaught
Heifer/Boys of Ballinahinch," one of the most enjoyable cuts.
"Master Crowley's/Crowley's #2," "The Four Courts/The Cuckoo," and "The Kesh/Morrison Jig/Donnybrook Fair" also are
inspired. **[LP, CS]**

NOTES: Ryan's Fancy have several lps, including <u>Dance
Around This One</u> (Boot 7217), <u>Irish Love Songs</u> (Boot 7232),
<u>Sea People</u> (Boot 7212), and <u>A Time with Ryan's Fancy</u> (Boot
7191).

THE KEANE FAMILY

112.   <u>Muintir Chatháin</u>. (1985)   Gael-Linn CEF 107

ARITSTS: Dolores Keane-vocals, background vocals;
Teresa Keane-vocals; Christina Mangan-vocals; Rita Keane-vo-
cals; Sarah Keane-vocals, fiddle; Seán Keane-vocals, flute,
whistle; Noel Keane-flute, accordion; John Faulkner-guitar,
bouzouki, fiddle; Pat Keane-vocals; Bridie Keane-vocals; Matt
Keane, Sr.-vocals; Matt Keane, Jr.-vocals; with Garry Ó
Briain-mandocello, piano; Tony Maher-Oberheim Synthesizer.
Produced by Dolores Keane.

CONTENTS: Cill Chais; The Faithful Sailor Boy;
Dónal Óg; Paddy Fahey's/Scotch Mary/Kitty the
Hare; Anach Cuain; The Bonny Labouring Boy; The
May Morning Dew; Seoladh na nGamhna; Tom Ward's
Downfall/Willie Coleman's; Louis Darcy; Seán Ó
Duibhir a Ghleanna; Scléip Na hOíche Aréir

The Keane Family has been closely involved with traditional
music for generations. Their home in Caherlistrane, County
Galway, is a stopping place for travelling musicians to share
tunes, songs, and stories with the family. This album,
produced by Dolores Keane, is a tribute to this talented
family and their contributions to Irish music. First rate
performances by various family members are many. Highlights
include Seán's excellent song, "The May Morning Dew,"
Dolores's vocals with "The Bonny Labouring Boy," Sarah and
Rita's duet, "Dónal Óg," the reel set, "Paddy Fahy's/
Scotch Mary/Kitty the Hare," and the jigs, "Tom Ward's Down-
fall/Willie Coleman's." Tasteful accompaniment is provided
on many selections by John Faulkner and Garry Ó Briain.
[LP]

NOTES: Sarah and Rita Keane recorded an album of
songs from the west of Ireland, <u>Once I Loved</u> (Claddagh CC4).

PADDY KEENAN

113.   <u>Paddy Keenan</u>. (1975)   Gael-Linn CEF 045

ARTISTS: Paddy Keenan-uilleann pipes, whistle; with
John Keenan-banjo; Thomas Keenan-whistle; Paddy Glackin-fiddle. Produced by Mícheál Ó Domhnaill.

CONTENTS: An Long Gaile ((The Steam-Packet)
and is also known as The Mountain Lark)/Cor
Mhic Leoid (McLeod's Reel); Braoiníní Brannda
(Drops of Brandy); An Fhuiseog 'sa Dumhach (The
Lark in the Strand); Pléaráca Bhaile Uí Cho-
naill (The Humours of Ballyconnell)/Scaipeadh
na gCleití (Toss the Feathers); Cornphíopa
Dhonnchaidh (Dunphy's Hornpipe)/An Árd-Mhín
(The High Level); Tarbolton/Bailitheoir Long-
phoirt (The Longford Collector); Barbara Allen;
Pinginí is Prás ((Coppers and Brass) also known
as The Humours of Ennistymon)/An Gabhal
Siúlach (The Rambling Pitchfork); A hAon sa Dó
na Píobaireachta (The Ace and Deuce of Piping);
An Londubh (The Blackbird); Obair an Aistir
(The Job of Journeywork); Slán le hÉirinn
(Farewell to Erin)/An Iníon is Óige (The Young-
est Daughter); Port Pheaidí Keenan (Paddy
Keenan's Jig); Drioball na Fáinleoige (The
Swallow's Tail); An tÉireannach Fiáin (The Wild
Irishman)/Boinéad an tSeoltóra (The Sailor's
Bonnet); Colonel Frazer/Tá mo Ghrá i Meiriceá
(My Love is in Amerikay)

Paddy Keenan's first solo album consists of mostly dance
tunes (jigs, reels, etc.). He is joined by his brothers,
John and Thomas, and his pal Paddy Glackin. Keenan, known
from his days as piper of the legendary Bothy Band, performs
skillfully throughout the album. He and Glackin blend well
on "The Humours of Ballyconnell/Toss the Feathers," and
Keenan's own harmony and syncopation with "Coppers and Brass/
The Rambling Pitchfork," is very polished. "The Wild Irish-
man/The Sailor's Bonnet" is a tour de force for Keenan and
his accompanists. Thomas and John Keenan also perform solos
on their respective instruments with "Tarbolton/The Longford
Collector" the best track. With liner notes written by the
renowned piper Séamus Ennis, production by Mícheál Ó Domhnaill, and the talents of Keenan and Company, Paddy Keenan is
indeed a delightful recording. [LP]

PADDY KEENAN

114. Poirt an Phíobaire. (1983)   Gael-Linn CEF 099

ARTISTS: Paddy Keenan-uilleann pipes, whistles; with
Arty McGlynn-guitar; Nollaig Bridgeman-drums; Brian Eoghain-
accordion.   Produced by Nicky Ryan.

CONTENTS: Condon's Frolics/The Eavesdropper;
The Factory Girl; Man of the House; The Maid
Behind the Bar/O'Rourke's/Eilish Brogan; The
Monaghan Twig/Collier's; The Ballintore Jig;
Marig ar Pollanton/Cahir's Kitchen; Máirseáil
Uí Néill (O'Neill's March); Jezaique; The Green
Gates/George White's Favourite; Cape Clear

Poirt an Phíobaire, the long awaited follow-up lp to Keenan's
first album, Paddy Keenan, (Gael-Linn CEF 045), is well worth
the eight year interlude. Keenan has returned in full force
with a more sophisticated and satisfying album. It is packed
with rich sounds of the pipes and whistles, and accompaniment
by the striking guitar of Arty McGlynn. Never are Keenan and
McGlynn better paired than on "The Monaghan Twig/Collier's"
and "Condon's Frolics/The Eavesdropper." Both sets are full
of verve and drive. With the innovative addition of Nollaig
Bridgeman on congas, "The Ballintore Jig" is given a Latin
beat. On the quieter side, Keenan is excellent with the
whistle solo, "The Factory Girl," whose wistful mood is a
contrast to the lively dance tunes. The album closes with
the lovely air, "Cape Clear," in which McGlynn takes the lead
on guitar following Keenan's whistle introduction. Keenan
rejoins him for a quiet, exquisite guitar and whistle duet.
[LP]

   NOTES: Paddy Keenan recorded Paddy and Paddy (Tara
2007), with fiddler Paddy Glackin. Andy McGlynn is currently
a member of Patrick Street

JAMES KELLY, PADDY O'BRIEN, DAITHÍ SPROULE

115.   Spring in the Air. (1982)   Shanachie 29018

   ARTISTS: James Kelly-fiddle; Paddy O'Brien-button
accordion; Dáithí Sproule-guitar, vocals. Produced by
Daniel Michael Collins and Richard Nevins.

   CONTENTS: Man of the House/Ryan's Rant; Brac-
   ken's/Mrs. Cooty's (also known as The Horse
   that Made a Haymes of His Winkers)/The Kinnegad
   Slashers; Jim Coleman's/Patsy Touhey's/Rodney
   Miller's; The Boys of Mullanghbawn; John Kel-
   ly's/The Green Cottage/Cuil Aodha; The Gravel
   Path/The Wild Irishman; Moving Cloud/Paddy
   Kelly's; Down the Hill; McCarthy's Favorite/
   Spring in the Air/Miss Emily; Hughie the
   Graeme; The Duke of Leinster's Wife/Boys of
   Ballisadare; John Doherty's/Kitty Come Down to
   Limerick (Donegal setting); Sarah's Delight/
   Sean Sa Cheo (Donegal setting)

Kelly, O'Brien, and Sproule, competent Irish musicians all,
perform an energetic collection of dance tunes and songs on
their second album. From reels, jigs, set dances to polkas,
each instrumental is simply yet skillfully played. The
collection includes well-known tunes utilizing the rare
Northern Irish variations, in addition to seldom recorded
pieces. Daithi Sproule rounds out this fine album with two
songs, "The Boys of Mullaghbawn" and "Hughie the Graeme."
[LP, CS]

   NOTES: Kelly, O'Brien, and Sproule's first lp is Is
It Yourself (Shanachie 29015).

KNOCK-NA-SHEE

116.   Last Night's Fun. (1979)   Shanachie 29017

ARTISTS: Marty Somberg-fiddle, guitar, vocals; Jo
Allen-flute; Mark Simos-guitar, fiddle, mandolin; with Johnny
"Ringo" McDonagh-bodhrán. Produced by Daniel Michael Col-
lins.

CONTENTS: Joe O´Dowd´s Mazurka/Scattery Is-
land/Limerick Lasses; Knocknagow Jig; Bouree
Carré/ Jim Keefe´s Polka; Maggy Walker Blues
(also known as The Girl I Left Behind)/Paddy
Kelly´s Jig; Miko Russell´s/Father O´Grady´s
Visit to Bocca; Aoibhneas Eilis Ni Cheal-
laigh/The Clare Jig; The Old Blackthorn/Jig
Away the Donkey; March of the King of Laois/
Planxty Morgan Magan; Lament for the Books/Mon-
aghan Jig; Ryan´s; Jacky Tar; The Mountain
Lark/The Cabin Hunter; The Tempest Reel

Last Night´s Joy is the only album recorded by Knock-Na-Shee.
The band, named for a mountain in Sligo, was formed on the
west coast, but moved to the northeast where this album was
made. Jo Allen, Marty Somberg, and Mark Simos are three very
talented non-Irish, American musicians with the ability to
play good Irish music. Their material is well-paced, tightly
arranged, and their performances are energetic and professional. Highlights include the ensemble dance set "Joe
O´Dowd´s Mazurka/Scattering Island/Limerick Lasses," the
guitar duet by Simos and Somberg, "March of the King of
Laois/Planxty Morgan Magan, which is performed in the style
of Dowland, and the "Lament for the Books," a flute and
fiddle duet from Allen and Somberg. Allen´s playing and
phrasing is excellent on this selection. [LP]

TOM LENIHAN

117.   Paddy´s Panacea. (1978)   Topic 12TS363

ARTISTS: Tom Lenihan-vocals and conversation. Produced by Jim Carroll and Pat MacKenzie.

CONTENTS: Paddy´s Panacea; Talk of Music at
Lenihan´s; A Wintry Evening; St. James Hospi-
tal; Talk of Thady Casey the Dancing Master;
The Lake of Coolfin; Talk of Fair Days in
Miltown Malbay; Pat O´Brien; Paddy, the Cockney
and the Ass; Talk of Straw Boys; The Holland
Handkerchief; The Bobbed Hair; Fair London
Town; Talk of Garrett Barry; Hurry the Jug

Paddy´s Panacea is a unique recording that provides a taste
of Irish country life through song and conversation. Tom
Lenihan, a farmer in Knockbrack, was in his seventies when he
recorded this album in the kitchen of his thatched roofed
cottage in County Clare. Lenihan collects his repertoire
from family, friends, printed collections, etc. He is even
able to trace some songs directly back four generations to
his great-great grandfather. Lenihan´s vocal style, common
to the west of Ireland, stresses a combination of subtle
phrasing and quality of tone. His naturalness in singing and
speaking is quite appealing. The album is an excellent

example of oral and music history of West Clare. Liner notes are included. **[LP]**

CHARLIE LENNON

118.   The Emigrant Suite. (1985)   Gael Linn CEF 112

ARTISTS: Charlie Lennon-fiddle, piano, viola; with Frankie Gavin-fiddle, flute, viola; Liam Og O'Flynn-uilleann pipes; Síle Ní Fhlaithearta-vocals; Pat O'Connell-guitar. Produced by Frankie Gavin and Charlie Lennon.

CONTENTS: Deora an Deoraí (The Emigrant Suite): The Gathering, The Piper's Turn, Round the House and Mind the Dresser, The Parting; Reels: Three Lovely Lassies-The Red Haired Lass/The Dairy Maid/The Primrose Lass; Hornpipes: The Harvest Home/Rossinver Braes; Reels: Early Breakfast/Colonel Frazer; Brídín Bhéasach; Reels: The Leitrim Lilter/The Twelve Pins; The Luckpenny Jig; Reels: The Two Maids-The Maid Behind the Bar/The Maid Behind the Barrel; The Stack of Barley Set; Reels: Tom Mulligan's Favourites-The Tobacco Leaf/The Blackberry Blossom/Touch Me if You Dare; Dónall Óg; The Parting

Charlie Lennon is well-known for traditional fiddling, piano accompaniment, and, of late, as a composer of original works in the traditional style. He has written several pieces for this album, including "The Emigrant Suite," an ambitious multi-part composition that depicts a house party with all the trimmings and a final farewell to the emigrant. The suite is performed on fiddles, flute, pipes, and viola, and contains a hornpipe, jig, reel, and slow march. Lennon is joined by Frankie Gavin of DeDanann, Liam O'Flynn formerly of Planxty, Pat O'Connell, and Síle Ní Fhlaithearta. In addition to the suite, other selections of note are the "The Three Lovely Lassies" set, "Rossinver Braes," and another set, "The Three Maids." **[LP]**

SEAN MCALOON AND JOHN REA

119.   Drops of Brandy. (1976)   Topic 12TS287

ARTISTS: Sean McAloon-uilleann pipes, fiddle; John Rea-hammered dulcimer. Produced by Robin Morton.

CONTENTS: The Maid in the Meadow/The Castlebar Races/Trip to the Cottage; The Mountain Lark/Crooked Road to Dublin; Jackson's Drum/ Jackson's Mistake/Jackson's Coagy; Blind Mary; Madame Bonaparte/O'Dwyer's Hornpipe; Crowley's No. 1/Crowley's No. 2; Moloney's/Paddy O'Brien's; First House in Connaught/The Copperplate; An Buachaill Caol Dubh (The Dark Slender Boy)/Drops of Brandy; Coil the Hawser/Lord McDonald's; Alexandria's/Higgin's; The Sligo Maid/Sheehan's; Wandering Minstrel/Katy

is Waiting/The Basket of Shamrocks; Tim the
Turncoat/The Quarrelsome Piper; The Old Siege
of Valencia/The Lark in the Morning

This duo from Ulster presents a unique blend of Irish music
on uilleann pipes and hammered dulcimer. With a light touch
Rea is able to effectively play the triplets, which often
appear in Irish music. Both solo and duet selections are
well-performed, but the album has a hollow sound quality,
which detracts from the overall performance. **[LP]**

NOTES: John Rea has recorded a solo album, <u>Irish
Music on the Hammer Dulcimer</u> (Topic 12TS373).

BILLY MCCOMISKEY

120.   <u>Makin´ the Rounds</u>. (1981)   Green Linnet SIF 1034

ARTISTS: Billy McComiskey-accordion; with Donny
Golden-step dancing; Pat Keogh-fiddle; Sean McGlynn-accor-
dion; Andy O´Brien-guitar. Produced by Mick Moloney and
Billy McComiskey.

CONTENTS: The Boogie Reel/The Controversial
Reel; The Independent/Rabbit in the Field; Bill
Hoare´s/Mick Flaherty´s; O´Donnell´s/Spellan
the Fiddler; Eddie Kelly´s Jig/Miss Casey´s;
Woods´ Lamentation; The Flowers of Brooklyn/The
Palm Tree; Peter Murphy´s/Mick Flaherty´s;
Johnny Allen´s/Sporting Nell; Planxty Davis;
Windsor Terrace/Sault´s Own Hornpipe; Dinny
Delaney´s/Set the Clock; The Wandering Min-
strel/The Millpond; Leave My Way/Chicago Reel

Billy McComiskey, one third of the popular Irish American
trio, the Irish Tradition, scores a hit with this solo lp.
Born in Brooklyn to Irish parents, he was the first American
to win the All Ireland Senior Accordion Championship (2nd
Place) in 1970. With fiddler, Brendan Mulvihill in 1977,
McComiskey was awarded first place in the Senior All-Ireland
Duets. (Mulvihill is also in the Irish Tradition). McComis-
key´s style is influenced by the sensitive, interpretive
Galway accordion style, the use of bass from accordion master
Paddy O´Brien, and the mentorship of Sean McGlynn, one of the
prominent accordion players in America. McGlynn joins McCo-
miskey on two excellent duets, "O´Donnell´s/Spellan the
Fiddler" and "Johnny Allen´s/Sporting Nell." The strongest
selections are McComiskey´s solos, "Dinny Delaney´s/Set the
Clock," "Eddie Kelly´s/Miss Casey´s," "Bill Hoare´s/Mike
Flaherty´s," and "Leave My Way/Chicago Reel." However, the
ensemble pieces are also well-mastered. **[LP, CS]**

CATHAL MCCONNELL

121.   <u>On Lough Erne´s Shore</u>. (1978)   Topic 12TS377

ARTISTS: Cathal McConnell-flute, whistle, vocals;
with Willie Johnson-guitar; Robin Morton-bodhrán. Produced
by Robin Morton.

CONTETNS: The Dark Woman of the Glen (Bean
Dubh an Ghleanna); The Maid Behind the Barrel;
Erin the Green; Johnny Going to Ceilidh/The
Gossoon that Beat His Father/The Long Slender
Sally; The Maho Snaps/Jenny Lind; The Wedding
of Molly/The Three-Hand Jig/Peter Flanagan´s;
Peoples´ Reel/Lady Montgomery; McConnell´s
Gravel Walk (also known as Granny´s Gravel
Walk)/The Laurel Tree; Andy Kerrin´s Set
Dance/McHugh´s Reel/The Primrose Road; The
Shannon Breeze (also known as The Lady´s Top
Dress and also as Roll Her in the Rye-
Grass)/Nugent´s Reel; St. Donard´s Cairn;
Edmund on Lough Erne´s Shore; Carolan´s Concer-
to; Big John´s Reel/Kitty the Hare; Siney´s
Jig/The Noon Lasses

Cathal McConnell, one half of the original Irish contingency
of Boys of the Lough, released his only solo album to date in
1978. Produced by Robin Morton (the other Irish half of Boys
of the Lough), the lp contains mostly unaccompanied tunes
from McConnell´s native County Fermanagh, which are played on
whistle and flute. His love for this music is unmistakable.
McConnell´s style is unpretentious yet polished and the album
aptly demonstrates his versatility as an instrumentalist and
singer. Notes on the selections are included. **[LP]**

CATHAL MCCONNELL & ROBIN MORTON

122. Underline An Irish Jubilee. (1976)   Topic 12T290

ARTISTS: Cathal McConnell-flute, whistle, vocals;
Robin Morton-concertina, bodhrán, vocals. Produced by Michael O´Donnell.

CONTENTS: Nil se na La (It´s Not Yet Day)/The
Humours of Winnington; The Hiring Fair at
Hamiltonsbawn; Three Out of One; Matt Hyland
(also known as Young Martiland); The Dusty
Miller/McDermott´s; On the Banks of a River
Near Blackwatertown; MacNamara´s/The Blue
Angel; The Gauger´s Song; Gather Round the
Fire/Brereton´s; Mary from Murroogh; Tiocfaidh
an Samhradh agus Fairsing Feir (Summer Will
Come with Planty of Hay); Planxty Reynolds;
Thousands are Sailing to Amerikay; Caoineadh Ui
Dhomhnaill (Lament for O Donnell); The Irish
Jubilee (also known as The Bundle of Lies)/The
Glass of Beer/The Longford Reel

This reissue of the 1970 Mercier Press recording successfully
captures the true wit and spirit of these Northern Irish
musicians, who later formed half of the popular Boys of the
Lough. A mixture of high caliber vocals and instrumentals
comprise the contents. Highlights include McConnell´s unaccompanied song, "Matt Hyland," Morton´s music hall piece,
"The Gauger´s Song," and their duet, "Thousands are Sailing
for Amerikay." In depth background notes on each selection
are included. **[LP]**

NOTES: Robin Morton is the author of <u>Folksongs Sung in Ulster</u> (Mercier Press, 1970) and <u>Come Day, Go Day, God Send Sunday</u> (Routledge & Kegan Paul, 1973), a biography of traditional singer, John Maguire of Co. Fermanagh. Morton currently heads Temple Records in Scotland and has produced many recordings.

ANDY MCGANN & PAUL BRADY

123.   <u>It's s Hard Road to Travel: Traditional Music of Ireland.</u> (1977)   Shanachie 29009

ARTISTS: Andy McGann-fiddle; Paul Brady-guitar. Produced by Daniel Michael Collins and Richard Nevins.

> **CONTENTS:** Crooked Road to Dublin (also known as Lady's Panteletts)/The Merry Harrier; Andy McGann's #42 Bunratty Reel/King of the Clans; Gold Ring/Carmen's Amber; Bonnie Kate/Jenny's Chickens; McDermotts/From Galway to Dublin (also known as Bonaparte Crossing the Rhine); Paddy on the Turnpike/Rocks of Cashel (also known as the Steeplechase and also as It's a Hard Road to Travel and also as Carrigaline); Dr. Gilberts/Mullian's Fancy (also known as the Flowers of Red Hill); The Banks/Galway Bay; Reel of Mullinavat/Pigeon on the Gate; Reevy's/ McFadden's Favorite; Monahan/Making Babies by Steam (also known as Larry O'Gaff); Boys of Ballisadare/Millstone (also known as Cottage Groves)

A solid performance from one of American's foremost Irish fiddlers! Andy McGann has been fiddling since he was seven years old in 1935 and as a young man he played with the venerable Sligo fiddler, Michael Coleman, who helped carve the Irish American music scene in New York City. This album contains jigs, reels and two hornpipes, some of which McGann learned in the 1940s at the Central Opera House, where Irish musicians informally gathered each month. McGann is also known for his membership in the 1950s with the New York Ceilidh Band, which unfortunately never recorded. This fine lp showcases McGann's flawless abilities. McGann is backed by the skilled guitar accompaniment of Paul Brady. The duo is splendid on each track, but especially with "Crooked Road to Dublin/Merry Harrier," which McGann learned from Coleman. In addition, "Bonnie Kate/Jenny's Chickens," has the potential of becoming monotonous due to endless repeating of phrases, but is rescued by McGann, who employs variations and some wonderful rolls and triplets. The other tracks are excellent and demonstrate McGann's true mastery **[LP, CS]**

NOTES: Andy McGann recorded an album with Paddy Reynolds (Shanachie 29004) and another with Joe Burke and Felix Dolan, <u>The Funny Reel</u> (Shanachie 29012).

SÉAMUS MCGUIRE, MANUS MCGUIRE, DÁITHÍ SPROULE

124.   <u>Carousel.</u> (1984)   Gael-Linn CEF 105

ARTISTS: Seámus McGuire-viola, fiddle; Manus
McGuire-fiddle; Dáithí Sproule-guitar, vocals; with Garry Ó
Briain-mandocello; Charlie Lennon-piano. Produced by Seámus
McGuire, Manus McGuire, Dáithí Sproule, and Garry Ó Briain.

CONTENTS: Gangar Baansul; Eddie Kelly´s/The
King of the Clan; The Carousel Waltz; Felix
Kearney´s/Andy McGann´s; Cumha An Fhile; The
Dean Brig of Edinburgh; An Cailín Bán; The
Controversial Reel (also known as Billy McComi-
skey´s Reel)/Andy Dixon´s; The Great Eastern/
Finbarr Dwyer´s Reel; Dónal Óg; The Whistling
Postman/The Chattering Magpie

This lovely, graceful album consists mostly of Irish tunes
and several songs. Séamus and Manus McGuire have a great
rapport with one another on dual fiddles and on fiddle and
viola. They execute melodious harmonies beautifully. Best
tunes include "Eddie Kelly´s/The King of the Clan," "Finbar
Dwyer´s," and "Gangar Baansal," a very stately and stunning
piece. In addition to supplying excellent guitar accompaniment for the instrumentals, Sproule offers three Irish songs,
of which "Cumha an Fhile" is the most impressive. Sproule´s
recent guitarwork on several albums proves him to be one of
the most skilled accompanists in the field today. [LP]

JOE MCKENNA AND ANTOINETTE MCKENNA

125.   Joe & Antoinette McKenna
        at Home. (1980)   Shanachie 29016

ARTISTS:´ Joe McKenna-uilleann pipes, whistle, accordion; Antoinette McKenna-harp, vocals; with Irene Hermann-
cello; Mick Moloney-bouzouki, banjo. Produced by Daniel
Michael Collins, Richard Nevins, Joe McKenna, and Antoinette
McKenna.

CONTENTS: Bird in the Tree/The Sunny Banks;
Willie Archer; Planxty Fanny Power; The Old
Bush/Within a Mile of Dublin; I´ll Give My Love
a Breast of Glass; Sean Bhean Bhocht/The Fancy
Fair; Waves are Rolling/The Monaghan Jig;
Reyardine; The Silver Spear/The Crooked Road to
Dublin; Sliabh Na Mban; The Travelling Slide/
The Old Favourite/Johnny Mickey´s

With a varied repertoire of dance sets and songs, plus
well-arranged accomapniment from Mick Moloney and Irene
Hermann, the McKenna´s second album on Shanachie is a
pleasurable experience. The record´s strongest asset is the
traditional and original instrumentals. Antoinette´s lovely
air, "Waves are Rolling," contrasts nicely with the accompanying jig. The whistle and cello accompaniment gives both
tunes in the set fullness. Joe contributes "The Travelling
Slide," the first of a trio of slides. One of the best
examples of the tight musical arrangements is the rousing
reel set, "The Silver Spear/The Crooked Road to Dublin," with
Joe on pipes and Mick Moloney playing banjo. [LP, CS]

NOTES: Joe and Antoinette McKenna have released a third album, <u>Farewell to Fine Weather</u> (Shanachie 79043), which features guest artists, Johnny McDonagh on bodhrán and Ciaran Curran on bouzouki.

JOE AND ANTOINETTE MCKENNA

126. <u>Traditional Music of Ireland:</u>
<u>Irish Pipes and Harp</u>. (1978)   Shanachie 29011

    ARTISTS: Joe McKenna-uilleann pipes; Antoinette McKenna-Irish harp, vocals. Produced by Richard Nevins and Daniel Michael Collins.

        CONTENTS: Travers Reels; Fred's Favorite/Coppers and Brass; The Eagle's Whistle; Fisher's/ The Groves; An Druimfhionn Donn Dilis (The Beloved Brown White-Backed Cow); Speed the Plow/The Lady's Pantelette's; The Lonely Boat; Jenny's Welcome to Charlie/Toss the Feathers; The Humours of Derrykissane/Pay the Reckoning/ Nancy Hynes; The Man of the House/The Dunmore Lasses/The Ivy Leaf; The Bank of Ireland/The Shaskeen; The Contradition; The Gartan Mother's Lullaby; Ride a Mile/Drops of Brandy

Both Joe and Antoinette McKenna were born into families heavily involved in traditional Irish music. Their debut lp coincided with their well-received American tour and exemplifies the McKenna's talents, their dedication to Irish music, and their delightful, youthful enthusiasm. The instrumentals are the album's strongest points with the pipes as the lead instrument. Antoinette's harp provides nice counterpoint on accompaniment. Of the fourteen tracks "The Eagle's Whistle," "The Lonely Boat," and "Jenny's Welcome to Charlie" are the most prominent. **[LP, CS]**

KEVIN MITCHELL

127. <u>Free and Easy</u>. (1977)   Topic 12TS314

    ARTISTS: Kevin Mitchell-vocals. Produced by Robin Morton.

        CONTENTS: Free and Easy; The Lurgy Streams; The Mickey Dam; Nancy Bell; The Boys of Mullaghbawn; Going to Mass Last Sunday; The Magherafelt May Fair; The Light Horse (also known as The Airy Bachelor and also as The Black Horse); The Moorlough Shore (also known as The Maid of Mourne Shore); Two Strings on a Bow (also known as The Bird's Courtship and also as The Leather Winged Bat); Seán Ó Duibhir (Sean O'Dwyer); The Oul' Grey Man

Kevin Mitchell recorded his only solo album to date after more than eighteen years of performing. Born in Derry, his unaccompanied repertoire consists mainly of ballads and songs from Ulster, especially the counties of Derry, Antrim, and

Donegal. Thirty-six when this record was recorded in Glasgow, Mitchell possesses a rich tenor voice and a confident,
lyrical style. All twelve songs are well-performed with
"The Mickey Dam," "Two Strings on a Bow," and "Seán Ó Duibhir" the best examples. Robin Morton provides in-depth liner
notes. [LP]

MATT MOLLOY

128.   Heathery Breeze. (1986)   Shanachie 79064

  ARTISTS: Matt Molloy-flutes; with Donal Lunny-
bouzouki, guitar, synthesizer; Mícheál Ó Domhnaill-guitar.
Produced by Donal Lunny with some basic tracks recorded and
produced by Nicky Ryan in his home.

  CONTENTS: Moving Cloud; The Bush in Bloom/
Drogheda Bay/Jenny´s Chickens; Heathery
Breeze/Long Strand; Slieve Russell/Jimmy Wards
J.G.; Drowsie Maggie; Silver Slipper/Frieze
Britches; The Hare in the Heather; Idir Deigh-
ric `Gus Breo´; The Contradiction/Yellow Tin-
ker; Fisherman´s/Ship in Full Sail/Out on the
Ocean; "Good Morning, Nightcap"?/"Bohola" (also
known as Martin Ainsborough´s); Spoil the Dance

This excellent second solo lp features Molloy accompanied by
ex-Bothy mates, Donal Lunny and Mícheál Ó Domhnaill. Together they perform a selection of jigs and reels ranging
from the contemplative "Heathery Breeze/Long Strand," the
soulful rendition of "Drowsie Maggie," the imaginative solo,
"The Hare in the Heather," and the sensitive accompaniment on
"Idir Deighric ´Gus Brea´" to the buoyant "Good Morning,
Nightcap?/Bohola," the high spirited "The Bush in Bloom/Drog-
heda Bay/Jenny´s Chickens," and the energetic "Silver Slip-
per/Frieze Britches." Another high class recording from this
marvelous musician. [LP, CS]

MATT MOLLOY

129.   Matt Molloy. (1984)   Green Linnet SIF 3008

  ARTISTS: Matt Molloy-flutes; with Donal Lunny-bouzouki, guitar. Produced by Dónal Lunny, Mícheál Ó Domhnaill,
and Matt Molloy.

  CONTENTS: The Boys of the Lough/The Tarbolton;
Maud Millar/Pol an Madra Uisce (The Otter´s
Holt); The Lament for Staker Wallace/The Green
Gowned Lass (also known as The Collegians of
Glasgow and sometimes as Martin Rochford´s
Reel); The Gold Ring; Patsy Tuohey´s/The Maid
Behind the Bar; Willie Coleman´s/Pull the Knife
and Stick It Again; Josie McDermott´s/Martin
Ainsboro´s; McDonagh´s/Toss the Feathers; The
New Policeman/The Dunmore Lasses; The Humours
of Ballyloughlin; The Templehouse; Travers´
Reels; The Groves; The Humours of Drinagh (also

known as Philip Martin's Jig)/The Mist on the
Mountain; The Bucks of Oranmore

There is not doubt that Matt Molloy is the leading flute
player in Irish music today. His performances as a solo
artist, as a duo with Seán Keane, as a part of the legendary
trio of Tommy Peoples, Paul Brady and Molloy, and as a member
of Planxty, The Bothy Band, and currently the Chieftains, are
legendary. This album was recorded in the mid-1970s for the
Mulligan label and remains a milestone in the art of fluting.
Molloy employs the most amazing intricate piping techniques
on flute. His breath control adds to the rhythm of a piece
without being choppy. Molloy also uses a piper's stutter
roll called cranning, which is highly unusual for the flute.
Two excellent selections exemplify this technique, "The Gold
Ring" and "The Humours of Ballyloughlin." Other top-notched
tunes include "The Templehouse," in which Molloy plays a Bb
flute on a slower version of this Sligo reel. The flowing
sounds makes this piece very beautiful. [LP, CS]

   NOTES: Molloy's third solo lp, <u>Stony Steps</u> (Green
Linnet SIF 3041), was released in 1987.

MATT MOLLOY AND SEÁN KEANE

130.   <u>Contentment is Wealth</u>. (1985)   Green Linnet SIF 1058

   ARTISTS: Matt Molloy-flute; Seán Keane-fiddle; with
Arty McGlynn-guitar. Produced by Brian Masterson.

   CONTENTS: Gorman's/The Dawn/Mrs. Crehan's
Reel; McGettrick's/McDonagh's/Tommy Gunn's;
Gillan's Apples/Up and About in the Morning;
Kitty in the Lane/Captain Kelly/The Green
Mountain; Caislean an Oir/The New Century; The
Gooseberry Bush/The Limestone Rock; The London
Lasses/Farewell to Ireland/The Piper's Despair;
The Sword in the Hand/The Providence Reel/The
Old Bush; George White's Favourite/The Virginia
Reel; Vincent Campbell's/The Swaggerin' Jig/The
Holly Bush; Dargai; The Marquis of Huntley/The
Mathematician; The Golden Keyboard/Mayor Har-
rison's Fedora; Seamus Ennis' Jig/Connie O'Con-
nell's; Dowd's #9/The First Month of Spring/The
Reconciliation

Chieftain members Matt Molloy and Seán Keane fly through a
wild concoction of jigs, reels, and hornpipes. Their dynamic
performances re-enforce the fact that they are masters of
their craft. From the first set of tunes to the last, the
album's material is well-chosen, fast paced, and festive. As
a trio with Arty McGlynn on guitar, one of the best sets is
"The Golden Keyboard/Major Harrison's Fedora." Keane and
Molloy shine as a duo on "Caislean An Oir." Molloy and
McGlynn team up with the wonderful "Kitty in the Lane/Captain
Kelly/The Green Mountain." Molloy's flute soars through the
set, easily gliding over difficult passages. A fine example
of Keane's prowess on fiddle is the unusual piece, "Dar-
gai/The Marquis of Huntley/The Mathematician." The first, a

lovely melody, builds to a wild crescendo by the end of the set. Nothing is sedate on this album. **[LP, CS]**

NOTES: Seán Keane recorded a solo lp, <u>Seán Keane</u> (Shanachie 79031).

MATT MOLLOY, PAUL BRADY, TOMMY PEOPLES

131. <u>Matt Molloy, Paul Brady,</u>
      <u>Tommy Peoples.</u> (1977)   Green Linnett SIF 3018

   ARTISTS: Matt Molloy-flute; Paul Brady-guitar, vo-cals; Tommy Peoples-fiddle. Produced by Donal Lunny with one track ("Mulqueeny´s Hornpipe/Out in the Ocean") produced by Paul Brady.

   > **CONTENTS:** Matt Peoples´; The Creel of Turf/Tom Billy´s; The Crosses of Annagh/McFadden´s Handsome Daughter; The Newport Lass/The Rambling Pitchfork; Shamrock Shore; Munster Buttermilk/The Connachtman´s Rambles; Speed the Plough/Toss the Feathers; The Limerick Lasses/The Foxhunters; Mick Finn´s/The Blackthorn; Fergal O´Gara/The Cloon; Mulqueeney´s/Out in the Ocean; The Rainy Day/The Grand Canal; The Scotsman Over the Border/The Killavil; John Brennan´s (also known as Silver Spire)/Drag Her Round the Road; The Graf Spee

A wonderful collection of dance tunes and a song from this superstar trio! The Irish musical history Molloy, Brady and Peoples represent is staggering. Names like the Johnstons, the Bothy Band, Planxty, and the Chieftains come to mind. Additionally all three artists are known as soloists. This vintage recording, originally released on Mulligan Records and domestically issued on Green Linnet in 1985, remains refreshing and vibrant. Matt Molloy on flute is marvelous. He shimmers throughout the lp. Tommy Peoples expertly accompanies him on fiddle. Molloy and Peopls are well-matched, complementing one another. Paul Brady joins the fray with guitar and also contributes an expressive version of "The Shamrock Shore," and a fine pair of reels on solo guitar. Excellent instrumentals from the trio include "Speed the Plough/Toss the Feathers" and "The Graf Spree." **[LP]**

MICK MOLONEY

132. <u>Mick Moloney with</u>
      <u>Eugene O´Donnell.</u> (1978)   Green Linnett SIF 1010

   ARTISTS: Mick Moloney-vocals, guitar, bouzouki, tenor banjo, mandolin; with Eugene O´Donnell-fiddle; Patrick Sky-tin whistle; Joe McKenna-uilleann pipes, tin whistle; Shelley Posen-concertina, vocals, guitar. Produced by Patrick Sky.

   > **CONTENTS:** Joseph Baker; John Dwyer´s/The Lasses of Castlebar; Killin´s Fairy Hill; The Limerick Rake; West Limerick Medley: The Clar Hornpipe/The Pride of Moyvane/The Humours of

Newcastle West; The Blackthorn Stick/The Poet
Carney; The Bantry Girl´s Lament; Alexander´s/
The Fairies´ Hornpipe; Winnie Greene´s/The
Boston Boys; John of Dreams; The Kilkenny
Races; Sean Reid´s/Toss the Feathers; Paddy
O´Brien´s/The King of Pipers; The Irish Maid
(also known as Erin´s Flowery Vale)

Mick Moloney has been active in folk music since his Dublin
college days with Donal Lunny in the Emmet Folk Group. He
played with the notable band, The Johnstons, in the late 60s
and early 70s, and has made a name for himself as a producer,
accompanist and solo artist. Derry fiddler Eugene O´Donnell
joins Moloney for this album. O´Donnell´s trademarks are his
skilled accompaniment and evocative playing of airs. Moloney
double tracks on banjo and guitar for the delightful reels
"John Dwyer´s/The Lasses of Casatlebar," and on the mandolin
and bouzouki for "The Clar Hornpipe/The Pride of Moyvane/The
Humours of Newcastle West." Joe McKenna joins him on pipes
for the spirited "Sean Reid´s Reel/Toss the Feathers."
O´Donnell is absolute wonderful on "Killin´s Fairy Hill" and
"The Kilkenny Races." He and Moloney are well-matched with
"Paddy O´Brien´s Jig/The King of Pipers." In addition to the
instrumentals Moloney offers five songs with "The Limerick
Rake" the most engaging. **[LP, CS]**

MICK MOLONEY

133.   <u>Strings Attached</u>. (1980)   Green Linnet SIF 1027

ARTISTS: Mick Moloney-tenor banjo, mandolin, guitar,
bouzouki; with Martin Fahey-piano on "Coyle´s Piano Reels, 1
and 2." Produced by Mick Moloney.

CONTENTS: My Love is in America/The Lisdoon-
varna Reel; Arthur Darley´s (also known as The
Swedish Jig)/Over the Hills to Runbush; Munster
Grass/Peacock´s Feather; The Gooseberry
Bush/Charlie Mulvihill´s Reels, 1 and 2; Shee-
hy´s/Taylor´s; Loftus Jones; Dunmore Lassies/
McFadden´s Handsome Daughter; Off to Puck Fair;
Ricky´s White Face/The Top of the Stairs;
Richard Brennan´s/The Bush on the Hill; The
Bellharbour Reel/Miss Lyon´s Fancy; Tom of the
Hill/Dwyer´s; Jackson´s Morning Brush/Paddy
Reynold´s Dream; Coyle´s Piano Reels, 1 and 2

Moloney´s second lp is an entirely solo effort. He expertly
performs all the selections on tenor banjo or mandolin,
accompanies himself with various instruments, and has produced this recording. The end result is an excellent statement on Moloney´s talent and dedication to Irish music.
Selections include jigs, reels, a set dance and one Carolan
composition, "Loftus Jones," wonderfully played on mandolin.
Other top-notched tunes include "Arthur Darley´s/Over the
Hills to Runbush" (on mandolin), "Gooseberry Bush/Charlie
Mulvihill´s 1 & 2" (on mandolin), Liz Carroll´s reels--"Ric-
key´s White Face/The Top of the Stairs" (on banjo), "Dwyer´s
Hornpipe" (on mandolin), and "Jackson´s Morning Brush" (on
banjo). Moloney´s musicianship is both competent, energetic,

and confident. In addition to his performing he has produced
at least 25 recordings of other artists in the last few
years, and is indeed an important proponent of Irish folk
music! [LP, CS]

MICK MOLONEY AND EUGENE O'DONNELL

134.   Uncommon Bonds. (1984)   Green Linnet SIF 1053

ARTISTS: Mick Moloney-guitar, mandolin, bouzouki,
tenor banjo, vocals, harmony vocals; Eugene O'Donnell-fiddle,
piano; with Nancy Blake-mandolin, cello; Norman Blake-guitar;
Rosalyn Briley-harp; Tim Britton-tin whistle; Saul Broudy-
harmonica, harmony vocals; Liz Carroll-fiddle; Bobby Clancy-
vocals; Paddy Clancy-vocals; Seamus Egan-flute; Donny
Golden-step dancing; Dennis Gormley-string bass, electric
bass, harmony vocals; James Keane-button accordion, concertina; Jimmy Keane-piano accordion; Billy McComiskey-button
accordion; Joe McKenna-uilleann pipes; Robbie O'Connell-guitar, harmony vocals; Mark Simos-guitar; Winnie Winston-pedal
steel guitar. Produced by Mick Moloney.

CONTENTS: St. Brendan's Fair Isle; The Road to
Dunmore; The Bow Legged Tailor/The Galway
Jig/April Fool/O'Lochlainn's Jig; Miss Fogar-
ty's Christmas Cake; Sean McGlynn's Mazurka;
Bonny Blue-Eyed Nancy; O'Hara, Hughes, McCreesh
and Sands; The Blackbird and the Hen/Keane's
Farewell to Nova Scotia; Mary in the Morning;
Farewell My Gentle Harp; Muldoon the Solid Man;
The Curlew's Reel/The Derry Reel/Hanly's; The
Bay of Biscay

Mick Moloney and Eugene O'Donnell are accompanied by the
cream of the crop of Irish and American folk artists, but
this does not alter this album's blandness. The instrumentals, while adroitly performed, lack the spark of other
Moloney productions. Even the vocals are low keyed. A lis-
tenable, but unexciting album. [LP, CS]

MICK MOLONEY, JIMMY KEANE, ROBBIE O'CONNELL WITH LIZ CARROLL

135.   There Were Roses. (1985)   Green Linnet SIF 1057

ARTISTS: Mick Moloney-tenor banjo, mandolin, guitar,
vocals, harmony vocals; Jimmy Keane-piano accordion, harmony
vocals; Robbie O'Connell-guitar, vocals, harmony vocals; Liz
Carroll-fiddle; with Jerry O'Sullivan-pipes; Eugene
O'Donnell-fiddle; Saul Broudy-harmonica, harmony vocals.
Produced by Mick Moloney.

CONTENTS: The Ballad of Jack Dolan; Alla-
strom's/Julia Clifford's; Drimin Donn Dilis
(The Dear Brown Cow); Redican's Mother/Gan
Ainm/A Blast of Wind; Almost Every Circum-
stance; Fuigfhidh Mise 'n Baile Seo (I Will
Leave This Town); There Were Roses; Caiseadach
Ban(Fair Haired Cassidy)/Paddy Gavin's/The
Priest's Boots/The Commodore/The Charleston

Reel; The Mickey Dam; Harvey Street Hornpipe/
The Birds/O'Connor's Frolics; Here I Am from
Donegal

Mick Moloney is a renowned traditional musician, living in
the States for over ten years. He contributes to the field
his own fine recordings and the production of numerous albums
from many other artists. On this outing Moloney shares lead
vocal duties with notable singer, guitarist and songwriter,
Robbie O'Connell, whose voice although similar and almost
interchangeable with Moloney's, possesses a unique style that
differentiates the two voices. Together, Moloney and O'Connell create sparkling harmonies, especially on the ballads
and songs, making these selections the album's highlights.
"There Were Roses," a song written by Tommy Sands and based
on an actual event in Northern Ireland, is outstanding.
O'Connell is at his best as the narrator of this very tragic
tale. Well-performed dance tunes round out this most exciting and entertaining album. **[LP, CS]**

NOTES: Liz Carroll has recorded Kiss Me Kate (Shana-
chie 29010), and A Friend Indeed (Shanachie 29013), and
Robbie O'Connell has a solo lp, Close to the Bone (Green
Linnet SIF 1038). Jerry O'Sullivan released a solo album,
The Invasion (Green Linnet SIF 1074) in 1987.

MOLONEY, O'CONNELL & KEANE

136. Kilkelly. (1987)   Green Linnet SIF 1072

ARTISTS: Mick Moloney-vocals, guitar, mandolin, tenor
banjo, tres; Robbie O'Connell-vocals, guitar; Jimmy Keane-
vocals, piano accordion, low whistle, Elkavoz, Yamaha DX-7,
CZ 101. Produced by Mick Moloney, Robbie O'Connell, and
Jimmy Keane.

> **CONTENTS:** Maids of Selma/Larry Redican's/
> Dancing Tables; Kilkelly; Horse Keane's Horn-
> pipe/The Kerry Huntsman (also known as Sten-
> son's Reel)/The Guns of the Magnificent Seven;
> Peter Pan and Me; The Green Fields of America:
> The Green Fields of America (Reel)/The Farewell
> Reel/The Sailor's Hornpipe/Leaving Tipperary/No
> Irish Need Apply/The Rambling Irishman/Paddy on
> the Canal/The Hod Carrier's Song/Miss McLeod's
> Reel/The Kellys/The Rocks of Cashel/Mrs. Reidy
> Johnson/The Likeable Lovable Leitrim Lad/Gar-
> ryowen/Nellie O'Morgan/Nellie Kelly/The Night
> that Paddy Murphy Died/The Wedding of Lottie
> McGrath/The Irish Washerwoman/Two-Shillelagh
> O'Sullivan

Kilkelly marks the second recorded collaboration of Mick
Moloney, Jimmy Keane, and Robbie O'Connell, who have been
performing together as a band since 1984. Filled with lively
tunes and dynamic songs, the recording imaginatively portrays
the Irish American experience. An ambitious medley, "Green
Fields of America," fills the entire second side. This piece
is taken from a variety of sources, including printed works,
radio, and old 78 rmp recordings. Songs are interspersed

with tunes in a tasteful presentation of emigration, arrival
in America, finding work, and life in the new country. The
animated jig set, "Maids of Selma/Larry Redican's/Dancing
Tables," is also notable. The showstopper is O'Connell's
captivating vocals on "Kilkelly," a sad, wistful song written
by Peter Jones, based on letters written for more than fifty
years to two emigrant sons from their father in Kilkelly,
County Mayo. This song realistically captures the Irish
emigrant experience. [LP, CS]

CHRISTY MOORE

Much has been written in praise of Christy Moore and his
contributions to Irish folk music since his first solo album
in 1969. He has even been heralded as the "Minstrel of
Ireland." Moore was instrumental in founding Planxty, one of
the most important bands in the resurgence of Celtic music in
the early 70s, and in 1980 he also formed Moving Hearts, a
group which combined the sounds of jazz, rock, and traditional Irish music. Since 1982 Moore has been primarily a solo
act. His work continues to be political in nature, but has
become more contemporary in sound with a close resemblence to
the American folk movement of the late 60s. In 1986 Green
Linnet Records domestically released four recent import lps
by Moore--Ordinary Man, The Spirit of Freedom, The Times Has
Come, and Ride On--which received mixed reviews. (They are
listed with critiques of two of the four picked at random).
In reviewing Moore's works, three time periods are addressed-
-the current 1980s albums listed above, the late 70s, and the
early 1970s, of which Prosperous is the best example. With a
vast number of albums to his credit, Christy Moore remains an
influential, if somewhat controversial figure in Irish
music.

137.   Christy Moore and Friends. (1981)   RTE 59

> ARTISTS: Christy Moore; with Stockton's Wing; Ralph
McTell; Planxty; Mary Black.

> CONTENTS: John of Dreams; The Maid Behind the
> Bar; Trip to Jerusalem; Streets of London;
> Patrick was a Gentleman; East of Glendart; The
> Good Ship Kangaroo; From Clare to Here; Sonny
> Brogan's; Anachie Gordon; Cliffs of Dooneen;
> The Crack was Ninety in the Isle of Man

This album was recorded from the RTE television program
"Christy Moore and Friends," in which Moore is joined by
outstanding musicians. Highlighted is the exquisite voice of
Mary Black, who, in addition to her solo lps, has recorded
with General Humbert and De Danann. Black's solo, "Anachie
Gordon," is breathtaking. Moore also performs well with
Planxty and on his own. [LP]

138.   The Iron Behind the Velvet. (1978)   Tara 2002

> ARTISTS: Christy Moore-guitar, bouzouki, bodhrán,
vocals; with Andy Irvine-mandolin, harmonica, valdolin,

dulcimer, bouzouki, vocals; Barry Moore-guitar, vocals; Noel
Hill-concertinas; Tony Linnane-fiddle; Gabriel McKeon-uil-
leann pipes; Jimmy Faulkner-electric guitar, acoustic guitar,
slide guitar; Rosemary Flanagan-cello. Produced by Brian
Masterson and Christy Moore.

> CONTENTS: Patrick was a Gentleman; The Sun is
> Burning; Morrissey and the Russian Sailor; The
> Foxy Devil; 3 Reels: The Newly Mowed Meadow/
> Farrell O Gara's Reel/(the third has no name);
> The Trip to Jerusalem/The Mullingar Races/The
> Crooked Road; 3 Reels: Tommy Coen's/The Young-
> est Daughter/Flax in Bloom; Patrick's Arrival;
> Gabriel McKeon's: Cailin Deas Cruaite Na
> mBo/Gilbert Clancy's (also known as The West
> Wind); Dunlavin Green; Joe McCann

Two reel sets highlight Moore's fifth solo lp. Accompanied
by an impressive collection of fine Irish musicians, Moore
and his accompanists perform skillfully and powerfully.
Vocally, "Trip to Jerusalem" and "The Sun is Burning" are his
best vocals. [LP, CS]

139.   Live in Dublin. (1978)   Tara 2005

> ARTISTS: Christy Moore-guitar, vocals; with Donal
Lunny-bouzouki, guitar, background vocals; Jimmy Faulkner-
lead guitar, slide guitar. Produced by Nicky Ryan.

> CONTENTS: Hey Sandy; The Boys of Barr Na
> Sraide; Little Mother; Clyde's Bonnie Banks
> (also known as The Blantyre Explosion); Pretty
> Boy Floyd; Bogey's Bonnie Banks; The Crack was
> Ninety in the Isle of Man; Black is the Colour
> of My True Love's Hair; One Last Cold Kiss

One of two post-Planxty lps released in 1978 on Tara Records,
Live in Dublin was recorded at various venues, including
producer Nicky Ryan's living room for one cut, "Clyde's
Bonnie Banks." Contents mix traditional and original compositions. Moore does justice to Woody Gutherie's "Pretty
Boy Floyd" with Jimmy Faulkner providing lively, twangy
accompaniment on slide guitar. Two traditional tracks, the
melodic "Black is the Colour of My True Love's Hair" and the
tragic "Clyde's Bonnie Banks," are the finest songs. This is
a charming and understated album; one of Moore's best. [LP,
CS]

140.   Ordinary Man. (1985)   Green Linnet SIF 3301

> ARTISTS: Christy Moore-guitar, vocals; with Arty
McGlynn-pedal steel guitar, guitar; Donal Lunny-guitar,
various keyboards, mandolins, bouzouki, vocals; Enya Ní
Bhraonáin-vocals; Liam Og O'Flynn-uilleann pipes, whistle;
Noel Eccles-percussion, chimes; Tony Molloy-bass; Noel
Bridgeman-accordion; Andy Irvine-mandolin; Nicky Ryan-
vocals. Produced by Donal Lunny.

> **CONTENTS:** Sweet Music Roll On; Delirium Tre-
> mens; Ordinary Man; Matty; The Reel in the
> Flickering Light; The Diamondtina Drover;
> Blantyre Explosion (also known as Clyde's
> Bonnie Banks); Hard Cases; Continental Ceili;
> St. Brendan's Voyage; Another Song is Born;
> Quiet Desperation

Ordinary Man is a popular album that appeals to audiences in
both Ireland and America. It is very contemporary, and while
this is not Christy Moore at his best, the record is enjoyable nonetheless. Moore has the ability to weave a tale and
easily entraps the listener with his humor, emotion, and
wit. This album does not have the political edge many of his
recordings possess, and frankly, the quality of the material
is uneven. Yet his sense of humor is evident throughout.
Just listen to "Delirium Tremens," Moore's look a the DT's,
and "Continental Ceili," which concerns the European invasion
of Ireland's summer music scene, for a taste of his biting
wit. [LP, CS, CD]

141. Prosperous. (1972)   Tara 2008

   ARTISTS: Christy Moore-guitar, vocals; Donal Lunny-
guitar, bouzouki; Liam Og O'Flynn-uilleann pipes, whistle;
Andy Irvine-mandolin, mouth organ; Clive Collins-fiddle; Dave
Bland-concertina; Kevin Conneff-bodhrán. Produced by Bill
Leader.

> **CONTENTS:** Raggle Taggle Gipsies/Tabhair Dom do
> Lámh (Give Me Your Hand); The Dark Eyed Sailor;
> I Wish I Was in England; Lock Hospital; James
> Connolly; The Hackler from Grouse Hall; Tribute
> to Woody; The Ludlow Massacre; A Letter to
> Syracuse; Spancillhill; The Cliffs of Dooneen;
> Rambling Robin

Prosperous is still considered one of Moore's best albums.
It was through these recording sessions that Moore, Lunny,
Irvine, and O'Flynn decided to perform together under the
name of Planxty. This album is a preview of that important
Irish band. Moore sings a refreshing variety of songs with
the subtle instrumentation of his accompanists. This blend
of the stringed instruments (guitar, mandolin and bouzouki),
Liam O'Flynn's pipes, and Moore's understated vocals would
become a Planxty trademark. The best examples are "I Wish I
Was in England" and "The Raggle Taggle Gypsies/Tabhair Dom Do
Lámh." Andy Irvine adds an additional layer to "Lock Hospi-
tal" and "Tribute to Woody" with a bluesy harmonica. Moore
proves his mettle as a skillful singer with "James Connelly,"
one of his finest selections. Prosperous is more than a cut
above Moore's more recent recordings. It is a diamond among
rhinestones. [LP, CS]

142. Ride On. (1984)   Green Linnet SIF 3302

   ARTISTS: Christy Moore-guitars, vocals; with Donal
Lunny guitar, bodhrán, Prophet V. Synthesizer, electric
bouzouki, bouzouki, vocals; Declan Sinnott-violin, electric

guitars, Spanish guitar, acoustic guitar, vocals.   Produced
by Donal Lunny.

>   **CONTENTS:** The City of Chicago; Ride On; Vive
>   La Quinte Brigada; Song of Wandering Aongus;
>   McIlhatton; Lisdoonvarna; Among the Wicklow
>   Hills; Sonny's Dream; The Dying Soldier; El
>   Salvador; Back Home in Derry; The Least We Can
>   Do

Backed by Lunny and Sinnott, Moore performs several pensive
songs, including ones about El Salvador and the Spanish Civil
War. One title which could have been quite dramatic, "The
Dying Soldier," just does not cut it. It falls short of
being memorable. The remainder of the tracks are appealing,
but nothing special. **[LP, CS, CD]**

143.   <u>The Spirit of Freedom</u>.   Green Linnet SIF 3304

>   **CONTENTS:** Forever on My Mind; No Time for
>   Love; The People's Own M.P.; Deportee; Michael
>   Gaughan; Grannie's Dustbin Lid; The Dying
>   Soldier; Boy from Tamlaghtduff; McIlhatton;
>   Jesus Christ and Jesse James; Galtee Mountain
>   Boy; Back Home in Derry **[LP, CS]**

144.   <u>The Time Has Come</u>.   Green Linnet SIF 3303

>   **CONTENTS:** The Knock Song; Faithful Departed;
>   Nancy Spain; Lanigan's Ball; All I Remember;
>   Lakes of Pontchartrain; Don't Forget Your
>   Shovel; The Wicklow Boy; The Time Has Come; Go
>   Move Shift; Curragh of Kildare; Sacco and
>   Vanzetti; Section 31; Only Our Rivers Run Free
>   **[LP, CS]**

>   **NOTES:** Other albums by Christy Moore include <u>Christy</u>
<u>Moore</u> (Polydor 2383 426), <u>Whatever Tickles Your Fancy</u> (Poly-
dor 2383 344), <u>Unfinished Revolution</u> (WEA 242-134), and
<u>Christy Moore</u> (Atlantic 81835), a compilation of his work
from the 1980s. Moore also contributed to <u>A Feast of Irish</u>
<u>Folk</u> (Polydor 2475 605).

MOVING HEARTS

145.   <u>Live Hearts</u>.*   Green Linnet SIF 3306

>   **ARTISTS:** Christy Moore, Donal Lunny, Davy Spillane,
> et al. Produced by Steve Turner.

>   **CONTENTS:** McBride's; 2-1 Freddie; Downtown;
>   All I Remember; Open Those Gates; Strain of the
>   Dance; What Will You Do About Me; Let Somebody
>   Know; Lake of Shadows

Recording quality is top-notched for this in concert album.
[LP, CS]

146. <u>Moving Hearts</u>. (1986)   Green Linnet SIF 3305

> **ARTISTS:** Christy Moore-vocals, guitar, bodhrán; Donal
Lunny-electric bouzouki, acoustic bouzouki, synthesizer,
vocals; Davy Spillane-uilleann pipes, low whistle; Declan
Sinnott-lead guitar, acoustic guitar, vocals; Eoghan O´Neill-
bass, vocals; Brian Calnan-drums, percussion; Keith Donald-
saxophones. Produced by Donal Lunny.

> > **CONTENTS:** Hiroshima Nagasaki Russian Roulette;
> > Irish Ways and Irish Laws; McBride´s; Before
> > the Deluge; Landlord; Category; Faithful Depar-
> > ted; Lake of Shadows; No Time for Love

Not folk music per se, but those involved with Moving
Hearts--Christy Moore, Donal Lunny, Declan Sinnot, Davy
Spillane--have musical roots steeped in the Irish tradition.
John Schaefer in his book, <u>New Sounds: A Listener´s Guide to
New Music</u> (Harper & Row, 1987), summed up this very popular
band perfectly. Moving Hearts is a "rock band with an Irish
twist." This lp, their first American release, contains some
wild, rambunctious saxophone, especially on "McBride´s." The
electric guitarwork is quite good, as is the combination of
sax and Irish pipes ("Category"). Most selections have an
upbeat, catchy, California mellow sound (i.e. Eagles, Jackson
Browne, etc). One slow song, "Irish Ways and Irish Laws,"
details a history of Ireland and its conquerors, and the
atrocities committed by these oppressors.
[LP, CS, CD]

147. <u>The Storm</u>. (1985)   Tara 3014

> **ARTISTS:** Davy Spillane-low whistle, uilleann pipes;
Eoghan O´Neill-fretless bass, bass; Donal Lunny-synthesizer,
bouzouki, bodhrán; Declan Masterson-uilleann pipes; Keith
Donald-soprano sax, alto sax, bass clarinet; Matt Kel-
leghan-drums; Greg Boland-guitar; with Noel Eccles-marimba,
congas, bongos, floor toms, gong, tambourine, crotales,
castanets, shakers, etc.. Produced by Donal Lunny.

> > **CONTENTS:** The Lark: The Lark in the Morning,
> > Earl the Breakfast Boiler, O´Broin´s Flight-
> > case, In the Mountains of Holland, Oh Hag!
> > You´ve Killed Me, Peter O´Byrne´s Fancy, Lang-
> > strom´s Pony; The Titanic: An Irishman in
> > Brittany, A Breton in Paris; The Storm: The
> > Storm in the Teashirt, The Staff in the Baggot;
> > Finore; Tribute to Peadar O´Donnell; May Morn-
> > ing Dew

Christy Moore left the band, but this outing contains tastefully performed instrumentals in a fusion of Irish folk/jazz/
rock. Prominent are the pipes and whistles of Davey Spillane. Highlights include Lunny´s "Tribute to Peadar O´Don-
nell," commissioned by University College in Galway, "The
Lark," which features a set of seven traditional dance tunes,
and "May Morning Dew," a traditional piece. **[LP, CS]**

> **NOTES:** Moving Hearts has one other lp, <u>Dark End of</u>

the Street (WEA 58 718). Davy Spillane recorded Atlantic
Bridge on Cooking Vinyl (009).

BRENDAN MULVIHILL

148.   The Flax in Bloom.   (1979)   Green Linnet SIF 1020

   ARTISTS: Brendan Mulvihill-fiddle; with Mick Moloney-
guitar, bouzouki, mandolin; Martin Mulvihill-fiddle. Produced by Mick Moloney.

      CONTENTS: The Flax in Bloom/The Honeymoon;
      Crabs in the Skillet; The Concertina/The Cir-
      cus; The Mullingar Races/Miss Thorton's; Lament
      for O'Donnell; John Grady's Downfall/The Flogg-
      ing Reel; The Pigeon on the Gate/Miss Monahan's
      Reel; Doctor O'Neill's; The Home Ruler/The
      Brigade; Fermoy Lassies/Bunker Hill; Hardiman's
      Fancy/Billy Rush's Own; The First House in
      Connaught/The Dairy Maid

Brendan Mulvihill, one third of The Irish Tradition, is the
son of Limerick fiddler and New York fiddler teacher, Martin
Mulvihill. Brendan was born in Ireland in 1954 and emigrated
to the States in 1965. He won the All Ireland Junior championship in 1972, was runner up for the Senior Championship
in 1974, and won the All Ireland Duet contest with band mate,
Billy McComiskey, in 1977. Mulvihill's playing style can be
described as energetic, inspired, and original. He is known
for his stutter roll embellishment, which can be heard on
"The Flogging Reel." Mulvihill plays a selection of dance
tunes and an excellent duet, "Femoy Lassies/Bunker Hill,"
with his father. Other tunes of note are "Pigeon on the
Gate," the sensitive, fluent air "Lament for O'Donnell,"
"Hardiman's Fancy," "The First House in Connaught," and
Mulvihill's solo "Crabs in the Skillet." **[LP, CS]**

MARTIN MULVIHILL

149.   Martin Mulvihill with
         Mick Moloney. (1978)   Green Linnet SIF 1012

   ARTISTS: Martin Mulvihill-fiddle; Mick Moloney-guitar, tenor banjo; with Dawn Mulvihill-fiddle; Gail Mulvihill-
tenor banjo. Produced by Mick Moloney.

      CONTENTS: The Road to Abbeyfeale/Lord Kitchen-
      er's Pipes; The High Road to Glin/The Low Road
      to Glin; Limerick is Beautiful; Paddy Scan-
      lon's/Buddy Furey's/The Kinard Polka; McAulif-
      fe's/Maggie Shanley's/Denis Enright's; Flynn's/
      Dillane's Hornpipe; Bridget Flynn's Reel/The
      Star of Munster; The Rathcrogan Reel/The Bag of
      Spuds/O'Connell's Trip to Parliament; The Pride
      of Moyvane/The Cross at the Wood; Breen's Horn-
      pipe/The Hangman's Rope; The Ballygoughlin Jig/
      Sean Duine Dóite; Mulhare's/The Morning Mist;
      The Vales of New Direen; The Queen of the
      Fair/Langstrom's Pony; Con Mullane's/Dando

Dillane´s; Wallace´s Cross/Tarmon´s/Pat
Enright´s

Martin Mulvihill, born in Co. Limerick in 1923, has resided
in New York City for more than twenty years. He is known for
his teaching abilities with young musicians, many of which
have won numerous competitions in American and Ireland.
Mulvihill´s son Brendan is also a well-known fiddler and
currently a member of the Irish Tradition. Mulvihill´s other
children are musicians, too. Gayle and Dawn accompany their
father on one cut, "Queen of the Fair/Langstrom´s Pony."
Mulvihill´s style has a lilting, gay quality. He performs
various traditional dance tunes (jigs, reels, hornpipes,
polkas) in addition to a few of his own compositions. Top
honors go to "Flynn´s Hornpipe/Dillane´s Hornpipe," "The High
Road to Glin/The Low Road to Glin," "Bridget Flynn´s Reel/The
Star of Munster," and "The Ballygoughlin Jig/Sean Duine
Dóite." [LP]

NA CASAIDIGH

150. Fead an Iolair. (1984)   Gael Linn CEF 108

ARTISTS: Aongus-bodhrán; Feargus-guitar; Seathrún-
bouzouki; Odhrán-uilleann pipes; Fionntán-fiddle; Caitríona-
harp. (Names and instruments taken from jacket photo).
Produced by P. J. Curtis.

CONTENTS: Thomas Burke; Caisleán Uí Neill; The
Monsoon Set; Dúil; Fead an Iolair; Mo Chleamh-
nas; Táim in Arrears; Pé in Éirinn I; The
Wedding at Ballyporeen; Molly St. George

Na Casaidigh or the Cassidys hail from Donegal, the same
birthplace of another family group, Clannad, which has a
similar dramatic sound. Vocally there is a resemblance with
the harmonies, although as a soloist Caitríona does not equal
Clannad´s Máire Ní Bhraonáin. Instrumentally Na Casaidigh
sounds more like the Bothy Band with its power and drive.
It has added lush synthesizer arrangements, which are also
prevelent in recent Clannad albums. Interesting performances
include the progressive title track, "Fead an Iolair." This
eerie tone poem utilizes synthesizers to create the mood and
the pipes for the melody. The country western rendition of
"Mo Chleamhnas" is a refreshing departure from the usual
traditional fare. Fine multipart harmonies run throughout,
but "Táim in Arrears" and "Pé in Éirinn I" are especially
good. This debut album shows a band with potential. [LP]

MAIRÉAD NÍ DHOMHNAILL

151. Mairéad Ní Dhomhnaill. (1976)   Gael-Linn CEF 055

ARTISTS: Mairéad Ní Dhomhnaill-vocals; with Noel
Hill-concertina; Kevin Burke-fiddle; Paddy Keenan-tin whistle; Mícheál Ó Domhnaill-guitar, harmonium; Tríona Ní Dhomh-
naill-harmony vocals. Produced by Mícheál Ó Domhnaill.

> **CONTENTS:** Éirigh Suas a Stóirín; Máire an
> Chúil Óir Bhuí; Fóill, Fóill a Shagairt; Lately
> Last Night (also known as The Nobleman's Wed-
> ding); Here's a Health (also known as Good
> Friends and Companions); Ar a dhul go Baile
> Átha Cliath Domh; Róisín Dubh; Amhrán Hiúdaí
> Phádaí Éamoinn; Barbara Allen; Seán Ó Duibhir
> an Ghleanna

Mairéad Ní Dhomhnaill, sister of Tríona and Micheál, has
recorded only one solo album. She easily sings in both
English and Irish with a more full-bodied soprano than
Tríona, yet the songs are still delicately beautiful. Album
highlights inlcude "Ar a dhul go Baile Átha Cliath Domh" with
evocative whistle accompaniment, the lilting quality of
"Fóill, Fóill a Shagairt" with accordion and concertina
background, and the delightful harmonies of both sisters on
the chorus of "Here's a Health." An enchanting album by a
singer who has not recorded heavily. Song lyrics are
included, but few of the notes are in English. **[LP]**

> **NOTES:** Mairéad Ní Dhomnaill was a memeber of Skara
> Brae, whose only record <u>Skara Brae</u>, released in 1971, has
> been domestically issued on Shanachie (79034). She also con-
> tributed to <u>Sailing into Walpole's Marsh</u> (Green Linnet SIF
> 1004).

TRÍONA NÍ DHOMHNAILL

152.   <u>Tríona</u>.   (1975)   Green Linnet SIF 3034

> **ARTISTS:** Tríona Ní Dhomhnaill-bodhrán, harpsichord,
> vocals; with Micheál Ó Domhnaill-guitar; Paddy Keenan-
> uilleann pipes; Paddy Glackin-fiddle; Declan McNeils-bass
> guitar; Mairéad Ní Dhomhnaill-vocals; Peter Brown-flute;
> Gerry Malone-uilleann pipes. Produced by Micheál Ó Domh-
> naill.

> > **CONTENTS:** When I was a Fair Maid; Na Gamhna
> > Geala; The Wee Lass on the Brae; O'Carolan's
> > Farewell to Music; Shíl Mé Féin; Turlough Óg
> > O'Boyle; Foinn Bhriotáineacha; As I Roved Out
> > from the County Cavan; Kitty from Ballinamore;
> > Stór a Stór a Ghrá; Here's to All True Lovers

Tríona Ní Dhomnaill has played an integral part in four top
Irish bands--Skara Brae, the Bothy Band, Touchstone, and
Relativity. Additionally, she participated with Stray Away,
an informal group that toured America in 1979 and included
fiddler Kevin Burke and her brother Micheál. This record,
originally released on Gael-Linn (CEF 043) and issued here on
Green Linnet in 1984, is still as hauntingly beautiful today
as it was more than ten years ago. Ní Dhomnaill's accompanying instrument, the harpsichord, offers both delicate melody
and driving rhythm. It gives the tunes a baroque quality,
especially the two instrumentals, "Carolan's Farewell to
Music" and "Fionn Bhriotáineacha." The remaining vocal
selections are the album's strength. Whether sung in English
or Irish, Tríona Ní Dhomnaill is an expert in interpretation

and delivery. She snares her audience and weaves the web of
her story. All the songs are excellent. Highlights include
the charming tale "When I Was a Fair Maid," the exquisite
"Here's to All True Lovers," and "Shíl Mé Féin," in which Ní
Dhomnaill's sister Mairéad joins in harmony. [LP, CS]

ROBBIE O'CONNELL

153.   Close to the Bone. (1982)   Green Linnet SIF 1038

ARTISTS: Robbie O'Connell-guitar, mandolin, vocals;
with Tommy Keane-uilleann pipes, tin whistle, low whistle,
mandolin, vocals; Roxanne O'Connell-vocals; Tom Phillips-
synthesizer. Produced by Tom Phillips.

CONTENTS: The Gay Old Hag; William Hollander
(also known as The Flying Cloud); A Week Before
Easter; The Earl of Murray; The Waterford
Waltz; With Kitty I'll Go for a Ramble; The
Torn Petticoat/The Rambling Pitchfork; I Know
Where I'm Going; Bobby's Britches; Sliabh na
mBan; Ferrybank Piper; Ham Sunday

Although the nephew of the venerated Clancy Brothers, with
whom he sometimes tours, Robbie O'Connell did not actually
begin to perform Irish material on a regular basis until he
emigrated to America in 1972. O'Connell is a storyteller,
humorist, and balladier, whose wit and warmth are evident.
Along with former bandmate Tommy Keane, O'Connell provides a
simple yet dynamic performance on this debut album. The
selections are mostly from or about Waterford and Carrick-
on-Suir, his family's home. Original compositions, "Ham
Sunday," "Ferrybank Piper," and "Bobby's Britches," are
descriptive and witty. They contrast with the more serious
works, such as the acapella "A Week Before Easter," which
includes O'Connell's wife Roxanne on vocal harmonies. The
album has both balance and depth. [LP, CS]

NOTES: Robbie O'Connell is now performing with Mick
Moloney and Jimmy Keane.

EUGENE O'DONNELL

154.   Slow Airs and Set
        Dances. (1978)   Green Linnet SIF 1015

ARTISTS: Eugene O'Donnell-fiddle; with Mick Moloney-
guitar, bouzouki, mandolin. Produced by Mick Moloney.

CONTENTS: The Downfall of Paris; The Scotsman
Over the Border/Hartigan's Fancy; The Lodge
Road; Da Auld Resting Chair/The Derry Hornpipe;
Barney Brallaghan/Ride a Mile; The Celtic
Lament; Planxty O'Donnell; Jockey to the Fair;
The Hunt; Ni Fheicim Nios Mó Thu A Mhúirnín (I
Won't See You Anymore, My Dear); The Three Sea
Captains; The Bonnie Lass of Bon Accord; Hurry
the Jug; Humours of Bandon/Planxty Maggie
Brown; Planxty Drury

O'Donnell was born in County Derry in 1932 and won six All
Ireland titles for his step dancing before his retirement at
age 26. It is due to his experience as a dancer that O'Donnell excells in playing set dances, which encompass over half
of this recording. O'Donnell is classically trained on
violin, but is a master of improvisation. He is also known
for his sensitive, contemplative playing of slow airs.
Accompanied by Mick Moloney, O'Donnell also provides his own
harmonies for several selections, including "The Bonny Lass
of Bon Accord," "Planxty Drury," "The Three Sea Captains,"
"The Downfall of Paris," and the lovely air "Da Auld Resting
Chair." Other notable tunes are "Hurry the Jug," "Planxty
O'Donnell," "Planxty Maggie Brown," and "The Celtic Lament."
Eugene O'Donnell is a consummate performer, who plays with
style, grace, and warmth. **[LP, CS]**

NOTES: O'Donnell released <u>The Foggy Dew</u> (Green Linnet
SIF 1084) with James McCafferty.

MARY O'HARA

155.   <u>A Song for Ireland</u>. (1985)   Shanachie 52009

ARTISTS: Mary O'Hara-Irish harp and vocals.

CONTENTS: My Lagan Love; Kitty of Coleraine; A
Soft Day; Óró Mo Bháidin (Óró My Little Boat);
Young Brigid O'Malley; Danny Boy; The Spanish
Lady; She Moved Through the Fair; The Gartan
Mother's Lullaby;. The Fairy Tree; Ailiú Éanai;
Bring Me a Shawl from Galway; Down by the Sally
Gardens; The Song of Glendun; An Peata Circe
(The Pet Hen); The Quiet Land of Erin

<u>A Song for Ireland</u> is a wonderful example of the talents of
Irish vocalist and harpist Mary O'Hara. O'Hara has been
playing harp since 16 and had her own radio program on Radio
Eireann soon after. She married American poet Richard Solig
at 20, and upon his death fifteen months later, entered a
Benadictine monastery for twelve years. O'Hara has resumed
her career and is billed as Ireland's favorite songstress.
This album is one of O'Hara's best. She accompanies herself
beautifully on Irish harp and sings with ease and grace in a
clear, operatic soprano. Top selections include "Ailiú Éanai," "The Spanish Lady," "My Lagan Love," and "Down by the
Sally Gardens." **[LP, CS]**

NOTES: O'Hara has published a book to accompany this
recording, <u>A Song for Ireland</u> (Merrimack, 1983), which contains lyrics of numerous songs, the author's memories of the
songs, and many lovely photographs.

MARY O'HARA

156.   <u>Traditional Irish
Folk Songs</u>.   Everest Records FS 344

ARTISTS: Mary O'Hara-Irish harp and vocals. Recorded
by David Hancock. Edited by Patrick Clancy.

CONTENTS: Haigh Didil Dum; Carraig Donn; The
Frog Song; Óró Mo Bháidin (Óró My Little Boat);
Jackets Green; Seoladh Na Ngamhna (Driving the
Calves); Wexford Mummer's Song; Sliabh Na Mban
(The Mountain of the Women); The Gartan Mo-
ther's Lullaby; Down by the Glenside; Maidrin
Ruadh (The Little Red Fox); Silent O Moyle
(also known as The Song of Fionnuala); Dia
Luain Dia Mairt (Monday, Tuesday); Farewell,
But Whenever; The Leprauchan; Na Leanbhai I
Mbeithil (The Children in Bethlehem); The
Famine Song; She Didn't Dance

This older recording is O'Hara's first American disc, but is
not as appealing as her more recent works. The production is
sparce and her vocals seem shrill in places. A Song for
Ireland is much more indicative of her talents. [LP]

NOTES: Other recording by Mary O'Hara include At the
Royal Festival Hall (Shanachie 52007), Mary O'Hara's Ireland
(Boot 4013), Mary O'Hara's Scotland (Boot 4509), Recital
(Boot 7237), Monday, Tuesday, and Other Children's Songs
(Boot 7203), and Sa Ghailearai Naisiunta (Gael-Linn CEF 118).

OISÍN

157. Bealoideas.   Tara 2011

ARTISTS: Seamus MacGowan-guitar, vocals; Tom
MacDonagh-bouzouki; Geraldine MacGowan-bodhrán, recorder,
vocals; Brian MacDonagh-12-string guitar, mandolin; Mick
Davis-fiddle, vocals; with Paul Brady-guitar, harmonium, tin
whistle. Produced by Paul Brady.

CONTENTS: Peata Beag Do Mhathair (Is trua gan
peata an mhaoir agam); The Star of Munster; The
Cow Ate the Piper; The Gold Ring; The Bonny
Irish Maid; The Rambling Soldier; The Irish
Girl; The Orphan/Tobin's Favourite; Fear an
Bhata; The Providence/Cooley's/The Moibhin

Combining a variety of songs and tunes, the group's choice of
material complements their strengths as solid instrumentalists and singers. "Fear an Bhata," a Scottish love song,
and "The Irish Girl," an unaccompanied song, both feature
Geraldine's pleasant voice. All instrumentals are tightly
blended and give fine examples of the band's talents. [LP,
CS]

OISÍN

158. The Jeanie C. (1982)   Tara 2013

ARTISTS: Anne Conroy-accordian; Mick Davis-fiddle;
Mick O'Brien-uilleann pipes, tin whistle; Seamus MacGowan-
twelve string guitar, vocals, harmony vocals; Geraldine Mac
Gowan-bodhrán, vocals, harmony vocals; Noreen O'Donoghueharp;
Paddy Glackin-fiddle; Tom MacDonagh-bouzouki; Ashling
Drury-Byrne-cello; Noel Bridgeman-percussion; Jimmy Slevin-

acoustic guitar, electric guitar, lead guitar, bass guitar;
Philip Begley-harmonium. Produced by Paddy Glackin.

>   CONTENTS: Hand Me Down the Tackle/The Drunken
>   Tinker/Chicago; Ellen Vanin; Lady Annes/Jackie
>   Coleman´s; Love and Freedom; The Echo/Walsh´s;
>   The Jeannie C; Battering Ram/Kinnegad Slashers/
>   Leg of the Duck; Faoileán; Salamanca Sister/
>   High Reel

The band´s current lineup includes Seamus MacGowan, Geraldine
MacGowan, Anne Conroy, and Mick Davis. A fifth member changes for each tour, and has included Davey Spillane, Donal
Lunny, Noreen O Donoghue, Janet Harbison, and finally, Maire
Breannach for winter 1987. Oisín toured Europe in fall 86
and are currently sponsored by the Guiness Brewing Co., which
has enabled the group to reach a larger audience. Their 1985
tours were undertaken as part of the European Music Year, a
most prestigious honor. The Jeannie C, Oisín´s most recent
recording, adds the driving accordion of Anne Conroy to the
band. "Hand Me Down the Tackle" and "Lady Anne´s/Jackie
Coleman´s" are the best examples of Conroy´s verve. Geraldine MacGowan sings two gems, "Ellen Vanin" and "The Jeanie
C," both songs of the sea. Noreen O Donoghue´s delicate
harp accompaniment on the first song makes it the album´s
best selection. [LP, CS]

OISÍN

159.   Oisín. (1976)   Tara 2010

>   ARTISTS: Geraldine MacGowan-bodhrán, recorder, vo-
> cals; Tony MacDonagh-bouzouki; Mick Davis-fiddle, vocals;
> Brian MacDonagh-mandolin; Seamus MacGowan-guitar, vocals;
> with Darach de Brun-whistle, pipes; Paul Brady-guitar; Pro-
> duced by Paul Brady.

>   CONTENTS: Doherty´s Jig/Donnybrook Fair;
>   Geordie; The Old Grey Goose; I Was a Young Man;
>   Oh Ro My Johnny/Terry´s Travels; Farewell to
>   Nova Scotia; The Maple Leaf/The Man of Arran;
>   The Peeler and the Goat/The Humours of Whiskey;
>   The Walk of the Fiddler´s Bride; Love is Teas-
>   ing; Cherish the Ladies

Oisín, a five member Irish band, performs a skillfully executed collection of songs and tunes on this impressive debut
lp. They show great potential, which has been proven in
subsequent albums. Highlighting the record is the band´s
multi-layered instrumentation on mandolin, guitar, bouzouki,
and fiddle. One of the best examples is "Doherty´s Jig."
The blending of the bouzouki and mandolin is marvelous.
Other choice tunes include "The Maple Leaf," "Oh Ro My Johnny," with the fine whistle of Darach de Brun, and the background instruments to the song, "Farewell to Nova Scotia."
Vocally Geraldine MacGowan is in fine form with the unaccompanied "Love is Teasing," and she offers bodhrán accompaniment to "I Was a Young Man," another good selection. [LP,
CS]

OISÍN

160. Over the Moor
      to Maggie. (1980)   Tara 2012

ARTISTS: Gerry Phelan-flute, whistle; Seamus MacGowan-guitar, vocals; Tom MacDonagh-bouzouki, guitar; Geraldine
MacGowan-vocals, bodhrán; Brian MacDonagh-mandola, guitar,
mandolin, bouzouki; Mick Davis-fiddle; with Paddy Glackin-
fiddle; Micheal O'Broin-pipes. Produced by Paddy Glackin.

CONTENTS: Over the Moor to Maggie/The Bird in
the Bush; Lady Le Roy; The Connaghtmans Ram-
bles/Paidin O Rafferty; The Bonny Light Horse-
man; Sonny Brogans Jigs; The Flogging Reel/The
Glass of Beer; The Bonny Labouring Boy; The
Flowing Tide/Reevey's Hornpipe; The Boyne
Hunt/Castle Kelly/The Humours of Scarrif; The
Next Market Day

Oisín's third outing continues the first rate tradition of
rousing instrumentals and striking vocals. The band's sound
is highlighted with well-blended stringed accompaniment and
the addition of Gerry Phelan's tin whistle. Top honors for
tunes go to "Sonny Brogan's Jig," "Over the Moor to Maggie,
and "The Flogging Reel/The Glass of Beer," in which Paddy
Glackin joins the band on fiddle. This last title is the
most vibrant instrumental. Geraldine MacGowan performs a
marvelous, unaccompanied vocal on "The Bonny Labouring Boy."
She is also good with "The Next Market Day," a song well-
accompanied vocally and instrumentally. [LP, CS]

NOTES: Geraldine MacGowan and Anne Conroy released
Winds of Change on Tara (2016).

SEÁN Ó RIADA

161. Ó Riada.   Gael-Linn CEF 032

ARTISTS: Seán Ó Riada-harpsichord; Martin Fay-fiddle;
Éamon de Buitléar-accordion; Peadar Mercier-bodhrán; Paddy
Moloney-uilleann pipes; Seán Ó Sé-vocals; Seán Ó Ceallaigh-
fiddle; Seán Ó Catháin-fiddle; Seán Potts-tin whistle;
Michael Tubridy-flute. Music arranged and directed by Seán Ó
Riada.

CONTENTS: Sí Bheag, Sí Mhór; M'uilleagán Dubh
Ó; Fead An Iolair ((The Eagle's Whistle) and is
also known as Mairseáil Uí Dhonncha (The March
of the O'Donoghues)); Tiarna Mhuigheo (Lord
Mayo); Planxty Maguire; Pléaráca na Ruarcach
(O'Rourke's Revelries); Fanny Power (also known
as Bean an Trínsigh (Mrs. Trench)); Planxty
Drury; Planxty Irwin; Sláinte Bhreá Hewlett (A
Fine Toast to Hewlett); Tabhair Dom Do Lámh
(Give Me Your Hand); O'Neill's Hornpipe

This lp is a tribute to Seán Ó Riada, released after his
untimely death in 1971 at the age of forty. Ó Riada, born

John Reidy in 1931, was classically trained and composed
numerous classical works. In the late 1950s he worked with
the Radio Eirann Symphony Orchestra, combining traditional
themes in an orchestral setting. While the Clancy Brothers
and other pub ballad groups were popular in the 1950s and
1960s, Ó Riada offered another dimension of Irish folk
music--the ensemble performance. He formed Ceoltóirí Chualann in 1960. This ensemble fulfilled Ó Riada's idea of an
Irish folk orchestra, a departure from the predominant solo
instrument performance prevalent in the Irish folk music
scene. Traditional music and harp tunes of Carolan were
played on traditional folk instruments with the addition of Ó
Riada's harpsichord that doubled for the metal-strung Irish
harp, which at that time was only a museum piece. Members of
Ceoltóirí Chualann included musicians, who would form the
Chieftains--Paddy Moloney, Seán Potts, Michael Tubridy,
Martin Fay, and Peadar Mercier. Another offshoot is Éamon De
Buitlear's Ceoltóirí Laighean.

All the selections on this live recording are excellently
performed, especially the three vocals by Ó Sé--"Fanny
Power," "Pléaráca na Ruarcach," and "M'uilleagán Dubh Ó. The
instrumentals are well-arranged with a chamber music feel to
them. The harpsichord seems heavy handed at times, but the
collection is most impressive. [LP]

     NOTES: Side One is from a Dublin concert recorded on
30 March 1969, while Side Two was recorded on 28 June 1970 in
Cork.

SEÁN Ó RIADA

162.   Ó Riada Sa Gaiety.* (1969)   Gael-Linn CEF 027

     ARTISTS: Seán Ó Riada-harpsichord; Seán Ó Sé-vocals;
Martin Fay-fiddle; Seán Ó Ceallaigh-fiddle; Seán Ó Cathain-
fiddle; Paddy Moloney-uilleann pipes; Seán Potts-whistle;
Michael Tubridy-flute; Éamon de Buitléar-accordion; Peadar
Mercier-bodhrán.

          CONTENTS: Marcshlua Uí Néill; Mná na hÉireann
          (The Women of Ireland); Planxty Johnson; Im
          Aonar Seal; Cnocáin Aitinn Liatroma (The Whinny
          Hills of Leitrim); Marbhna Luimní (Limerick's
          Lamentation or Lament for Limerick); Do Bhí
          Bean Uasal (also known as Carrickfergus); An
          Ghaoth Ó nEas (South Wind); Máirséail Rí Laoise
          ((March of the King of Laoise) and is known as
          Rory O'Moore); An Chéad Mháirt de'n Fhômhar/Na
          Gamhna Geala; Iníon an Phailitínigh (The Pales-
          tine's Daughter); Ríl Mhór Bhaile an Chalaidh

This is considered Ó Riada and Ceoltóirí Chualann at their
best. Recorded live at the Gaiety Theatre in Dublin. [LP]

     NOTES: Seán Ó Riada and Ceoltóirí Chualann's recor-
dings include Reacaireacht An Riadaigh (Gael-Linn CEF 10),
Playboy of the Western World (Gael-Linn CEF 12), Ceol n
Nuasal (Gael-Linn CEF 15), Ding Dong (Gael-Linn CEF 16),

Seán Ó Riada (Gael-Linn CEF 76), Mise Eire (Gael-Linn CEF 80), and Aifreann (Gael-Linn CEF 81).

PATRICK STREET

163.   Patrick Street. (1987)   Green Linnet SIF 1071

   ARTISTS: Kevin Burke-fiddle; Jackie Daly-accordion; Andy Irvine-harmonica, vocals, bouzouki, mandolin; Arty McGlynn-guitar; with Donal Lunny-keyboards, bodhrán. Produced by Donal Lunny.

   CONTENTS: Patrick Street/The Carraroe Jig; Walter Sammon's Grandmother/Concertina Reel/Brendan McMahon's; The Holy Ground; The Shores of Lough Gowna/Contentment is Wealth/ Have a Drink with Me; French Canadian Set "La Cardeuse"; Loftus Jones; The Dream/Indiana; Martin Rochford's Reel/Roll Out the Barrel/The Earl's Chair; Mrs. O'Sullivan's Jig/Caliope House; The Man with the Cap

No one could ask for a better recording from these stellar musicians. The group's debut lp contains ten masterfully performed selections. The energetic tunes tastefully blend strings, accordion, and keyboards. "French Canadian Set: 'La Cardeuse,'" and "The Carraroe Jig" provide examples of the band's outstanding arrangements. Additionally Andy Irvine sings four songs. One can hope that this is only the beginning of a long association. **[LP, CS, CD]**

   NOTES: A sequel by Patrick Street, No. 2 Patrick Street, was released in 1988 by Green Linnet (SIF 1088).

TOMMY PEOPLES

164.   The High Part of the Road. (1976)   Shanachie 29033

   ARTISTS: Tommy Peoples-fiddle; with Paul Brady-guitar. Produced by Richard Nevins and Daniel Michael Collins.

   CONTENTS: The Oak Tree/Pinch of Snuff; Kid on the Mountain/O'Farrell's Welcome to Limerick; Wheels of the World/Toss the Feathers; The High Part of the Road/Monk's Jig; Bank of Ireland/ Dairy Maid; Nine Points of Roguery/Mistress on the Floor; Green Groves of Ireland/Pigeon on the Gate; Old John's Jig/Queen of the Fair; Salamanca/Lucy Campbell; Silver Slipper/Old Hag in the Kiln; Farewell to Ireland (Air and Reel); McCahill's Reels

Touted as one of the finest Irish fiddlers today, Tommy Peoples' first solo lp proves the accolades to be true. He performs a standout selection of classic Irish dance tunes with dazzling guitar accompaniment by Paul Brady. The album is a prominent example of fiddling at its best. **[LP, CS]**

TOMMY PEOPLES

165.   The Iron Man.   (1985)   Shanachie 79044

    ARTISTS: Tommy Peoples-fiddle; with Dáithí Sproule-
guitar. Produced by Daniel Michael Collins and Richard
Nevins.

        CONTENTS: Reavy's/Merry Sister's; Tom Billy's/
        Out on the Ocean; Sunny Brogan's Favorite/
        Drunken Landlady; Kit O'Connor's; The Iron
        Man/William Marshall's; Carrigaline/Belles of
        St. Louis; Crowley's Reel/Sweeny's Dream; John
        Doherty's Fancy/Brogan's Ferry; Tell Her I Am/
        Chorus Jig; O'Dowd's/Chicago Reel; Woman of the
        House/Morning Star; Kitty O'Shea; O'Callahan's/
        Scarta Glen

Backed brilliantly by Dáithí Sproule, Tommy Peoples, formerly
with the Bothy Band, excels in a collection of mostly Irish
dance tunes, representing various fiddling styles and
regional influences. Outstanding selections include "Brogan's Ferry," "Kitty O'Shea," "The Iron Man/ William Mar-
shall's Strathspey," and "Tom Billy's Jig/Out on the Ocean."
This record is a triumph for both Peoples and Sproule. [LP,
CS]

PLANXTY

The catalyst for forming Planxty was the gathering of three
musicians, Donal Lunny, Liam O'Flynn, and Andy Irvine, to
accompany Christy Moore on his album, Prosperous (Tara 2008).
Upon completion of the lp in 1972 the quartet began performing as Planxty, a group which revolutionized the norm of
Irish music. With its combination of traditional and original compositions and multi-layered, intricate instrumental
harmonies, the band presented a new, dynamic sound. Planxty
also introduced into its arrangements instruments, such as
the bouzouki and the hurdy gurdy, not traditionally played in
Celtic music. In the three years as a band, Planxty reached
a large audience in Europe and the United States, demonstrat-
ing the great potential for innovation in Irish music with
the creativity and originality in its arrangements and performance. This inventiveness is still felt today by other
groups of musicians who have emulated Planxty's style.

Planxty officially split in the fall of 1975. Lunny was
replaced by Johnny Moynihan in 1973 and went on to pursue
contemporary, original music. He would later be an important
part of the Bothy Band, another innovative Irish group.
Moore left Planxty in 1974 to work as a solo artist and was
replaced by Paul Brady, formerly of the Johnstons. This
lineup (Brady, Moynihan, O'Flynn, and Irvine) would never
record together, although they did perform a farewell tour.
Planxty reunited for subsequent "reunion" albums, but the
magic of its first lps has never waned. Shanachie Records
keeps these three fabulous titles in print, allowing Planxty's innovative statement to remain vital.

166. Cold Blow and the
         Rainy Night. (1974)   Shanachie 79011

    ARTISTS: Liam O'Flynn-uilleann pipes, tin whistle;
Andy Irvine-mandolin, mandola, hurdy gurdy, dulcimer; Christy
Moore-guitar, bodhrán, harmonium; Johnny Moynihan-bouzouki,
fiddle, tin whistle; with Donal Lunny-guitar, bouzouki,
portative organ, bodhrán. Produced by Phil Coulter.

       CONTENTS: Johnny Cope (song and hornpipe);
       Dennis Murphy's Polka/The 42 Pound Cheque/John
       Ryan's Polka; Cold Blow and the Rainy Night;
       "P" Stands for Paddy, I Suppose; The Old Torn
       Petticoat/The Dublin Reel/The Wind that Shakes
       the Barley; Baneasa's Green Glade/Mominsko
       Horo; The Little Drummer; The Lakes of Pont-
       chartrain; The Hare in the Corn/The Frost Is
       All Over/The Gander in the Pratie Hole; The
       Green Fields of Canada

The final original Planxty lp introduces new band member
Johnny Moynihan, who replaces Donal Lunny. Moynihan is
credited with introducing the Greek bouzouki into Irish
music. Album highlights include the showstopper "The Lakes
of Pontchartrain" and "The Green Fields of Canada," a
poignant emigration song in which the protaganist realistically accepts his fate and hopes for a better life in
America. "Banesea's Green Glade" and "Mominski Horo," a
Bulgarian dance, exemplify Irvine's Balkan influences. [LP,
CS]

167. The Planxty
         Collection.   Shanachie 79012

    ARTISTS: Christy Moore, Donal Lunny, Andy Irvine,
Liam O'Flynn, Johnny Moynihan. Produced by Phil Coulter,
with the exception of "Cliffs of Dooneen," which is produced
in mono by Planxty.

       CONTENTS: The Jolly Beggar/Reel; Merrily
       Kissed the Quaker; The Lakes of Pontchartrain;
       The Blacksmith; The Hare in the Corn/The Frost
       is All Over/The Gander in the Pratie Hole;
       Cliffs of Dooneen; Cúnla; Pat Reilly; Bean
       Phaidín; Raggle Taggle Gypsy/Tabhair Dom Do
       Lámh; Denis Murphy's Polka/The 42 Pound
       Cheque/John Ryan's Polka; As I Roved Out

A greatest hits collection orignally on Polydor (2383 387),
this recording is culled from Planxty's three albums--Planxty
(Polydor 2383 186), The Well Below the Valley (Polydor 2383
232), Cold Blow and the Rainy Night (Polydor 2383 301). It
also includes extensive notes and a layout of various news
clippings from Planxty's heyday. [LP, CS]

168. Planxty. (1972)   Shanachie 79009

    ARTISTS: Christy Moore-vocals, guitar, harmonica,
bodhrán; Andy Irvine-vocals, mandola, mandolin, hurdy gurdy,

harmonica; Liam O'Flynn-uilleann pipes, tin whistle; Donal
Lunny-vocals, bouzouki, guitar, bodhrán. Produced by Phil
Coulter.

> **CONTENTS:** Raggle Taggle Gypsy/Tabhair Dom Do
> Lámh (Give Me Your Hand); Arthur McBride;
> Planxty Irwin; Sweet Thames Flow Softly; Junior
> Crehan's Favourite/ Corney is Comin'; The West
> Coast of Clare; The Jolly Beggar/Reel; Only Our
> Rivers; Sí Bheag, Sí Mhor; Follow Me Up to
> Carlow; Merrily Kissed the Quaker; The Black-
> smith

Planxty, the band's debut lp, contains rousing dance tunes
with O'Flynn in lead on the pipes and vocals from the other
three members. "Planxty Irwin," a Carolan harp tune, is
given a stately feeling on hurdy gurdy and pipes. Quite a
departure from the harp! A perennial favorite, "Raggle
Taggle Gypsy," adroitly segues into Rory Dall O Catháin's
"Tabhair Dom Do Lámh," a tune now closely associated with the
Chieftains. Vocally, the songs are all gems. The nostalgic,
bittersweet "The West Coast of Clare" was inspired by
Irvine's memories of Miltown Malbay. The wistful whistle and
mandolin/bouzouki/guitar give it a melancholy tone. This is
indeed the lp's best song! "Only Our Rivers," a sad commentary on the state of Ireland, "Follow Me Up to Carlow, com-
memorating the Irish victory in 1580 over Lord Grey de Wilton
and the Crown's forces, and the oft-recorded and well-known
song, "The Blacksmith," are outstanding. **[LP, CS]**

169.   The Well Below
        the Valley. (1973)   Shanachie 79010

   ARTISTS: Christy Moore, Andy Irvine, Donal Lunny,
Liam O'Flynn. (No instruments are listed). Produced by Phil
Coulter.

> **CONTENTS:** Cúnla; Pat Reilly; The Kid on the
> Mountain/An Phis Fhliuch; As I Roved Out (Tun-
> ney); The Dogs Among the Bushes/Jenny's Wed-
> ding; The Well Below the Valley; Hewlett; Bean
> Phaidín(The Woman of Páidín); Fisherman's
> Lilt/Cronin's Hornpipe; As I Roved Out (Rynne);
> Humours of Ballyloughlin; Time Will Cure Me

Liam O'Flynn soars through several tunes on the pipes, including the reels "The Dogs among the Bushes/Jenny's Wedding,
two slip jigs, "The Kid on the Mountain/An Phis Fhliuch," and
his solo jig, "Humours of Ballycoughlin." Planxty also
presents an unusual combination of songs, two of which have
the same title (an indexer's nightmare), but are vastly
different. "As I Roved Out," performed by Irvine, was
learned from Paddy Tunney. It concerns the jilting of a
man's true love for the capital gains offered by another
lady. The second "As I Roved Out," learned from Andy Rynne
and sung by Moore, portrays a crafty soldier. The lilting
"Cúnla," first heard from Kevin Conneff, who ran the Tradition Club in Dublin at the time, is also notable. The most
fascinating and unusual selection is the title cut, "The Well
Below the Valley," a story of Christ at the well. It has a

very deliberate rhythm and mesmerizing sound. The liner
notes state that many old time singers would not perform this
song due to its subject of incest. **[LP, CS]**

   NOTES: Reunion albums by Planxty include Words and
Music (Shanachie 79035), After the Break (Tara 3001), and The
Woman I Loved So Well (Tara 3005). Solo recordings by Plan-
xty members include The Brendan Voyage (Tara 3006) and The
Pilgrim (Tara 3011) by Liam O'Flynn, Andy Irvine's Rainy
Sundays... Windy Dreams (Tara 3002), Donal Lunny (Gael-Linn
CEF 133) by Donal Lunny, and a multitude of lps by Christy
Moore, which include his latest, Christy Moore (Atlantic
81835).

RELATIVITY

170.   Gathering Pace. (1987)   Green Linnet SIF 1076

   ARTISTS: John Cunningham-fiddle, vocals; Mícheál Ó
Domhnaill-guitar, vocals; Phil Cunningham-accordion, whistles, synthesizers, vocals; Tríona Ní Dhomhnaill-clavinet,
synthesizers, vocals; with William Bell, Colin Berwick, and
Andy McPherson-drummers. Produced by Relativity.

   CONTENTS: Blackwell Court/Highland Laddie/
   Gillies' Taxis/The Double Rise; Gathering Pace;
   Rosc Catha Na Mumhan; Miss Tara MacAdam/ The
   First Train to Kyle; Má Théid Tú 'un Aonaigh;
   Siún Ní Dhuibhir; When She Sleeps; The Monday
   Morning Reel/Cutting a Slide/Robert the Min-
   now/Hogties' Reel; Ceol Anna/A Ríbhinn Óg Bheil
   Cuimhn' Agad

The brothers Cunningham and the siblings Ó Domhnaill have
created an even more dynamic recording than their debut,
Relativity (Green Linnet SIF 1059). Gathering Pace
contains both contemporary material written by the band and
traditional tunes and songs. Arrangements are imaginative
and use a liberal amount of electronics (guitars, synthesizers, etc.), which enhance the overall sound. A mixture of
traditional tunes and compositions by John and Phil Cunningham comprises the eleven exciting instrumentals. The
energetic "Miss Tara MacAdam/The First Train to Kyle" is a
showstopper. On the quieter side, both John's "When She
Sleeps" and Phil's "Ceol Anna," a composition auctioned to
benefit needy children, are haunting and beautiful. Also
electrifying is the rip-roaring set that includes "Hogties
Reel," which is accompanied by members of the First Battalion
Black Watch Pipes and Drums. The Ó Domhnaills provide the
vocals on the mostly traditional songs. Their duet "Rosc
Catha Na Mumhan," written by 17th century poet Piaras Mac
Gearailt, is outstanding. The Cunninghams join in for "A
Ribhinn Òg Bheil Cuimhn' Agad," a song from the Isle of
Lewis. Each member sings a verse and the quartet the chorus.
Tríona offers "Gathering Pace," a song she wrote in her
teens, and the evocative "Má Théid Tú 'un Aonaigh," one of
her father's favorites. Relativity has successfully blended
its Celtic roots with contemporary arrangements and instru-
mentation into a satisfying, provocative recording. **[LP, CS]**

RELATIVITY

171.   Relativity. (1985)   Green Linnet SIF 1059

   ARTISTS: Johnny Cunningham-fiddles, harmony vocals;
Tríona Ní Dhomhnaill-clavinet, vocals; Mícheál Ó Domhnaill-
guitar, keyboards, vocals; Phil Cunningham-accordion, keyboards, whistles, bodhrán, harmony vocals. Produced by John
Cunningham, Phil Cunningham, and Mícheál Ó Domhnaill.

   CONTENTS: The Hut on Staffin Island/Sandy
   MacLeod of Garafad; The Soft Horse Reel; There
   Was a Lady; Gile Mear; Gracelands; When Barney
   Flew Over the Hills; Leaving Brittany/The
   Pernod Waltz; An Seanduine Dóite; John Cun-
   ningham's Return to Edinburgh/Heather Bells/
   The Bell Reel/The Limerick Lasses; Úr-Chill an
   Chreagáin

What do you get when you mix the vocal strength of Ireland's
Bothy Band with the instrumental force behind the Scottish
group, Silly Wizard? Relativity! This outstanding album by
two pairs of siblings begins with a fine trio of dance tunes
composed by Phil Cunningham, and ends with a lovely duet from
Mícheál and Tríona, which laments the demise of the Gaelic
aristocracy. The other selections include several instrumentals, such as "John Cunningham's Return to Edinburgh," written orginally for bagpipe by brother Phil, and a song of
requited love, "There Was a Lady," performed by Tríona.
Mícheál's driving version of "Gile Mear," a song about Bonny
Prince Charlie, is a gem. Tríona's harmony and Mícheál's
forceful guitar make this tune one of the album's best. [LP,
CS]

   NOTES: Solo recordings by the Cunnningham brothers
include Phil Cunningham's Airs and Graces (Green Linnet SIF
3032) and John Cunningham's Fair Warning (Green Linnet SIF
1047).

SKARA BRAE

172.   Skara Brae. (1971)   Shanachie 79034

   ARTISTS: Mícheál Ó Domhnaill, Tríona Ní Dhomhnaill,
Mairéad Ní Dhomhnaill, Dáithí Sproule.

   CONTENTS: An Cailín Rua; An Suantraí; Bán-
   chnoic Éireann Óighe; Angela; Táim Breoite go
   Leor; Inis Dhún Rámha; An Saighdiúir Tréigthe;
   Cad é Sin don Té Sin; An Chrúbach; Casadh an
   tSúgáin; Caitlín Óg; Aird a' Chumhaing; Tá Mé
   'mo Shuí

A few years before the birth of the Bothy Band the siblings
Ó Domhnaill (Mairéad, Tríona, and Mícheál) and their cousin
Dáithí Sproule recorded as Skara Brae. The members were
still in college but showed a keen maturity in their music,
creating thirteen gems on this album. Vocal harmonies are
exquisite especially on the a capella "Bán chnoic Éireann
Óighe." Another fine example, "Táim Breoite go Leor,"

employs alternating two part harmonies between the women and men. Instrumentally, Sproule and Mícheál Ó Domhnaill add bluesy guitar to "Angela" and "Aird a´ Chumhaing," making both excellent and innovative selections. The meeting of jazz and folk was quite experimental at this time, and Ó Domhnaill, a pioneer in the sound, would take this fusion to the Bothy Band. This album is the first to feature the Ó Domhnaills and Sproule, who have become a prominent force in Irish music. The wealth of material, vocals, and inventive instrumentation have not lost their impact in the years since the initial release of this record. [LP, CS]

BOB STEWART AND FINBAR FUREY

173. <u>Tomorrow We Part</u>. (1976)   Crescent ARS 110

ARTISTS: Bob Stewart-psaltery, cittern, guitar; Finbar Furey-uilleann pipes, whistles; with George Furey-guitar, cittern, bodhrán; Stuart Gordon-fiddle, bodhrán.

CONTENTS: Bird in the Tree; Anach Chuain/ Brian Boru´s March; The Chance/The Old Pipe on the Hob/The Mad Cat; A Ramble to the West; Kiss the Maid Behind the Barrel; Slievenamon/Garrett Barry´s Jig; La Volta; Morning on a Distant Shore; The West Wind; Over the Cliff/Denver the Dancer; Down by the Glenside/Cork City; Regulation Reel; Tomorrow We Part

The psaltery, an ancient stringed instrument of the zither family, and the uilleann pipes are a unique and innovative musical combination, which makes <u>Tomorrow We Part</u> an exciting and intriguing album. Finbar Furey, a stalwart figure in traditional Irish music for over ten years, is joined by Bob Stewart, an accomplished musician, author, and instrument designer. This album, the result of a two day recording session in Bath, England, includes both traditional and original pieces arranged by the duo. The overall performance is very good, especially the instrumental duets, "Down by the Glenside/Cork City," "A Morning on a Distant Shore," and "Anach Chuain/Brian Boru´s March." What is surprising is the tasteful blend of two very different instruments. Each complements the other, no matter which is in the lead. The haunting, delicate quality of the psaltery and the more forceful sound of the pipes are a winning blend. [LP]

NOTES: Albums by Bob Stewart include <u>The Unique Sound of the Psaltery</u> (Argo ZDA 207), and <u>The Wraggle Taggle Gypsies O</u> (Crescent ARS 105). Stewart has also published <u>Pagen Imagery in English Folksong</u> (Humanities Press, 1977).

ALAN STIVELL

174. <u>Harpes Du Nouvel Age</u>. (1986)   Rounder 3094

ARTISTS: Alan Stivell-electro-acoustic harp, nylon sting electro-harp, electric harp, Celtic harp. Recorded and mixed by Fabrice Sauré.

CONTENTS: Musique Sacrée: Tremen´ra pep tra
(All Things Pass), Pedenn Ewid Breizh (Prayer
for Brittany), Tremen´ra pep tra, Spered Santel
(The Spirit); Dor I: Taol-arnod (Experimental
music); Piberezh: Cumh Chlaibhers, Lament for
the Children, McDonuill of the Isles; Dor II:
(Taol-prim) Improvisation; Rory Dall´s Love
Tune (also known as Tabhair Dom Do Lámh (Give
Me Your Hand)); Kervalan; Luskellerezh; Dihun´
ta (Awaken!); En Dro Inis-Arzh (Around the Isle
of Arzh); Dans Fanch Mitt; Suite Ecossaise; Dor
III: Harp´ Noun! (Help Me!)

The long awaited sequel to Stivell´s monumental success,
Renaissance of the Celtic Harp (Rounder 3067), does not hold
a candle to its predecessor. It is strange that when Renaissance... was recorded it was considered folk music, and for
years continued to be referred to as such, but for the last
couple of years Stivell has been heralded as a "new age"
artist, a very successful label in contemporary adult music.
Harpes du Nouvel Age is a pleasant album, recorded digitally
and released also on compact disc. Stivell uses the harp in
many ways, including percussion, but this album just does not
have the magic of its prequel. The appeal to the yuppie
kingdom may foster interest in Stivell´s more traditional
recordings. [LP, CS, CD]

                        ALAN STIVELL

175.   Renaissance of the Celtic Harp. (1971)   Rounder 3067

   ARTISTS: Alan Stivell-Celtic harps, Irish flute,
Scottish bagpipes, Breton bombardon; with Michel Delaporte-
percussion, tablas; Guy Cascales-drums; Gerard Levasseur-
bass guitar; Gerard Salkowsky-bass guitar; Dan Ar Bras-elec-
tric guitar, acoustic guitar; Gilles Tinayre-organ; Yann-
Fanch Ar Merdy-Scottish drums; Mig Ar Biz-bombardon; Alan
Kloatr-bombardon; Jean Huchot-cello; Henri Delagarde-cello;
Manuel Recasens-cello; Stephane Wiener-viola; Gabriel Beau-
vais-viola; Paul Hadjaje-viola; Pierre Cheval-viola; Jean-
arc Dollez-double bass; Anne Germain, Claude Germain, Jean-
Claude Briodin, Francois Wall, Jacques Hendrix, Daniele
Bartolletti-background vocals.   Produced by Franck Giboni.

CONTENTS: Ys; Marv Pontkellec; Ap Huw/Penllyn;
Eliz Iza; Gaeltacht: Caitlin Triall (Irish
melody), Port Ui Mhuirgheasa (Irish Jig), Airde
Cuan (Irish Melody), Na Reubairean (Scottish
melody), Manx Melody, Heman Dubh (Isles of
Hebrides songs), Gaelic Waltz (traditional
Scottish waltz), Struan Robertson (Scottish
strathspey), The Little Cascade (Scottish
reel), Braigh Loch Iall (Scottish melody), Port
An Deorai (Irish jig)

Alan Stivell Cochevelou has been instrumental in the renaissance of the Celtic harp. Stivell, Derek Bell of Ireland,
Charles Guard from the Isle of Man, and American Patrick Ball
are considered masters of the instrument. Born in 1944 in
Gourin, Brittany, Stivell´s family moved to Paris, where he

began to learn the piano at five. Soon he would begin to
study the harp under the direction of his father, Jord. The
elder Cochevelou built one of the first modern day Breton
harps, based on designs from the sixteenth century. His
creation was first heard in 1953, played by Alan. This
performance was the first time an authentic Celtic harp had
been played in four centuries. Alan Stivell performed at the
Olympia in Paris at eleven, and recorded two albums shortly
thereafter. He studied the traditonal music of the Celts
(Ireland, Scotland, Wales, Brittany), and expanded his musical abilities to include the Scottish bagpipe, bombardon,
flute, dulcimer, and penny whistle. He has experimented with
pop and rock music, integrating rhythms and electric instruments into his arrangements.

However, Alan Stivell is known worldwide first as a premier
harper and Renaissance of the Celtic Harp is a wonderfully
exquisite recording. This classic, released as an import in
1971 on Fontana, was issued domestically on Rounder Records,
which also recently released the compact disc version. The
recording contains five pieces, all imaginatively arranged
with luxurious textures and haunting resonance. The entire
second side is a medley of tunes taken from the traditions of
Ireland, Scotland, the Isles of Hebrides and the Isle of Man.
Dedicated to the late Seán O Riada, "Gaeltacht" is the 'piece
de resistance' of the recording. This nineteen minute excur-
sion features Irish jigs, Scottish dances, and tunes from the
Hebrides and the Isle of Man. These numerous pieces are
seamlessly interwoven to perfection. If one can only own one
harp album, this is the one. **[LP, CS, CD]**

  NOTES: Other recordings by Alan Stivell include
Celtic Symphony (Rounder 3088/89), Journee A La Maison (Rounder 3062), which has been released on CD, From Celtic Roots
(Fontana 6325 304), A Langannet (Fontana 6325 332), A L'Olympia (Fontana 6399 005), Live In Dublin ((Bocaccio Records ES
129) This is a recent Spanish release). The album was originally on Fontana (9299 547), Legende (Celtic Music CM 022),
Reflections (Fontana 6399 008), Terre des Vivants (Disc' AZ 2
373), and Trema'n Inís (Disc' Az/2 374). The Fontana items
are almost impossible to locate, but with foreign issues,
such as Live in Dublin, becoming available, perhaps other
titles will so be obtainable.

STOCKTON'S WING

176.   American Special.* (1984)   Tara 4001

  ARTISTS: Paul Roche-flute, whistle, vocals; Maurice
Lennon-fiddle, viola, vocals; Kieran Hanrahan-banjo, man-
dolin, bouzouki, harmonica; Mike Hanrahan-guitar, vocals;
Tommy Hayes-bodhrán, bones, Jew's harp.

  CONTENTS: Boys of the Lough/Star of Munster;
  Sonny Brogan's/Charlie Lennon's; Lucy Camp-
  bell's; Fiddler John; Bill Harte's/Going to the
  Well for Water; Chicago Set; Dirt Track to the
  Sky; The Frost is All Over/Queen of the Rushes;
  The Belltable; Take a Chance; Queen of the
  Fair; My Darling's Asleep/Sonny Brogan's

In honor of Stockton's Wing's first American tour, this album
was specially released to reach American audiences unfamiliar
with the band's previous three albums. No new material is
offered, but this provides a good compilation of some of its
best material. **[LP, CS]**

STOCKTON'S WING

177.   <u>Light in the Western Sky</u>. (1982)   Tara 3009

     ARTISTS: Maurice Lennon-fiddle, viola; Mike Hanrahan-
guitar, vocals; Kieran Hanrahan-mandolin, banjo, harmonica;
Tommy Hayes-taburka, bodhrán, percussion; Paul Roche-whistle,
flute; with Steve Cooney-bass, guitar, Didgeridoo, mandolin,
rhythm guitars; Fran Breen-drums, finger bells, percussion;
The Winglettes-backing vocals, handclaps; James Delaney-syn-
thesizer; Aíne O Connell-backing vocals; Brian Masterson-rol-
ling wave, water drip; Jonathan Ryan-voice; Mick Berry-
chimes; Aisling Drury-Burns-cello; P. J. Curtis-wind chimes,
tambourine; Charlie Lennon-piano. Produced by P. J. Curtis.

     CONTENTS: Walk Away; The Belltable; Beneath
the Shade; Dirt Track to the Sky; Lucy Campbell's/Francis John McGovern's; The Chicago
Set; Beautiful Affair; Trip to London; Promenade Love; The Golden Stud: Tommy Peoples'
Jig, The Golden Stud, The Morning Dew, excerpt
from <u>The Journals</u> by Henry David Thoreau

The band's third studio album continues Stockton's Wing's
move toward a more contemporary sound. The songs written and
performed by Mike Hanrahan are uninspired for the most part.
He does not have the depth of Paul Brady or the appeal of
Christy Moore. American country and western music heavily
influences Hanrahan's vocals and compositions, and although
the songs are pleasant, their overall weakness detracts from
the appeal of this record. Tight arrangements and the innovative use of the American banjo, Jew's harp, and harmonica
play a part in the group's instrumental strength. Top dance
tunes include "The Chicago Set," "The Belltable," and "Lucy
Campbell's." The Australian aboriginal didgeridoo provides a
most unusual accompaniment on "The Golden Stud." **[LP, CS]**

STOCKTON'S WING

178.   <u>Stockton's Wing</u>. (1978)   Tara 2004

     ARTISTS: Kieran Hanrahan-banjo, bouzouki, harmonica,
mandolin, vocals; Tony Callanan-guitar, bouzouki, vocals;
Tommy Hayes-bodhrán, Jew's harp, vocals; Paul Roche-flute,
tin whistle, vocals; Maurice Lennon-fiddle, vocals. Produced
by Stockton's Wing.

     CONTENTS: The Humours of Tulla/The Bucks of
Oranmore; The Maid Behind the Bar; Padriag
O'Keefe's; No Man's Land; The Green Gates/The
Boy in the Gap; The Drops of Brandy; The Con-
cert Reel; The High Road to Linton; Pleasant
and Delightful; Queen of the Fair; Sonny Bro-

gan's/Charlie Lennon's; Bold Donnelly; Lord
McDonald's/The Wild Irishman

Stockton's Wing offers an excellent introduction to this
multi-talented band of All-Ireland champions. The group
combines its youthful enthusiasm with outstanding musical
abilities. The material is only a sample of the variety of
Stockton's Wing's repertoire. Dance tunes (jigs, reels,
slip-jigs, and mazurkas) are all progressively arranged, but
remain traditional. The band possesses a full sound highlighted by the combinations of stringed instruments. The
Jew's harp produces a most unusual but charming accompaniment
on "The Drops of Brandy" and "Queen of the Fair." It gives
both tunes a lighthearted appeal. Three songs round out the
selections. The most outstanding is the delightful "Bold
Donnelly" with its wild rhythms punctuated by the bodhrán.
[LP, CS]

STOCKTON'S WING

179.   Take a Chance.* (1981)   Tara 3004

   ARTISTS: Mike Hanrahan-guitar, vocals; Tommy Hayes-
bodhrán, Jews harp, bones, spoons; Paul Roche-flute, whistles, low whistle, vocals; Maurice Lennon-fiddle, viola,
vocals; Kieran Hanrahan-banjo, manodlin, bouzouki, guitar,
harmonica.

   CONTENTS: My Darling Asleep/Sonny Brogans;
   Boys of the Lough/Star of Munster; Cameron
   Highlander's; Take a Chance; Bill Harte's/
   Going to the Well for Water/Fiddler John; The
   Frost is All Over/Queen of the Rushes; The Post
   Man; Ten Thousand Miles; Austin Tierney's;
   Hughie Travers/Jenny's Chickens

Not as successful as the band's debut lp, Take a Chance does
contain tightly arranged instrumentals that come alive with
the fiddle of Maurice Lennon. In contrast the songs are
disappointing and never seem to hit their mark. [LP, CS]

   NOTES: Other albums by Stockton's Wing include Take
One - Live (Tara 4002), Full Flight (Polydor 831 183-1), and
Celtic Roots Revival (Raglan RGLP 6).

SWEENEY'S MEN

180.   Sweeney's Men. (1968)   Transatlantic TRASAM 37

   ARTISTS: Andy Irvine-vocals, mandolin, harmonica,
guitar; Johnny Moynihan-vocal, bouzouki, tin whistle; Terry
Woods-vocals, 6-string guitar, 12-string guitar, 5-string
banjo, concertina. Produced by Bill Leader.

   CONTENTS: Rattlin' Roarin' Willy; Sullivan's
   John; Sall Brown; My Dearest Dear; The Exhiles
   Jig; The Handsome Cabin Boy; Dicey Riley; Tom
   Dooley; Willie O'Winsbury; Dance to Your Daddy;
   The House Carpenter; Johnston; Reynard the Fox

It is difficult to believe that Sweeney's Men recorded this
lp in 1968, as it is very progressive and innovative for its
time. Ireland was just beginning to tear itself away from
the pub ballad songs performed by the Clancy Brothers and
others. A new, subtler music was breaking away from this
norm. Sweeney's Men (and later Planxty) was one of the first
groups to experiment with this type of music. The blending
of bouzouki and mandolin was something new. Johnny Moynihan
is credited with introducing the instrument into Irish music.
Terry Woods helped bring to Sweeney's Men's repertoire American and English songs, like "Tom Dooley" and "House Carpenter." The band was not easily labeled and did not fit
into one category or another. Being ahead of its time, the
group did not receive the full attention its talents war-
ranted. Sweeney's Men called it quits in late 1969 after
recording two lps. Andy Irvine left the group after this
album to live in Romania, but would later team up with Moynihan as part of Planxty. This Balkan influence would appear
in Planxty's music. Irinve was replaced by Henry McCullough,
who later joined Paul McCartney in Wings. Terry Woods formed
Steeleye Span, one of the most successful electric folk bands
of the 70s.

This self-titled album is the best of the Sweeney pair.
Irvine, Moynihan, and Woods alternate lead vocals, and all
contribute to vocal harmonies. The intricate instrumentation, unique for its time, is vibrant yet subtle. All thirteen cuts are gems with the sea shanty "Sally Brown," "The
Exhiles Jig," and "Dance to Your Daddy" three of the best
selections. **[LP]**

SWEENEY'S MEN

181.   The Tracks of Sweeney.   Transatlantic TRASAM 40

   ARTISTS: Andy Irvine, Terry Woods, Johnny Moynihan.
Produced by Bill Leader.

       CONTENTS: Dream for Me; The Pipe on the Hob;
       Brain Jam; Pretty Polly; Standing on the Shore;
       A Mistake No Doubt; Go By Brooks; When You
       Don't Care for Me; Hiram Hubbard; Hall of
       Mirrors

This 1977 reissue sampler on Transatlantic, the band's second
album, was probably recorded in late 1968 or early 1969, but
an exact date is not listed. Although Andy Irvine is said to
have left the group after the first album, he is credited
with the original composition "Hall of Mirrors." His
replacement, Henry McCullough, is not even mentioned in the
liner notes. Tracks of Sweeney contains mostly original
material written by the band and four traditional tunes,
"Pipe on the Hob," "Hiram Hubbard," "Pretty Polly," and
"Standing on the Shore", which are quite good. The overall
album is less satisfying than the group's first record. **[LP]**

TOUCHSTONE

182.   Jealousy. (1984)   Green Linnet SIF 1050

ARTISTS: Tríona Ní Dhomhnaill-clavinet, piano, synthesizer, accordion, vocals; Claudine Langille-tenor banjo, mandolin, vocals; Mark Roberts-flute, whistle, banjo, bodhrán; Skip Parente-fiddle, viola; Zan McLeod-acoustic guitar, electric guitar, mandocello, bouzouki, electric bass; with Mícheál Ó Domhnaill-guitar, synthesizer; John "Snake" Larson-drums. Produced by Mícheál Ó Domhnaill.

> **CONTENTS:** The Mooncoin Jig/The High Reel/The
> Plover's Wing; Cuach Mo Lonndubh Buí/The Three
> Sea Captains; The Last Chance; The Lonely
> Wanderer; The Primrose Lass/The Keel Row/Green
> Grow the Rushes O; Garcon Á Marier/Orgies
> Nocturnes/Dans Fisel; Jealousy (You Better Keep
> Your Distance); The King's Favourite/The Cook
> in the Kitchen/Din Turrant's Polka; Invisible
> Wings/Faoileán; The Green Gates/The Pinch of
> Snuff; White Snow

Jealousy, the second album by this Celtic American band, is a more confident, boisterous recording than its debut album, The New Land, (Green Linnet SIF 1040). From the rousing American banjo tune, "The Last Chance," to the mesmerizing Breton melodies, "Garcon Á Marier/Orgies Nocturnes/Dans Fisel," Touchstone presents an impressive richness and diversity. In addition to traditional Celtic and American tunes, the group also performs three original compositions. Claudine Langille sings her own song, the powerful "Jealousy." Tríona Ní Dhomnaill, late of the Bothy Band, offers several of her own compositions. One of the most interesting is "Faoileán," originally written in English with added Irish lyrics by poet Michael Davitt. Ní Dhomnaill is definately the nucleus of the band with her lovely vocals and the clavinet, which gives both robust and beautiful accompaniment. However, each band member takes the spotlight, making for a balanced performance. **[LP, CS]**

NOTES: Zan McLeod and Mark Roberts left the group in 1985.

TOUCHSTONE

183.   The New Land. (1982)   Green Linnet SIF 1040

ARTISTS: Tríona Ní Dhomhnaill-vocals, clavinet, synthesizer, harmony vocals; Claudine Langille-mandolin, tenor banjo, vocals; Mark Roberts-flute, 5-string banjo, tin whistle, bodhrán; Zan McLeod-bouzouki, guitar, mandocello, electric guitar; with Mícheál Ó Domhnaill-guitar. Produced by Mícheál Ó Domhnaill.

> **CONTENTS:** The Killmoulis Jig/The Maid at the
> Spinning Wheel; Jack Haggerty; The Flowing
> Tide/Cooley's Hornpipe; Susanna Martin/Sweeney's Buttermilk; The Flying Reel/My Maryann/The Game of Love; Casadh Cam Na Feadarnaigh; Three Polkas; Farewell to Nova Scotia;
> Song in F; Bolen's Fancy/The Dunmore Lasses/The
> Maid Behind the Bar/The Glass of Beer; The New
> Land

The band's award winning debut album successfully blends
traditional Irish music with American bluegrass and
"old-timey" music. This combination yields an innovative
sound dominated by the energetic performances of the band's
two women artists. Claudine Langille is an impressive
instrumentalists on banjo and mandolin. Although an American
by birth, she has mastered the mandolin playing styles of
both the Irish and the Scots. Her performances are outstanding. Vocally, she provides two songs including the excellent
"Farewell to Nova Scotia." Her husky, strong voice contrasts
with Ní Dhomnaill's more distinctive and delicate style.
Tríona Ní Dhomnaill, well-known from her days with The Bothy
Band, Skara Brae, and Strayaway, is the focal point of the
Celtic tradition for Touchstone. Her family is renowned for
its collection of tunes from the Gaelic tradition in Donegal.
For The New Land she has included "Casadh Cam Na Feadar-
naighe," in addition to an original composition, "Song in
F." Ní Dhomnaill also provides rhythm and sometimes a
baroque accompaniment to the album's selections. [LP, CS]

GERALD TRIMBLE

184. Underline Flight. (1983)   Green Linnet SIF 1043

    ARTISTS: Gerald Trimble-cittern, guitar, mandolin;
with Mícheál Ó Domhnaill-guitar; John Cunningham-fiddle,
synthesizer; Clair Connors-piano; Terry Teachout-bass, piano;
Dave Brown-bodhrán; David Agee-bones; Colleen Williams-
flute; Doug McBain-tenor saxophone, soprano saxophone; Dan
Leonard-tenor banjo; Joel Higgins-side drums. Produced by
John Cunningham.

        CONTENTS: Paddy O'Brien's/Scatter the Mud/
        Arthur Darley's (also known as The Swedish
        Jig); Lady Hamilton of Dalrymple/ Johnny's
        Wedding/Nellie O'Donovan/Last Night's Joy; War
        Hent Kerrigouarch (On the Road to Kerrigouarch/
        Gavotte de Scignac; The York Reel/Dancing
        Feet; Martin Wynne's #2; The Sailor's
        Return/The Return to Camdentown/The Maid Behind
        the Bar; The Captain's Hornpipe/The First
        Flight of Geese; Mr. Webster/Miss Jane
        MacInnes-Dandeleith; The Three Men of Brit-
        tany/The Wild Man of Steel/Elizabeth's Air; The
        Pumpherston Hornpipe/Open the Door to
        Three/The Judge's Dilemma

Gerald Trimble, an exciting artist from Kansas City, Missouri, has created a vibrant blend of traditional and original tunes on this impressive debut album. First Flight is
the first recording to feature the 10-string cittern, a
relative of the Greek bouzouki, as the lead instrument.
Trimble's innovative use of the cittern on melody, rhythm,
and harmony produces a wonderful array of sounds. Produced
by Silly Wizard's fiddle wizard, John Cunningham, the album
is a collection of old and new tunes, performed by Trimble
and other musicians of caliber. As a soloist Trimble is
excellent on two strathspeys, "Mr. Webster" and "Lady Hamilton of Dalrymple." Brilliant cittern ornamentation is found
on "The York Reel/Dancing Feet," reels originally written for

the Highland pipes. The best ensemble selection is the delicately melodic "Martin Wynne's #2," a reel played as an air.
Trimble's intricate fingerpicking highlights "Elizabeth's
Air," which contrasts with the two forceful reels in the
set. [LP, CS]

GERALD TRIMBLE

185.   Heartland Messenger.* (1984)   Green Linnet SIF 1054

ARTISTS: Gerald Trimble and others.

CONTENTS: The Kail Pot/The Fisher's Rant/The
Morayshire Farmer's Club/General Lonstreet's
Reel; Miss Wharton Duff/Miss Wharton Duff's
Jig; Coates Hall/The Amazon; Miss Stewart's
Jig/Mrs. Rose of Kilravock's Jig/Donald
MacLean; Ostinelli's/Miss Gunning's Fancy Reel;
Heartland Messenger Trilogy: Heartland Waltz,
The Battle of Pea Ridge, Heartland Messen-
ger/Missouri Stubborn/The Air of Drawn Dag-
ger/The Jig of Boone County/The Solar Wind/Liz
Carroll's/The Spirit of the House

Trimble musically explores his Missouri roots, culminating
with a three part suite, "The Heartland Messenger Trilogy,"
which includes a Scots waltz, a Civil War song, and a set of
Irish and Scots dance tunes written by Midwestern musicians.
The remainder of Trimble's second album is devoted to jigs
and reels from his vast repertoire. [LP, CS]

NOTES: Gerald Trimble has recorded a third album,
Crosscurrents (Green Linnett SIF 1065).

PADDY TUNNEY

186.   The Stone Fiddle: Traditional
Songs of Ireland. (1982)   Green Linnet SIF 1037

ARTISTS: Paddy Tunney-vocals. Produced and recorded
by Mick Moloney.

CONTENTS: The Green Fields of America; The
White Steed; The Cool Winding Ayr; Erin the
Green; An Bunnan Bwee (The Yellow Bittern);
Lovely Annie; Tam Brown; The Temptation Song;
The Banks of the Bann; Highland Mary; Good
Friends and Companions (also known as Here's a
Health)

For more than fifty years Paddy Tunney has been singing
traditional songs from a tremendous and varied repertoire.
Born in Scotland in 1921 Tunney was raised in Ulster and has
lived in many parts of Ireland. Most of the selections on
this recording are from County Fermanagh in Ulster or were
collected there. Tunney's sean nós or old style singing is
full of rich ornamentation and embellishments. An entire
record of solo singing can be tedious, but with patience the
listener will enjoy the songs and Tunney's grand performance.

Standout selections are "Good Friends and Companions," "The
Temptation Song," and "Erin the Green." Tunney has included
historical notes on each title, but a lyric sheet would be
helpful. **[LP]**

NOTES: Tunney wrote The Stone Fiddle: My Way to
Traditional Song (Gilbert Dalton, Dublin, 1979), in which he
tells his own life story along with songs and their origins.
A wonderful accompaniment to this album.

JOHN WHELAN & EILEEN IVERS

187.   Fresh Takes.   (1987)   Green Linnet SIF 1075

ARTISTS: John Whelan-button accordion; Eileen Ivers-
fiddle; with Tríona Ní Dhomhnaill-clavinet, synthesizers;
Mark Simos-guitar, piano. Produced by Mick Moloney.

CONTENTS: Castle Kelly's; Tom Fleming's/Kit-
ty's Wedding/Sean McGuire's; Lorraine's Waltz;
Blackberry Blossom; Jenny's Welcome to Char-
lie/Father Francis Cameron; Kevin Burke's; The
Gypsy; The Red-Haired Lass/Paddy O'Brien's/The
Scholar; Desaunay/The Petticoat I Bought in
Mullingar; Trip to Skye; Darach DeBrun's

A refreshing collection of tunes, fluidly arranged with a
mixture of both evocative and thundering instrumentals!
Whelan and Ivers play mostly duets with the expert accompaniment of Mark Simos and Tríona Ní Dhomhnaill. The pair also
takes turns soloing. Ivers plays fiddle with "Jenny's Welcome to Charlie/ Father Francis Cameron," and mandolin for
the first part of "The Gypsy." Whelan wrote several tunes
("Desaunay," "Lorraine's Waltz," and "Trip to Skye") and
plays solo accordion with "Desaunay/The Petticoat I Bought in
Mullingar." Together Whelan and Ivers create magic. "Castle
Kelly's," "Sean McGuire's," and "Blackberry Blossom" are the
tastiest cuts. **[LP, CS]**

WILDGEESE

188.   Celtic Music of the
           Northwest.   Wildgeese Cassette

ARTISTS: Randal Bays-fiddle; Bill Bulick-flutes,
whistles; Kate Power Burns-lead vocals, harmonium, percussion; Barry Crannell-guitar, mandolin; Jim Chapman-bouzouki,
harmonium, whistles. Produced by Mícheál Ó Domhnaill.

CONTENTS: Planxty Charles O'Connor/Kitty's
Wedding/Sonny Brogan's; I Wish My Love Was a
Red, Red Rose; Star Above the Garter/Saint
Patrick's Day; Anach Cuain/The Blacksmith; The
Bush in Bloom/Maud Miller/Russ' Favorite/John
in the Fog; Bridget O'Malley; Ryan's/Scotch
Mary/Sweeney's Dream; Undressed Melody; Mist
Covered Mountain/Monaghan's Jig; Verdant Braes
of Screen; Wheels of the World/Maid in the
Cherry Tree/Speed the Plow

Wildgeese, not to be confused with the late 1970s Irish band
of the same name, is a group of young musicians residing in
the Pacific Northwest. This cassette, produced by Mícheál Ó
Domhnaill, contains a variety of dance tunes and several
songs from Kate Power Burns. The band executes well the
lively instrumentals and Power Burns has a throaty voice that
easily performs the songs. "The Blacksmith" and "Verdant
Braes of Screen" are her best numbers. Of the many dance
medleys "Wheels of the World/Maid in the Cherry Tree/Speed
the Plow" is one of the most satisfying. **[CS only]**

   NOTES: Other examples of young, regional performers
include the The Martin Mulvihill School-Irish Music: The
Living Tradition (Green Linnet SIF 1009), and Irish Music:
The Living Tradition, Volume 2 (Green Linnet SIF 1022). Both
lps are professionally performed by musicians between the
ages of nine and nineteen, who have been taught by Mulvihill
in New York City.

                         JOEMY WILSON

189.   Carolan's Cup: Music of Turlough
       O'Carolan on the Hammered
       Dulcimer. (1984).   Dargason Music DM 102

   ARTISTS: Joemy Wilson-hammered dulcimer, fretted
dulcimer; with the Carolan Consort: Anisa Angarola-guitar;
Valarie King-flute, piccolo, alto flute, bass flute; Miamon
Miller-violin; Sylvia Woods-Celtic harp. Produced by Joemy
Wilson and Scott Fraser.

       CONTENTS: Sheebeg and Sheemore; Colonel John
       Irwin/George Brabazon, (Second Air); Hewlett;
       Betty MacNeill/Planxty Burke; Hugh O'Donnell;
       Carolan's Concerto; Eleanor Plunkett; #179/
       Lord Inchiquin/Carolan's Cup; Dr. John Hart;
       Sir Charles Coote/Lady Blayney; #171; Blind
       Mary/Beauty in Tears/Bridget Cruise, (Third
       Air)

Turlough O'Carolan, the late seventeenth, early eighteenth
century blind harper, wrote a multitude of harp tunes in his
distinctive style, a combination of Gaelic traditions with
Italian baroque, whose composers such as Vivaldi, Carolan
greatly admired. Carolan's Cup contains well-known and
lesser known pieces primarily performed on the hammered
dulcimer by Joemy Wilson with accompanying musicians forming
the Carolan Consort. Arranged by Wilson, the selections
range from lively baroque melodies, such as "Carolan's Concerto," to the Irish air "Bridget Cruise." The accompaniment
on all the cuts is well-arranged and well-performed, with
"Sheebeg and Sheemore" a prime example. Traditionally played
on the harp, Carolan's compositions do not suffer at the
hands of Wilson and her dulcimers. These instruments provide
an interesting contrast to the more traditional Irish harp.
[LP, CS]

   NOTES: Joemy Wilson and her Carolan Consort recorded a
second volume of Carolan tunes, Carolan's Cottage (Dargason
Music DM 104). She also released Gifts (Dargason Music DM

103) and Gifts, Volume 2 (Dargason DM 105), both feasts of
traditional Christmas carols. Sylvia Woods, who accompanies
Wilson on both recordings, is no stranger to Celtic music.
She won the All-Ireland Championship on harp in 1980, the
first American to win. Woods performed and recorded with
Robin Williamson and His Merry Band for several years, and
has been instrumental in reviving the American interest in
the Celtic harp from her Los Angeles headquarters. Her
albums include 3 Harps for Christmas (Tonmeister Records TNLP
1225), and The Harp of Brandishwhiere (Tonmeister Records
TNLP 1213), an originally composed suite for Celtic harp.
With Robin Williamson and His Merry Band, Woods recorded
Journey's Edge (Flying Fish FF 033), American Stonehenge
(Flying Fish FF 062), and A Glint at the Kindling (Flying
Fish FF 096).

THE WOLFE TONES

The Wolfe Tones formed over twenty years ago in Dublin. With
more than ten albums to date to its credit, the band has
gained national and international accolades. The Wolfe Tones
has played Carnegie Hall (the first time in 1972), the Olympia in Paris, and London's Albert Hall. The group's musical
style combines the sounds of the Kingston Trio, the Clancy
Brothers, plus a little instrumentation à la the Chieftains
for good measure. Its repertoire embraces Irish republican-
ism and varies between Irish standards and original compositions.

Listed alphabetically below are the band's albums and each
record's contents. Since the members have not changed, they
and their instruments will be listed once. (A special thanks
to Oliver Barry Artiste Management for providing access to
the Wolfe Tones' albums and background info on the band).

190.   Across the Broad Atlantic (1976)   Triskel TRL 1002

    ARTISTS: Noel Nagle-tin whistle, uilleann pipes
vocals; Tommy Byrne-lead vocals, guitar; Derek Warfield-man-
dolin, vocals; Brian Warfield-tin whistle, Irish harp, guitar, banjo, vocals.

    CONTENTS: The Rambling Irishman; Paddy on the
    Railway; The Great Hunger; Many Young Men of
    Twenty; Sweet Tralee; Shores of America; A
    Dream of Liberty; Paddy's Green Shamrock Shore;
    Goodbye Mick; Spancil Hill; The Fighting 69th;
    The Boston Burgler; Farewell to Dublin [LP]

191.   As Gaeilge.   Triskel TRL 1008

    CONTENTS: Caoine Cill Cais; Sí Finn; Amhran Na
    Mbreac; Thugamar Féin An Samhradh Linn; Braba-
    zons; Cáit Ní Dhuibhir; Cuan Bhantrai; Rosc
    Catha Na Mumhan; I nGarán Na Bhfile; Éamonn An
    Chnoic; Siun Ní Dhuibhir; Tá Na Lá; Reels; An
    Dórd Feinne (Óró 'Se Do Bheatha Abhaile) [LP]

192.   Belt of the Celts.   Triskel TRL 1003

        CONTENTS: Misty Foggy Dew; Quare Things in
        Dublin; The Fairy Hills; Connaught Rangers;
        Bold Robert Emmet; The Hare in the Heather; Tá
        Na Lá; Some Say the Divil is Dead; General
        Monroe; Hurlers March; The West's Asleep; The
        Boys of Bárr Na Sráide; The Rose of Mooncoin;
        Rory O Moore **[LP]**

193.   Irish to the Core. (1976)   Triskel TRL 1001

        CONTENTS: Botany Bay; The Water is Wide; The
        Irish Brigade; Grain Waile; Whelan's Frolics;
        The Night Before Larry was Streched; Fiddlers
        Green; Vale of Avoca; The Limerick Races; The
        Jackets Green; Cook in the Kitchen/The Rambling
        Pitchfork; Kevin Barry; Rock on Rockall **[LP]**

194.   Let the People Sing. (1972)   Triskel TRL 1007

        CONTENTS: Snowy Breasted Pearl; Sean South of
        Garryowen; Twice Daily; James Connolly; Don't
        Stop Me Now; Táim in Arrears; Come Out Ye Black
        & Tans; On the One Road; The Men Behind the
        Wire; For Ireland I'd Not Tell Her Name; Paddy
        Lie Back; The First of May; Long Kesh; A Nation
        Once Again **[LP]**

195.   Live Alive-Oh!   Triskel TRL 1005

        CONTENTS: Botany Bay; Slievenamon; Whelan's
        Frolics; Twice Daily; Some Say the Divil is
        Dead; Rock On Rockall; Highland Paddy; Travel-
        ling Doctor's Shop; Princess Royal; Sean South
        of Garryowen; The Boys of Fair Hill; Snowy
        Breasted Pearl; On the One Road; The Boys of
        the Old Brigade; Banna Strand; Paddy's Dream;
        Broad Black Brimmer; Big Strong Man; James
        Connolly; Fiddlers Green; Tri Coloured Ribbon;
        God Save Ireland; Get Out Ye Black & Tans; A
        Nation Once Again **[LP]**

196.   Rifles of the I.R.A.   Triskel TRL 1010

        CONTENTS: Slievenamon; A Row in the Town (Erin
        Go Brath); God Save Ireland; The Sun is Bur-
        ning; Big Strong Man; I nGarran Na Bhile; Four
        Seasons; Rifles of the I.R.A.; Skibbereen;
        Sweet Carnlough Bay; Ships in Full Sail; Sean
        Tracy; Holy Ground; Uncle Nobby's Steamboat
        [LP]

197.   Spirit of the Nation   Triskel TRL 1006

        CONTENTS: Dingle Bay; No Irish Need Apply;
        Down by the Glenside; Bold Fenian Men; Paddle

Your Own Canoe; Padraic Pearse; The Lough
Sheelin Eviction; Song of the Celts; Butterfly;
Protestant Men; Only Our Rivers Run Free; Saint
Patrick Was a Gentleman; Ireland Unfree; Caro-
lan's Concerto; Streets of New York **[LP]**

198.   'Till Ireland a Nation. (1973)   Triskel TRL 1011

CONTENTS: Highland Paddy; Travelling Doctor's
Shop; My Green Valleys; The Boys of the Old
Brigade; Children of Fear; The Boys of Fair
Hill; Bodenstown Churchyard; The Grandfather;
The Blackbird of Sweet Avondale; The Broad
Black Brimmer; Laugh and the World Laughs with
You; A Soldiers' Life; Give Me Your Hand; Must
Ireland Divided Be; Ireland Over-all **[LP]**

NOTES: One other Wolfe Tones' album, A Sense of
Freedom (Triskel TRL 1012), was not available for analytics,
although it is still in print.

VARIOUS ARTISTS

Under this heading are recordings listed by title. There is
no single artist given as the main performer. All the
artists in this category will be listed in the Artist Index.

199.   Celtic Folkweave. (1974)   Polydor 2908 013

ARTISTS: Mick Hanly-guitar, dulcimer, vocals; Mícheál
Ó Domhnaill-guitar, vocals; Liam Óg O Floinn-Uilleann pipes,
whistle; Donal Lunny-bodhráns; Matt Molloy-flute; Tommy
Peoples-fiddle; Declan McNeils-bass; Tríona Ní Dhomhnaill
harpsichord. Produced by Donal Lunny.

CONTENTS: Bíodh Orm Anocht; The Bold Princess
Royal; The Banks of Claudy; Éirigh's Cuir Ort
Do Chuid Éadaigh; An Bothán a Bha'ig Fionnghu-
ala; The Heathery Hills of Yarrow; Breton
Dances; The Hiring Fair at Hamiltonsbawn; Bríd
Óg Ni Mháille; The Glasgow Barber; (No Love Is
Sorrow) Songbird

Songsters Mick Hanley and Mícheál Ó Domhnaill perform a fine
collection of works from Ireland, Scotland, Brittany, and
England. Joining them are musicians, who at the time of this
recording were basically unknown. However, they are some of
Ireland's top performers today. Material on Celtic Folkweave
consists of songs sung individually by Hanly or Ó Domhnaill,
duets from the pair, and a set of Breton dance tunes. The
most unusual selections are the enjoyable nonsense rhymes,
"Bíodh Orm Anocht," a mixture of Scottish and Donegal Gaelic,
and "An Bothán aBhu'ig Fionnghuala," Gaelic mouth music from
the western Scottish Isles. (The latter tune was later
popularized by the Bothy Band under the title "Fionnghuala"

from their second album, <u>Old Hag You Have Killed Me</u> (Green
Linnet SIF 3005)).

The selection of material is the strength of the album.
Hanly provides the stories: "The Bold Princess Royal," "The
Glasgow Barber," and "The Hiring Fair at Hamiltonsbawn,"
while Ó Domhnaill contributes songs from his native County
Rannafast, Donegal: "The Banks of Claudy," "Bríd Óg Ni
Mháille," and "The Heathery Hills of Yarrow," a sorrowful
piece of love and death, which Mick Hanly recently re-recor-
ded in a shortened version on <u>As I Went over Blackwater</u>
(Green Linnet SIF 3007). <u>Celtic Folkweave</u> has withstood the
hands of time and is still an excellent recording. **[LP]**

    NOTES: Mick Hanly and Mícheál Ó Domhnaill once
performed under the name Monroe.

200.   <u>Cherish the Ladies: Irish
       Women Musicians in America</u>. (1985)   Shanachie 79053

    ARTISTS: Liz Carrol-fiddle; Mick Moloney-guitar; Joan
Madden-flute, tin whistle; Kathy McGinty-fiddle; Mary McDonagh-accordion; Lori Cole-piano; Patty Bronson-flute; Laura
MacKenzie-flute; Dáithí Sproule-guitar; Bridget Fitzgerald-
vocals; Paulette Gershen-tin whistle; Gerry O'Beirne-guitar;
Eileen Ivers-fiddle; Mark Simos-guitar; Eileen Clohessey-tin
whistle; Maureen Doherty-tin whistle, flute; Patricia Con-
way-accordion; Pauline O'Neill-flute; Mary Rafferty-flute;
Rose Conway-fiddle; Treasa Uí Cearúil-vocals; Mary Coogan-
guitar; The Maureen Glynn School of Irish Music: Sheila
McGuire-flute, Karen Foyes-fiddle, Deirdre McDermott-fiddle,
Rosemary Clarke-fiddle, Kathleen McQuillan-fiddle, Patricia
Sullivan-whistle and flute, Cara Early-whistle and flute,
Bridget Harte-whistle and flute, Mary Foynes-flute, Deirdre
Connolly-flute, Ann-Marie Doherty-accordion, Michael Fee-
bodhrán and drums, Ed McDonagh-accordion, Eileen Callaghan-
accordion. Produced by Mick Moloney.

       CONTENTS: Miss McLeod's/Wissahickon Drive/Fer-
       moy Lassies/Morse Avenue; The Tempest/Smash the
       Windows/Lad O'Beirne's; Johnny Doherty's/The
       Cock and the Hen/The Humours of Whiskey; Tá ná
       Páipéir dhá Saighnéail (The Papers are Being
       Signed); Jig Away the Donkey/Josie McDermott's;
       Dear Lisa/The Maid of Ardagh; The Orphan (also
       known as Miss Casey)/Paul Montague's; The
       Galtee Rangers/Gan Ainm; Cherish the Ladies;
       The Lads of Laois/The First Month of Summer;
       Sagart na Cúile Báine (The Fair Haired Priest);
       The Burren/Kilty Town; The Shaskeen/ Gan Ainm;
       Toss the Feathers; The Pride of Rockchapel

Mick Moloney has produced a gem! <u>Cherish the Ladies</u> and its
companion volume, <u>Fathers and Daughters</u> (Shanachie 79054),
are fascinating studies of the Irish American music scene.
More women of all ages are now playing Irish music in America
than prior to 1970, when the field was male dominated.
<u>Cherish the Ladies</u> is a salute to these talented musicians,
who reside in various parts of the U.S. Containing both old
and new tunes, the album presents varied musical styles from

more than twenty performers and accompanists. Outstanding
selections include Liz Carroll's opening reel set, "Miss
McLeod's/Wissahickon Drive/Fermoy Lassies/Morse Avenue", of
which she wrote the second and fourth tunes, Bridget Fitz-
gerald's sean nós singing on "Tá na Páipéir dhá Saighneáil,"
"The Orphan/Paul Montague's" performed by Eileen Ivers and
Mark Simos, and the rousing title cut, "Cherish the Ladies."
The remaining tracks also are excellently performed. Exten-
sive liner notes, lyrics, photos, bios on the artists, and
notated tunes are included. A most innovative recording!
Bravo to Moloney and Shanachie Records for its creation.
[LP, CS]

NOTES: This album was made possible by grants from
the New York State Council on the Arts and the Folk Arts
Programs of the National Endowment for the Arts, and is a
project of the Ethnic Folk Arts Center, New York.

201. Fathers and Daughters: Irish
     Traditional Music in America. (1985) Shanachie 79054

ARTISTS: Joe Madden-accordion; Joan Madden-flute;
John Fitzpatrick-accordion; Maureen Fitzpatrick-fiddle; Kevin
Carroll-accordion; Liz Carroll-fiddle; John Cahill-bodhrán;
Kevin Henry-flute; Maggie Henry-flute; Martin Mulhaire-accor-
dion; Laura Mulhaire-piano; Sheila Mulhaire-flute; Mattie
Connolly-uilleann pipes; Deirdre Connolly-flute; Mike Raf-
ferty-flute; Mary Rafferty-accordion; Martin Mulvihill-
fiddle; Gail Mulvihill-tenor banjo; Dawn Mulvihill-fiddle;
Tom Doherty-melodeon; Maureen Doherty-flute. Produced by
Mick Moloney.

CONTENTS: Cottage in the Grove/The Blackthorne
(also known as The Eel in the Sink); Lad
O'Beirne's/Dinny Delaney's (also known as
Follow Me Down); The Dancing Table/Lightly
Tripping/Gan Ainm; Down the Broom/The Gatehouse
Maid; The Ceilier/The First House in Connaught;
The Rambling Pitchfork (also known as The
Fisherman's Widow)/The Bride's Favorite; The
Sunny Banks/Callahan's (also known as Kate
Kelly's Fancy, also as The Ravelled Hank of
Yarn, and also as Nellie O'Donovan); The Kil-
dare Fancy/Sean Ryan's Hornpipe; The Maid
Behind the Bar (also known as The Green Moun-
tain); Tom Ward's Downfall (also known as
Mourne Mountain)/The New Policeman (also known
as Duffy's Reel); Sean Ryan's/Gallagher's
Frolics/The Bush on the Hill (also known as
McGlinchey's Jig); The Shaskeen/The Knotted
Cord (also known as Junior Crehan's Favorite);
The Three Sisters; Sean Ryan's/The Cliffs of
Moher; Roaring Mary/The Banshee (also known as
The Willing Hand and also as McMahon's Reel);
Paddy O'Brien's Jigs; Laura's Favorite/Fahey's;
The Hare's Paw (also known as Jim Kennedy's
Favorite)/Castlekelly

Fathers and Daughters continues the high quality performances
by Irish American musicians. For this lp the women are

paired with their fathers to form duets and trios. All the
groupings play delightfully with standout performances by Liz
and Kevin Carroll, Martin, Gail, and Dawn Mulvihill, Martin,
Laura, and Sheila Mulhare, and Tom and Maureen Doherty. This
is a most admirable recording accomplishment by both Shanachie and Mick Moloney, the producer of both records. [LP,
CS]

NOTES: This album was a project of the Ethnic Folk
Arts Center, New York, and was funded by grants from the Folk
Arts Programs of the National Endowment for the Arts and the
New York Council of the Arts.

202.   The Irish Rebellion Album.   Folkways FH 5415

ARTISTS: Harvey Andrews-guitar, vocals; Willie Camp-
bell-vocals; Brian Clark-guitar, vocals; Tommy Dempsey-
vocals; John Dunkerley-accordion, banjo; Paddy Mahone-vocals;
Barrie Roberts-accordion, guitar, vocals; John Swift-lute.

CONTENTS: God Bless England; Lonely Banna
Strand; Bold Jack Donahue; Foggy Dew; Sandbags
and Trenches; Tricolor Ribbon; Bold Fenian Men;
Patriot Game; John Mitchell; Dunlaven Green;
Sean South; Belfast Brigade; Smashing of the
Van; Wearing of the Green; Kelly, the Boy from
Killane; Corrig Dun; Follow Me Up to Carlow;
Join the British Army

Just one of many outstanding albums from Folkways, an American independent record label. This delightful record is a
collection of songs that realistically captures the history
and emotions of the Irish people. Six singers offer six
different vocal styles to songs that range from the satirical
to stories of the bitter conflict in the North. Liner notes
give the lyrics and historical backgrounds for each selection. [LP]

203.   Sailing into Walpole's
       Marsh. (1977)   Green Linnet SIF 1004
       ARTISTS: Seán Corcoran-vocals; Mairéad Ní Dhomhnaill-
vocals; Maeve Donnelly-fiddle; Eddie Clarke-harmonica.
Produced by Lisa Null and Patrick Sky.

CONTENTS: The Girl that Broke My Heart/Sailing
into Walpole's Marsh; Bold Doherty; Two Reels;
Barbara Allen; Music in the Glen/The Green
Fields of America; Johnny and Molly; The Hu-
mours of Drinagh/Down the Back Lane; The Mice
Are At It Again; Ranntaí Fheilinidh na Fidile
(The Song of Phelim the Fiddler); Two Jigs;
Johnny Scott; The Morning Star/The Mountain
Top; Nobleman's Wedding

The four featured musicians participated in the Bicentennial
Festival of American Folklife sponsored by the Smithsonian
Institute in 1976. Their performances were some of the
highlights of this event and are commemorated on this pleasant album. Seán Corcoran of County Lough sings in the

northern style with ornamentations and embellishments. His
finest contribution is the humorous "The Mice Are at It
Again." The solo fiddle of Maeve Donnelly, County Galway,
is excellent. "The Humours of Drinagh/Down the Back Lane is
her best selection. Eddie Clark joins Donnelly on harmonica
for two great duets, "The Girl that Broke My Heart/Sailing
into Walpole's Marsh" and "Two Jigs." Finally, Mairéad Ní
Dhomhnaill, who sings three songs, is known for her work with
her siblings, Mícheál and Tríona. All the Ó Domhnaills
perform songs collected mainly by their aunt Neilí and their
father from Donegal. Mairéad's most impressive song is
"Nobleman's Wedding." **[LP]**

204. <u>Singing Men of Ulster</u>. (1977)   Green Linnet SIF 1005

     ARTISTS: Liam Andrews; Colm O Boyle; Cathal O Boyle;
Packie Manus Byrne; Robert Cinnamond; Frank Donnelly; Johnny
Doherty; Paddy Tunney. Produced by Diane Hamilton and Pat-
rick Sky.

     CONTENTS: The Verdant Braes of 'Screen; The
     Heroes of Comber; The Boys of Mullaghbawn; The
     Old Man Rocking the Cradle; Molly Bawn; Tander-
     agee; The Rambling Boys of Pleasure; The Frog's
     Wedding; Lovely Willie; The Blackbird of Mul-
     laghmore; Caoine na dTri Muire; Bean á tí; The
     Dark Eyed Gypsies; You and I in the One Bed Lie

This album is an excellent example of oral history collected
from field recordings. Made by Diane Hamilton and Sean O
Boyle between 1956 and 1962, the selections focus on English
and Gaelic songs from Northern Ireland. These tunes were
influenced by the migration of laborers between Ulster and
Britain (England and Scotland). This migration is still
prevalent today. Songs in English are well-known by Ulster
singers and are included along with Irish Gaelic songs in
their repertoires. It is interesting to note that many songs
are not sung with their original melodies. Quite often the
Irish singer will substitute his or her favorite air for the
song's melody. It is also common to spice up the stories
with emotional comments on the tale, which is not an unusual
practice in the Irish singing tradition. The combination of
the British and Irish styles create some very interesting
songs.

Variety is this album's main strength. Some of the best
songs include Johnny Doherty on vocals and fiddle with "The
Old Man Rocking the Cradle," "The Boys of Mullaghbawn" sung
by Colm O Boyle, the lighthearted "Tanderagee" with Paddy
Tunney on vocals, and "The Frog's Wedding" by Packie Manus
Byrne. The selections are all interesting and provide examples of various styles of the Ulster sound. Extensive
liner notes on the songs and the performers are included.
[LP]

205. <u>The Wheels of the World</u>. (1976)   Shanachie 33001

     ARTISTS: Edward Mullaney-uilleann pipes; Patrick

Stack-fiddle; Michael Coleman-fiddle; Patrick "Patsy" Touhey-
uilleann pipes; J. P. "Páckie" Dolan-fiddle; Liam Walsh-uil
leann pipes; James Swift-fiddle; Tom Ennis-uilleann pipes;
Michael J. Cashin-fiddle; Tom Doyle-flute; James Morrison-
fiddle.

> **CONTENTS:** Maid in a Cherry Tree; Stack of
> Barley; Steam Packet/Morning Star/Miss McCleod;
> Lasses of Donnibrook; Billy Taylor's Fancy;
> Hough's Favorite/What Ails You; Mullin's Fancy;
> The Three Little Drummers/The Connachtman's
> Rambles/The Joy of Life/Nancy Hynes; Tar Bol-
> ton/Longford Collector/The Sailor's Bonnet; The
> Maid on the Green/Jackson's Jig/A Drink of
> Water; The Kerry Reel/Shannon Shores; Rakish
> Paddy/The Wheels of the World

One of Shanachie Records' best offerings is <u>The Wheels of the
World</u>, a survey of the Irish American music scene in the
1920s and 1930s. Most selections were collected from rare 78
rpm records, which present some of the top performers of that
era who influences succeeding musicians to this day. Legends
such as Michael Coleman, Patsy Touhey and James Morrison
perform at their recorded best. Overall sound quality is
quite good and the variety of artists is commendable. A must
for anyone interested in the roots of Irish music. **[LP, CS]**

> **NOTES:** Other Shanachie albums of the masters include
> <u>The Legacy of Michael Coleman</u> (SH 33002), <u>Paddy Killoran's
> Back in Town</u> (SH 33003), <u>The Pure Genius of James Morrison</u>
> (SH 33004), and <u>Michael Coleman, Volume 2</u> (SH 33006).

Glossary

AIR A melody or tune for a song. Usually consists of a lead vocal or lead instrument and accompaniment.

AISLING A popular type of vision poetry from the 18th century, in which Ireland or Eire is disguised, usually as a woman or young girl. Example: "For Ireland I′d Not Tell Her Name."

BODHRÁN A single-headed hand drum usually made of goatskin. Pronounced bo-ran, it is played by a double-ended beater.

BOUZOUKI A 19th century Greek long-necked lute with a carved wood bowl resonator, which has 3 or 4 double courses of metal strings and is played with a plectrum. Johnny Moynihan is credited with introducing the bouzouki into Irish music while a member of Sweeney′s Men in the 1960s.

HORNPIPE Played more deliberately than a reel, the hornpipe has a more defined first and third beat in each measure. This dance, originally from England, has been written in its present common time (4/4) since the middle 1700s. It was utilized as an interlude between acts and scenes of English theatre.

JIG The jig is considered the oldest form of dance music. Three types of jigs are used: a) single jig in 6/8 and occassionally 12/8 time; b) double jig (6/8 time); and slip jig or hop jig (9/8 time). The majority of Irish jigs were composed by fiddlers and pipers of the 18th and 19th centuries.

PLANXTY   A sportive and animated harp tune, which moves
                 in triplets. It is slower in pace than a jig
                 and not intended to be adapted to lyrics.
                 Carolan wrote planxties as songs of praise in
                 honor of his patrons. The origin of the word
                 is not known, but the late Seán O Riada
                 believed that the term planxty to be a adult-
                 eration of the Irish word "Sláinte" or "Good
                 Health."

POLKA   A rapid tempo dance in 2/4 time that utilizes
                 duple meter. The polka originated in Eastern
                 Europe and then spread throughout Europe and
                 America. Ireland's County Kerry is known for
                 its polkas.

REEL   An ancient and lively indigenous British dance,
                 probably of Celtic origin, the reel is in
                 common time (4/4), but sometimes is played in
                 6/4 or 2/4 time. Chiefly danced in circular
                 motion, it is performed by two couples in
                 Scotland and by three in England. Irish reels
                 have been borrowed and naturalized from Scot-
                 land.

SEAN NÓS   An old style song tradition in the Irish
                 language, which is characterized by its com-
                 plex, subtle ornamentation and embellishment.

SET DANCE   Music to which special dancing steps were set.

STRATHSPEY   An mid-18th-century Scottish dance written in
                 common time, which was conceived for the
                 fiddle. It is a slower tempo reel that allows
                 for more elaborate steps.

**TIN
WHISTLE**   Small, high-pitched flute that is played like a
                 recorder (endblown). It has six fingerholes
                 and is usally made of metal. Also called a
                 penny whistle.

TIOMPÁN   An ancient Irish instrument similar to a
                 hammered dulcimer. It can be plucked like a
                 psaltery or played with mallet.

**UILLEANN
PIPES**   Uilleann (pronounced illyun) pipes or elbow
                 pipes date from the late 1600s. They contrast
                 with the Scottish Highland bagpipes in two
                 ways. First, the uilleann pipes are powered by
                 bellows driven by the player's elbow as opposed

to using the lungs.   Secondly, the Irish pipes
are more quiet and mellow, enabling them to be
played with other instruments in an ensemble
fashion.   Also called union pipes or Irish
pipes.

Directory

Several sources for obtaining Irish folk music recordings are listed below. Most reputable record stores will special order specific titles for customers, but recordings are available directly from record labels or through mail order businesses. (The author has personally used the mail order firms listed.)

The Directory is divided into two parts: 1. Mail Order Establishments; and 2. Record Labels. Record labels send catalogs upon request and some accept mail orders. Labels also are prime sources for information on musicians, recordings, and concert dates.

MAIL ORDER ESTABLISHMENTS

ANDY´S FRONT HALL. P.O. Box 307 Voorheesville, NY 12186. (518) 765-4193.

Andy Spence runs both a mail order business and a record company, Front Hall Records, which has more than 30 titles to date. Andy´s Front Hall provides access to a multitude of folk labels, both domestic and import, which cover various aspects of traditional music from America and abroad. They also carry books, magazines, songbooks, instruments, instrument kits, and even folk toys. Reasonable prices, timely delivery, and accepts credit card orders. An annual catalog with periodic updates is published, which is free with a purchase. For first class mailing, send $1.00 per year. Accepts telephone orders using Mastercard and Visa.

DOWN HOME MUSIC, INC. 13041 San Pablo Avenue El Cerrito, CA 94530. (415) 525-1494.

Owned by Chris Strachwitz and Frank Scott, who also own Arhoolie Records, Down Home is both a record store and mail order catalog business. Their newsletter, which contains both new record listings and record reviews, is published

approximately eight times per year and is free of charge by
third class mail. For first class the cost is $3.00 per year
domestically, and $10.00 per year for overseas air mail.
Down Home also publishes various specialized catalogs on a
periodic basis. These include the areas of blues and gospel,
vintage rock and roll, and country music. Catalogs for
Arhoolie Records, Charly Records, City Hall Record Distributors, Bayside Record Distributors, and Japanese Chess, Fire
and P-Vike labels are also available for purchase. Down Home
carries both domestic and import labels in a wide variety of
music types. Magazines and books are also available.
Reasonable pricing, prompt shipping, and accepts credit
cards. Will back order items not immediately available.
Credit card telephone orders are accepted.

GREEN LINNET RECORDS, INC. 70 Turner Hill Road New Canaan,
CT 06840. (203) 966-0864.

The "Green Linnet" was the name given to Napoleon Bonaparte
by the Irish, when he was at war with England and thought to
sympathize with the Irish freedom cause. Green Linnet Records is one of two major Irish folk music labels in the
United States. Their artists include Christy Moore, Dolores
Keane, the Bothy Band, Silly Wizard, and Mick Moloney among
many others. They have also domestically released titles
from the catalog of the now defunct Mulligan Records, an
Irish label. Green Linnet's mail order service offers low
prices and quick delivery. They accept Mastercard and Visa
by mail and take telephone orders. A yearly catalog with
descriptive information and excerpts from published reviews
is produced. Concert information and announcements of new
releases also are sent to regular customers.

ROUNDUP RECORDS. P. O. Box 154 North Cambridge, MA 02140.

Roundup Records carries over 10,000 titles on more than 350
record labels (domestic and import). The Record Roundup,
their newsletter, is published six times a year. It is sent
free via third class mail to customers making a purchase
every six months, and is sent first class for $6.00 per year.
Each Roundup gives a listing of new releases and record
reviews of selected titles. Areas of music covered include
bluegrass, folk, country, blues, gospel, rhythm, and blues,
Celtic, British Isles, Cajun, Zydeco, jazz, rock, reggae, new
age, and children's. Records are arranged by type of music
for easy browsing. A comprehensive Artist Catalog is published yearly. Quick service. Mastercard and Visa accepted
by mail, but no telephone orders. Will not back order items
out of stock.

SHANACHIE RECORDS CORPORATION. P. O. Box 208, Newton, NJ
07860.

Shanachie Records is both a record label and mail order
service, which carries many types of music--Celtic, reggae,

blues, and jazz. Major Irish labels include Gael-Linn, Claddagh, Tradition, Green Linnet, and Tara. Shanachie's spora-
dic publication that announces and reviews new releses has
evolved from the Shanachie Newsletter of several years ago to
the Shanachie Bulletin to the revised Shanachie Review, which
has in-depth record reviews. Shanachie does not back order.
Credit card and telephone orders are not accepted.

RECORD LABELS

BOOT RECORDS, LTD. 1343 Matheson Blvd. East Mississauga, ON
L4w 1R1.

CLADDAGH RECORDS, LTD. Dame House Dame Street Dublin 2,
Ireland. (U. S. representative is Shanachie Records Corporation).

DARA RECORDS (Distributed by Dolphin Traders) 56 Moore
Street Dublin 1, Ireland.

FLYING FISH RECORDS 1304 West Schubert Avenue Chicago, IL
60614.

FOLKWAYS RECORDS 632 Broadway New York, NY 10012.

FORTUNA RECORDS P. O. Box 1116 Novato, CA 94947.

FRONT HALL RECORDS P. O. Box 307 Voorheesville, NY 12186.

GAEL-LINN RECORDS 26 Merrion Square Dublin 2, Ireland.

OUTLET RECORDS (Homespun Recording, Inc.) 13 A/B Conyngham
Road Dublin 8, Ireland.

PHILO RECORDS, INC. **(SEE ROUNDER)**

POLYDOR GROUP (Polygram Records, Ltd.) 130 Slaney Road
Dublin 11, Ireland.

ROUNDER RECORDS CORPORATION 1 Camp Street Cambridge, MA
02140.

TARA RECORDS 4 Anne's Lane Dublin 2, Ireland.

TOPIC RECORDS, LTD. 50 Stroud Green Road   Finsbury Park
London N4 3EF, England.

WEA RECORDS (IRELAND), LTD. 130 Slaney Road   Dublin 11,
Ireland.

Artist Index

NOTE: Numbers in this index refer to the discography entry numbers, not the page numbers. The names of groups, individual artists in a band, principal solo musicians, guest artists on a recording, and the producers are included. A "P" adjacent to the entry number differentiates a producer from the musicians.

Title Index

Note: Numbers in this index refer to the entry numbers not to page numbers. Included are all titles found in the contents' section of the discography. Many selections are known by more than one title. If these alternative titles are given in the liner notes or on the disc, these will be included in the index with a SEE ALSO reference to additional titles. No attempt has been made to decide on a definitive title for these selections. However, in the case of foreign titles, the English language equivalent is used if given in the liner notes. A SEE reference refers users to the English title. No attempt has been made to translate foreign titles.

About the Compiler

DEBORAH L. SCHAEFFER currently is a public services librarian and social sciences/humanities bibliographer on the faculty of California State University, Los Angeles. She earned a Master's of Library Science Degree from the University of California, Los Angeles and a Bachelor's Degree in geography at California State University, Long Beach. Ms. Schaeffer avidly has collected recordings of traditional music from Ireland and the British Isles for nearly fifteen years. She is an FCC licensed radio announcer. During her tenure in Bozeman, Montana, Ms. Schaeffer hosted a radio program of early rock and roll music and later produced and hosted "The Celtic Tradition," a weekly show primarily focusing on the folk music of Ireland.

www.ingramcontent.com/pod-product-compliance
Lightning Source LLC
Chambersburg PA
CBHW070444100426
42812CB00004B/1203